Individuals, Groups and Business Ethics

T0304296

Routledge Studies in Business Ethics

Individuals, Groups and Business Ethics

Chris Provis

Routledge
Taylor & Francis Group

LONDON AND NEW YORK

First published 2012
by Routledge

2 Park Square, Milton Park, Abingdon, Oxon OX14 4RN
711 Third Avenue, New York, NY 10017, USA

Routledge is an imprint of the Taylor & Francis Group, an informa business

First issued in paperback 2016

Library of Congress Cataloging in Publication Data
Provis, Chris.
Individuals, groups, and business ethics / by Chris Provis. -- 1st ed.
p. cm. -- (Routledge studies in business ethics ; 4)
Includes bibliographical references and index.
ISBN 978-0-415-89194-3 (alk. paper)
1. Business ethics. 2. Social responsibility of business. 3. Interpersonal
relations. I. Title.
HF5387.P768 2011
174'.4--dc22
2011003391

ISBN13: 978-0-415-89194-3 (hbk)
ISBN13: 978-1-138-20313-6 (pbk)

Typeset in Sabon
by Taylor & Francis Books

Contents

Acknowledgments

In preparing this book I have received assistance and encouragement from many people, too many for me to be able to acknowledge each by name. In particular, I am grateful for the deep and collegial support of members of the Association of Industrial Relations Academics of Australia and New Zealand, of the Australian Association of Professional and Applied Ethics, and of the Ethics Centre of South Australia. I have benefited from support by the School of Management of the University of South Australia, and from editorial assistance by Kate Leeson of the university's Hawke Research Institute, as well as from the friendship of individual colleagues. In late stages of preparing the typescript I was given invaluable additional support and hospitality by the Graduate Institute of International Human Resource Development at National Taiwan Normal University.

Individuals whom I must mention are Silvia Pignata, Rob Neurath, Tony Norris and Stephen McKenzie, who each read the entire draft manuscript at one stage or another. For comments on specific parts of the draft I am also grateful to Joanne Ciulla, Ed Freeman and Stephen Cohen. For comments on earlier works of mine that were directly relevant to this work, I thank Dave Buchanan and Ian Davey.

At several places in the book I draw on material that has been published elsewhere in journal articles. These are acknowledged by footnotes or in-text references, but I must also acknowledge that in a number of cases, the articles and points I have drawn from them have benefited from comments and advice from the journal editors and reviewers.

Lastly, but above all, I express appreciation for the many forms of support given to me by my family.

Introduction

This book is about obligations that arise in our membership of social groups. It examines ethical dimensions of our relationships with family, friends and workmates, the extent to which we have obligations as members of teams and communities, and how far ethics may ground our commitments to organisations, corporations and countries.

Most of the discussion in the book is about situations where we may have some difficulty in seeing what we ought to do. It does not dwell on situations where we fail to do what we ought to out of laziness or greed or some other character failing. Nor does it deal greatly with situations where the greed or aggression of others causes us distress. There are certainly many cases where such moral weaknesses can cause problems, but it is too easy to imagine that all of our moral problems are so simple. In particular, I will suggest in the book that self-interest is over-rated as an explanation for people's actions, and that it is important to achieve a more balanced view about people's capacity for ethical behaviour. In this respect, the book runs counter to trends that have been associated with neoliberalism and managerialism since the 1980s, as they have sought to extend market mechanisms and technocratic decision making at the expense of moral argument and discussion.

In the concluding chapter of the book I discuss general shortcomings I see in those views compared with the approach taken here. Overall, I suggest that good decisions need to be based on reflective moral judgment, informed by understanding the logic of our obligations in group situations. Articulating that logic is the main aim of the book. Differences amongst different types of groups have significant implications for what is required of us. Our situation is different in a small, face-to-face group than it is in a large business organisation. The latter poses distinctive problems.

For example, the idea of corporate social responsibility has become prominent in discussions of business and business ethics, but accepting that corporations have social and ethical responsibilities does not necessarily make it clear how particular responsibilities devolve to individuals within corporations. Suppose a manager makes decisions in the face of constraints and on the basis of information provided by others. How much responsibility for the corporate action lies with that manager, and how much with those who have provided the information or imposed the constraints?

In many situations, our destiny seems to be in the hands of faceless, impersonal organisations, and we have difficulty in finding real individual human persons whom we can identify and address as having moral responsibility for the problems we encounter. Often, others who make decisions that affect us are responding to situations that are not of their own making and that are not situations they would choose to be in, but which place moral constraints on them, so that we cannot condemn them for the decisions they make, even though we dislike those decisions. A worker facing a shift change may be the victim of her manager's situation, as the manager tries to cope with client needs and other workers' illness in the face of limited resources. Who is responsible? The manager may have no other option, if she is to meet obligations to clients, who may have pressing needs. Perhaps we can examine the decisions about resource allocation. But those decisions themselves may have been made by other managers with limited options. In the face of this situation, we may be inclined to say that the problem is the fault of the organisation, but that merely shuffles aside the question how corporate responsibility is related to the responsibilities of individuals.

In considering how individuals' actions are tied to corporate social responsibility, I shall suggest that they need to be evaluated partly by whether they support or restrain corporate actions. However, the evaluation still has to take account of multiple, often conflicting demands. Some of these are obligations to family or colleagues, while others seem to be duties to the organisation. In this context, organisations are groups, and my account rests on identifying ethical differences amongst three different types of groups. There are smallish groups whose members are known to one another and who have personal relationships with one another, which are referred to as common-bond groups. There are abstract groups that exist only as mental categories, which are called common-identity groups. Finally, there are large groups that rely on institutionalisation and role relationships for their existence. These may be referred to as institutions, institutionalised groups, or organisations.

From this analysis of the different classes of groups, I will argue that we can distinguish three classes of putative obligations: one, obligations we have towards other concrete individuals as a result of relationships we have with them; two, obligations we have because of roles we play; and, three, putative obligations to abstract groups of which we are members, which under ethical analysis turn out not to be genuine obligations at all.

In organisations, I argue that role obligations are a specific instance of the first sort of obligations mentioned, namely obligations we have toward other individual persons as a result of relationships we have with them. In this case, however, the relationships are not necessarily close or enduring ones: they may be transient, but emerge from expectations that individuals have of one another. My account revolves around the proposition that others' expectations frequently generate obligations for us, and may sometimes do so even in contexts where we are not responsible for them having those expectations. In short, part of my argument is that our social obligations are based on personal relationships rather than relationships to abstract groups.

As well as a wish to clarify how our roles create obligations for us in complex organisations, another motivation I have in writing is a concern that I think many of us share, about the influence that abstract groups have on us. We are very familiar with the loyalties that are summoned up by national, ethnic and religious groups. It can be hard to see how these commitments are different from the commitments to sporting teams that result in soccer hooliganism and other violence. Ingroup–outgroup conflicts are everywhere, and are constant sources of aggression and hatred, as supporters rally behind flags that represent an infinite variety of groups: men, women, Christians, Muslims, Catholics, Protestants, Americans, Iraqis, Manchester United followers, Bolton Wanderers supporters – all combining with those whose social identity they share, to combat others.

Sometimes, members of an identity group may rightly feel a sense of oppression or injustice, and in these cases they or other individuals may have genuine rights or obligations to remedy such injustice. In many other cases, though, moral obligations that seem to stem from identity group membership are illusory, and derive instead from the basic psychological need to develop self-understanding by categorising ourselves and others, and then basing our decisions and actions on the identity groups we form by doing so. Such impulses are well-known, and the novelty here emerges only from considering their ethical implications. My analysis allows us to see why we may have a sense of obligation to an abstract group, but at the same time suggests that the sense is illusory: genuine obligations revolve around commitments to other human beings, not to abstract groups like white people, Catholics, or Bolton Wanderers supporters.

As a white Catholic Bolton Wanderers supporter, I say this with some feeling, since I experience a tug from each of those abstract groups. Nevertheless, I see no genuine obligations that emerge from membership of an abstract group of white persons, and it is hard to see who might think I did have any. It may seem more plausible to suggest that I have obligations as a Catholic, but I believe that the genuine obligations I have as a Catholic are not based on membership of an abstract identity group, but from membership of a human community whose members have a network of personal relationships with one another. As a Bolton Wanderers supporter, I might have obligations if I had joined an organised supporters' club, but those obligations would be partly contractual, based on conditions of membership, and partly personal, based on personal relationships with others. Since I am not actually a member of such a club, my obligations are minimal.

So, that is also part of my background motivation for writing: a suspicion of obligations grounded in membership of abstract groups. That concern ties together with the desire to explore the ways in which our individual obligations and responsibilities are related to the responsibilities of corporations and other institutionalised groups. Both of these motives draw my account toward a focus on individuals and their obligations, and the idea that role obligations are grounded in expectations that individuals have of one another.

One implication that arises in the book is that we ought to be careful of situations where people are induced to have expectations of others, not only because these situations may be demanding and stressful for those of whom things are expected, but because such situations may generate multiple, potentially conflicting obligations. We encounter the moral 'dirty hands' problem, where individuals have to renounce some obligations if they are to fulfil others. If the account given here is sound, the situation is bad for the individuals directly affected, but also can numb our sensitivity to obligations we all may have in social situations. There are clear moral reasons to avoid constructing such situations so far as we can and, when such situations do occur, dealing with them is easier if we have an analysis of the logic of our obligations. The account I will provide shows how we can explain some relationships amongst obligations that may seem to be of different types, like personal obligations and role-based obligations. On this account, it is then unsurprising that we face conflicts of obligations, but we can see what we may try to do to in order to avoid the occurrence of such situations. We can also see that the obligations are not vastly different in their character, even if they do pull in different directions, and decisions may be easier, even if there is no routine, rule-based way to make them.

In this book I also identify a number of problematic situations that may arise in work organisations. Apart from cases of conflicting obligations, there are cases where individuals may be exploited through meeting their obligations to one another. An example is the case where people's obligations to workmates yield benefit to third parties like shareholders. There are a number of other cases that come up in work organisations, including questions about loyalty, conscientious action, and questions of how judgment about social situations is tied to evaluating obligations.

I am not suggesting that these issues only arise in work organisations. For example, people may be influenced through appeals for loyalty to many abstract identity groups, including not only corporations but other groups like nations and racial or religious groups. Work organisations are the recurring focus of discussion in the book, but much of the discussion aims to be generally applicable to a wide variety of groups. The picture that is painted in the book revolves around daily lives where we have choices to make, projects to complete and relationships to maintain, and the issues addressed can arise in all parts of our lives. The world depicted is one where we have to think of the effects our actions have, of our commitments to others, of our ideals and goals. In this world, most of us think about what we ought to do, as well as what we would like to do. We think of ourselves as having obligations to others for many reasons: commitments we have made, opportunities to help others, as a matter of simple fairness, and many more. There may be some art to balancing these obligations with our own projects and goals, to let neither side take over completely. However we do that, we acknowledge some importance for those moral obligations.

The book is an effort to untangle some of the logic of these obligations, beginning from obligations that we acknowledge to other individuals, and moving to obligations we may have in contexts where groups and corporations are salient. I explore the relationship between this ethical life-world and the world of impersonal corporate forces that impact so heavily on us but seem at the same time to be so remote from us. If my analysis is correct, it suggests two things. One is a tragic dimension to human social existence. However far we try to meet our obligations, there will be occasions when we must fail. That is not a new point. It is familiar enough in drama and literature. Second, however, I suggest that we may be able to ameliorate those tragic demands by amending and tempering the social structures that create them. It is no novelty to argue that we have reasons to amend our social structures. If there is novelty here, it lies in the suggestion that our social structures create the arrays of obligations that we have to deal with in our ethical life-world, and by seeing detail of the logic of our social obligations, we can avoid those tragic situations of conflict and exploitation that undermine our goodwill and moral inclinations.

CHAPTER OUTLINE

Chapter 1 identifies ethical principles to be used in subsequent chapters. They include basic general principles like benevolence, fairness and respect, with a derivative principle that is important subsequently: that others' expectations may create obligations for us. Another principle that is important later in the book is the idea that we are obliged not to help others do bad actions. I also consider some issues about ethical decision making, including the sort of situation typified by the 'dirty hands' problem, and the idea that we can best account for moral choice in such situations as a process of pattern recognition rather than calculation or step-by-step rule following.

In Chapter 2, I note that individuals' interests and identities are established in relationships. Common-bond groups are held together by close personal relationships usually involving reciprocal interaction and linked individual identities. Common-identity groups are constituted out of individuals' shared social identity but may involve no mutual acquaintanceship. Common-bond groups may have interests or rights that impact on individuals' obligations, but pressures of loyalty towards common-identity groups do not create genuine obligations.

Chapter 3 adds the point that institutionalised groups involve linked roles, bringing a new dimension to the obligations that individuals have in group contexts. Role requirements stem from scripts that embody people's expectations. Violating those expectations can generate confusion and harm for others. However, role requirements are not absolute. Individuals have obligations not to assist in bad actions by groups, just as we have such obligations with regard to bad actions performed by other individuals. These obligations must be set alongside obligations generated from role requirements, neither subordinate to them in all cases nor over-riding them in all cases.

The special importance of that last point is taken up in Chapter 4. Role prescriptions can have a force that goes beyond genuine ethical requirements. There are enormous pressures on organisational members to conform to group expectations, beyond any genuine ethical requirements. Added to the psychological pressures of group identification, there are tendencies to conform with group norms, and with authority that is perceived as legitimate. The account given here helps us to distinguish our genuine ethical obligations – loyalty to small groups, assistance to organisations or meeting others' expectations – from other conformity pressures.

In Chapter 5, I extend points from previous chapters to analyse ethical issues using a series of related hypothetical case situations set in a complex work organisation. One situation highlights the contrast between loyalty to abstract groups and commitments to other individuals. Another combines issues about involvement in groups with issues about persuasion and con-scientious action. The complexity of the situation emphasises the need to use *phronēsis*-like intuitive judgment in making some ethical decisions. Another situation shows how competitive environments can exacerbate tendencies towards social conformity and identification with a group, while a fourth illustrates problems of conflicting responsibilities.

Those sorts of situations of moral conflict are important in organisations, because of the multiple sources of obligations within them. Chapter 6 focusses on that problem. Given that we cannot avoid all conflicts of obli-gations, how may they be dealt with? Often, we must rely on the obvious fact that some obligations are more important than others, and in considering judgments about which are more important we see the weakness of views that reduce decision making to calculation or routine. It is consistent with this that organisations can take steps to assist people with decision making in difficult situations. It is a shortcoming when they fail to do so, even more when they ignore such problems or establish systems of incentives that make conflicts more likely.

Examples can be seen in some cases of team-based production, where people's mutual obligations are contrived or used for others' benefit. In others, people are influenced by appeal to obligations of loyalty they perceive themselves to have to the abstract group, even though such obligations are illusory. In Chapter 7, I suggest that dealing with these cases hinges on respect for people as responsible agents, and on the nature of moral decision making. In particular, it requires understanding of the sources of obligations in group contexts, and that some apparent obligations have no real moral force.

Chapter 8 sets all the preceding discussion in a more general context. Recent years have been dominated by a network of views including rational choice theory, managerialism and neoliberalism. These views all hinge on the idea that maximisation of individuals' preference satisfaction is the key to rational action. Such views fail to account for the importance of dialogue, reflection and development of moral judgment. The difficulty can be seen quite clearly when individuals' conscientious actions run counter to official organisational authority. Neoliberal emphasis on market-based approaches to problems cannot deal with such cases. It also tends to reject collective solutions to social problems in favour of individualistic approaches. The present account shows we can recognise the importance of individuals vis-à-vis large, abstract groups, but also recognise the importance of institutionalised groups in sustaining people's welfare. The chapter concludes with a summary of all the main points in the book.

1 Ethical principles and ethical decision making

Ethics can often be an area of dispute and contention. Nevertheless, there are some areas of wide agreement. In the next section of this chapter, I set out some generally accepted principles, to establish ethical common ground for subsequent analysis of obligations we have in various group settings. Such principles include requirements of beneficence, justice and fairness, respect, honesty and good faith. In the following section, I emphasise the fact that sometimes these principles can make others' expectations of us an important source of our obligations, a point that will be important later, especially when we consider individuals' role requirements in organisations. I shall then turn to consider some secondary ethical principles, which may modify or refine application of the general principles. These include provisions to do with self-defence, coercion and 'help and hindrance'. The last will also be important when we examine the responsibilities that individuals have in organisations. Then the chapter will turn to some issues about how these principles figure in decision making, with a basic account of moral conflict and the intuitive processes of ethical decision making.

Setting out some general, basic principles will serve to draw our attention to issues that have sometimes been pushed aside in recent years, in a social and political climate that has moved away from ethical principles and obligations and placed emphasis instead upon processes and outcomes. The last decades of the twentieth century saw a series of connected moves in social and economic policy, often referred to collectively as neoliberalism. These included efforts to extend competition and market mechanisms as widely as possible, with a mistrust of bureaucracy and government. One aspect of these moves has been emphasis on the results of what is done rather than how it is done (see e.g. Osborne and Gaebler, 1992: 14). This approach has had many benefits, but has also taken attention away from ethical demands we have on us in our social lives. Issues of efficiency and effectiveness have overshadowed issues of ethics. Analysis has primarily been about ways to improve competition and eliminate waste, rather than about different types of obligations.

It was argued some years ago that modern ethical theory had focussed too much on obligations (see e.g. Anscombe, 1958; Crisp and Slote, 1997), but it is also possible to focus too little on our obligations. Such discussion is especially important when there are pressures on us that present themselves as though they are obligations, even though they are not real obligations. Some social pressures are like that. Even though we may feel pressures to conform, nevertheless these pressures have no genuine ethical force. Some allegiances that we feel may not be genuine obligations, whether they be commitments of patriotism or merely allegiances to football teams and sporting clubs.

On the other hand, some of the social obligations we feel are quite genuine, and we ought to make room in our lives to heed them. Most communities in history have believed that people have special obligations to parents and children, and I shall suggest that these relationships do indeed create genuine obligations. But where do they stand in modern times when workers in advanced economies face challenges of 'work–life balance'? How do we weigh obligations to families against obligations to employers and workmates? The answer is not easy, but the question is more tractable if we can see more clearly what the sources of these obligations are.

In seeing the roots of some of those obligations, we may also see more clearly how genuine obligations emerge from social structures and institutions that we create. If we are not careful, we may create obligations for ourselves that we have difficulty in meeting. In that case we run risks of uncertainty, stress and anxiety, challenges in leading ethical lives, and the temptation to push aside ethical concerns as just too hard to deal with. We shall turn to such issues in some later chapters of the book.

The first step, then, is to consider the sources of our social obligations. I noted that most communities in history have believed that people have special obligations to parents and children, but we cannot rely on common opinion. For example, obligations of patriotism have also been widely accepted, but I shall argue that these are often of questionable force. The fact that communities accept one thing or another does not go very far in helping us to see sources of obligations. The goal of the book is to address prescriptive or normative questions, rather than descriptive questions. In that respect, it must be distinguished from studies in a number of other areas. Historians have given accounts of the norms and values of past societies, their evolution and development; sociologists and anthropologists have considered the mores and customs found in a wide variety of different communities; while psychologists and evolutionary biologists have given explanations about rules of behaviour and moral perceptions. I shall allude to work in some of those areas, but all of those studies are essentially descriptive, in the sense that they address questions about what people do and what they believe or perceive, rather than directly addressing the question of what we ought to do. This book aims directly at prescriptive ethical questions about what we ought to do, and touches on descriptive issues only in order to move towards answers to those prescriptive questions (for useful discussion of the difference between the sorts of questions, see Cohen, 2004: ch. 1). There is room for worthwhile discussion and analysis of prescriptive issues, and such analysis is essential if we are to distinguish genuine obligations from other pressures on us that masquerade as obligations but have no real moral force.

In this chapter I therefore set out some ethical principles that most readers will agree to, and which can be used as a partial basis for some further discussion. In doing so, I adopt Aristotle's methodological view that 'our treatment of this science will be adequate, if it achieves that amount of precision which belongs to its subject matter' (Aristotle, 1934: I, iii, p. 7). The principles are imprecise, but meaningful enough to allow us to draw worthwhile conclusions in the rest of the book. In setting them out, I emphasise some in particular that will be important later.

SOME ETHICAL PRINCIPLES

The idea of a principle must be distinguished from the idea of a rule. In discussing principles, I do not mean well-defined rules that form criteria against which to evaluate decisions and actions. As I will note further, ethical decision making often is not based on such rules or algorithms. The moral principles mentioned here can identify sorts of considerations that often are relevant to making decisions and explaining them, but they function by identifying the sorts of considerations that we accept as reasons for actions, not as well-defined measuring devices (cf. Scanlon, 1998: 197–202; Raz, 2000: 56–57; Herron and Gilbertson, 2004).

Because ethical principles are not precise rules, there is considerable overlap amongst them, and there are various arguments that some ethical principles may in fact be reduced to others. So far as possible I shall avoid those arguments. Instead, I will be examining a series of ethical principles and asking how they apply to us as members of groups. Do we have obligations to avoid harming groups, as we do to avoid harming individuals? Do groups have an independent existence that can be impacted upon through our principled or unprincipled behaviour? Do we have obligations of loyalty to groups as we may have to individuals? I shall call on the general ethical principles to address such questions.

One widely accepted principle is that we ought to pay attention to the consequences of what we do, seeking good outcomes and avoiding harmful ones. We may refer to this as the principle of beneficence. The idea is a natural one, with some very old versions: the Hippocratic Oath includes the statement 'I will prescribe regimens for the good of my patients according to my ability and my judgment and never do harm to anyone.' Many notable social obligations are grounded in this principle. In a simple case, for example, if others are relying on us to play our part in social arrangements, they may suffer if we fail to do so.

Extending ideas of beneficence, some theorists argue that all ethical obligations can be accounted for by reference to consequences of actions, like the good or suffering created for others. The general view is most often known nowadays as 'consequentialism'. In modern times, it can be traced back to Jeremy Bentham's utilitarianism (Bentham, 1962 [1789]). Consequentialism is controversial, and some have argued that different ethical principles like principles of justice or good faith should have an ethical weight independent of their resulting consequences (see e.g. Scheffler, 1988). Consequentialist moral theory has been associated historically with laissez-faire economic doctrine, and it is no coincidence that neoliberalism may have fallen into the error of focussing too much on consequences, in outcome-based approaches to social policy.

However, there is little disagreement that consequences of actions are often relevant to their ethical evaluation. Our later discussion will touch on some questions about consequentialism, but initially what will loom larger is whether the sorts of consequences in question concern individual human beings, or if their effects on groups should have some separate weight of their own. We know well enough what is harmful or beneficial to individuals. Can we separately harm or benefit groups in their own right, in ways that are ethically significant? In Chapter 2 I will take up this question in more detail.

We may set some other principles alongside beneficence. One is justice. There is widespread acceptance that justice is a relevant consideration for ethical evaluation. Principles of justice are at the foundation of some notable social obligations. Issues of justice can often be phrased as issues of fairness (cf. Rawls, 1972). So I shall speak of 'fairness', rather than using the word 'justice', but that does not mean to imply a distinction between justice and fairness. I shall take it that ethics often requires us to have regard for what is fair, even though it is sometimes contentious what that involves. For example, there is likely to be contention amongst people who argue that justice requires equal treatment for different individuals, and others who say that justice requires analysis of what different people deserve, taking into account factors like the amount of effort they have put in, and the amount of disadvantage they have to contend with. Those different considerations of fairness will sometimes be in tension, and they may also be in tension with regard for consequences. The possibility of such moral conflicts is important below.

The same sort of tensions can arise from another ethical principle, 'respect'. Just as it is not always possible to state a rule for 'justice' that specifies what to do in any situation, neither is it always possible to state the ethical principle of 'respect' in a unique, well-defined way. Indeed there is considerable overlap between the two conceptions. Kant expressed the idea of respect for persons by saying 'act in such a way that you always treat humanity, whether in your own person or in the person of any other, never simply as a means, but always at the same time as an end' (1964: 96). Such an idea may be tied to ideas of justice and the fair treatment of persons. However, as I have said, we are not engaged in the task of trying to untangle those ties, nor do I wish to strengthen them so as to assert that justice and respect are one and the same. The principle of 'respect for persons' will be used as a guide in assessing what ethics requires of us, without us having to determine whether justice and respect are distinct considerations. As with all the principles, we are mostly interested in how these principles apply in situations where individuals' membership of groups is a prominent factor. We may consider how individuals' obligations are shaped by requirements to consider groups' welfare, or be fair to groups or respect them, and we may ask how being a group member shapes requirements towards other individuals, whether these are requirements of beneficence, fairness or respect.

Like considerations of beneficence, justice and respect, there is wide acceptance also that requirements of honesty and good faith are ethically important. Once again, I shall avoid questions about whether these require-ments are separate and independent, or somehow reducible to those others. For our purposes it is more important to notice the link that such requirements have with others' expectations. Because others' expectations are especially connected with the ethics of roles we play in groups, let me explore this area in more depth.

Obligations and expectations

A prominent form of honesty is honesty in communication, and that is tied to respect for persons, since respecting others involves consideration for them as autonomous agents with scope to make responsible decisions, with a need for an understanding of the world that is as accurate as our own. There will be many situations where the implications are not just to do with out-right lying, but with deception by other means, giving a false impression, withholding some relevant information, and so on (Provis, 2010a).

Linked with the general requirement of honesty that emerges from the obligation to respect others is the need to have regard for their expectations. A similar consideration underpins the requirement to act in good faith, the obligation to keep promises, to stand by one's word. Just as our obligations of honesty go beyond the requirement to refrain from explicit lies, so obli-gations of good faith go beyond keeping explicit promises. I shall argue that requirements to meet others' expectations are often an important factor in assessing our social obligations. Scanlon has compared this sort of consideration with the accepted need to keep one's promises:

> there are many other ways in which one can behave wrongly in regard to other people's expectations about what one will do: one can fail to take care about the expectations one leads others to form, fail to warn them that their expectations are mistaken or (without promising anything) intentionally lead others to form false expectations when their doing so is to one's advantage. Not every action falling under the last two descriptions is wrong, but many are. There are no familiar and widely taught principles – analogous to 'Keep your promises' – that cover these

cases. Yet once the question arises we are able to see the wrongness of these actions in much the same way that we see the wrongness of breaking a promise or of making a promise that one does not intend to keep.

(Scanlon, 1998: 202)

If I lead others to have certain expectations, this may create just as much of an obligation on me whether I do so by explicit statement, or in some other way. Legal obligations are not always a perfect guide to moral obligations, but certainly the law acknowledges that obligations can be incurred through inducing expectations in others by means other than explicit statements.

For example, in *Schneider v. Heath* (1813) 3 Camp. 505, a ship was sold with 'all faults' (in other words, the seller did not warrant its soundness). There was a defect in the bottom of the ship which the seller prevented the buyer from discovering by taking the ship out of dry dock and keeping it afloat. In these circumstances, the seller was held liable. On the same footing, in the Canadian case of *Gronau v. Schlamp Investments Ltd* (1975) 52 DLR (3d) 631, the vendor of a house concealed some cracking in a wall with temporary brick work, and this was held to amount to actionable fraud.

(Duggan et al., 1994: 29)

In this sort of case, the obligations we have as a result of inducing expectations in others overlap with the obligations we have not to deceive them, and we see here cases where our obligation not to deceive others is wider than the obligation not to tell them explicit lies.

The overlap between our obligations to be honest with others and our obligations to keep faith with them grows out of the 'double aspect' of obligation inherent in any statement of intent. Suppose that I give people to understand what I intend to do. In my initial communication to them, my obligation is to not deceive them about what I shall do. Subsequently my obligation is to do what I have indicated. I can fulfil my obligation either by getting my message to conform to my intention, or my subsequent action to conform to my message. Whichever the case, my obligation, when I have induced expectations in others, is fairly clear, and the principle that we have an obligation to meet others' expectations when we have created them seems unexceptionable. There may be circumstances where the obligation is reduced or removed, for example when it becomes clear that there will be previously unanticipated consequences. If this does not occur then I have a clear obligation to indicate truthfully what I will do, and to do what I have said.

But are there cases where I have obligations to meet others' expectations even when it is not I who have induced those expectations? The answer seems to be yes, at least in some cases. This kind of situation will be important in some of our subsequent discussion. While our obligations are all the stronger if we have some responsibility for others' expectations, as some writers have noted (e.g. Scanlon, 1998: 296–309), the expectations alone create some obligations for us, if failing to conform to them will indeed result in others' harm or discomfiture. They may not be simple obligations to do what is expected, but they are significant obligations nonetheless.

An example is where you have expectations of me as a result not of what I have said or done but as a result of what someone else has said or done. If my son tells the neighbour's children that I will take them all to the beach, perhaps more in a spirit of optimism than on the basis of any indication I have given, I may feel some obligation when they arrive with towels and swimwear. Is my felt obligation a real one? Is there some obligation on my part because I shall sadden them by refusal? Of course, even if I do have some obligation, it may well be over-ridden by other commitments I have, or countered by rights I have to carry out plans of my own. Perhaps my son has to accept blame if the trip does not go ahead, for raising the others' expectations unreasonably. There are various factors like these that we could look at more closely. Nevertheless, in some such cases we have real obligations, and I may have some obligation as a result of the expectations my son has given to the neighbour's children. Often, we do not welcome obligations created for us by others, but some such there are, and we shall discuss more weighty examples in later chapters.

To a large extent the obligations we have to others to meet their expectations are obligations based in considerations of respect, but to some extent they are also based in considerations of beneficence. Others may suffer if they have made plans that rely on us playing our part in social arrangements. There are certainly cases when one individual incurs an obligation through inducing an expectation in others: promising is the basic case, and has attracted so much analysis by moral philosophers just because it is such a basic case. But knowing that others have expectations and doing nothing to discourage them can equally leave us with obligations, in many circumstances, and obligations may emerge from others' expectations about our behaviour, even when we have not instilled those expectations.[1] The example of my son and the neighbour's children is not a major obligation, but some cases are much more substantial. In cases where others have expectations of us based on social conventions we may sometimes do great harm if we ignore those expectations.

This is important throughout our social lives, since we are constantly interacting with others who have expectations of us. Sometimes, we have obligations because we have created those expectations. Sometimes, however, they have expectations of us because of the sorts of established scripts, routines and conventions that we shall discuss in Chapter 3, and then we can still have obligations as a result, even though we have done nothing to establish those scripts, routines or conventions. Perhaps this is the fundamental

---

1 Feinberg (1984: ch. 4), has given an extended discussion about obligations we have to others to prevent them coming to harm, although most of Feinberg's discussion is more directly about the extent to which such obligations ought to be enforced by criminal law.

insight in theories that ground obligations in the notion of a hypothetical 'social contract'. Such theories have been criticised on the basis that such contracts are pure fiction (e.g. Dworkin, 1989). However, the constant to-and-fro interaction of our social lives does in fact bring us constantly into contact with others who have expectations of us, some of which we have engendered more or less directly, some of which we have not, but with varying degrees of obligation resulting for us in either case.

So far, then, I have suggested several principles that I believe will be widely accepted as guides for ethical action. One, the principle of beneficence, is that we should aim to achieve good outcomes from our actions and avoid harmful ones. Another, which we might refer to as the principle of justice, is that we should treat people fairly. A third we might call the principle of respect for persons, a fourth the principle of honesty, and a fifth the principle of good faith. There are clear connections and overlaps amongst these, such as the relationship between the principle of respect for persons and the principles of honesty and good faith. Other authors have of course given such lists of duties or principles (see e.g. Ross, 1930: 20–21), and this list does not purport to be more complete or otherwise superior, but only to identify principles that will be relevant to our later discussion. On that basis, we may also accept as a principle that others' expectations can form a significant moral consideration in deciding what we ought to do. The last point will be especially important in some group contexts.

We shall primarily be interested in how these principles apply to individual persons. Even though our discussion revolves around people's membership of groups, I am not primarily interested in how the principles themselves apply to groups, except to the extent that that question is relevant to the obligations that individuals have. However, my argument about individuals' obligations will have to touch on issues about how far some moral considerations apply to groups. For example, the extent to which they have interests will affect the extent to which we as individuals may have obligations towards groups, such as obligations not to harm them or obligations of loyalty towards them.

Secondary principles and moral discretion

The principles I have set out so far are mainly useful for the initial identification of ethical behaviour: in other words, we can use them to draw at least a tentative conclusion without first having to consider what other principles apply. There are some other principles that play a slightly different role in moral appraisal. These are 'secondary' in the sense that they have application only in conjunction with those more primary principles above. For example, they identify mitigating factors, which may free us from obligation or blame that we would otherwise attribute on the basis of those primary factors.

A well-known example is the principle of self-defence. This, we may take it, is the principle that we have a right to take actions to preserve ourselves from harm in the face of actions by others that they take to harm us. This principle can free us from blame for doing what often would be wrong. For example, it may on some occasions provide some justification for lying. If someone seeks information from us to use to our detriment, then morally we have a right to conceal that information, and if the only way to conceal it is to lie, then we may have that right, depending perhaps on the magnitude of the harm we are threatened with and the other person's overall intentions.

Another secondary principle that identifies mitigating factors is that people's liability to praise or blame for what they do may be lessened to the extent to which it is done against their will. It is clear that physical coercion frees one from much praise or blame for what one does. Some other cases are less clear: for example, when I am addicted to drugs or another person plays on my weaknesses. Some such influences diminish the extent to which we can be held morally responsible for what we do (Feinberg, 1965; Murphy, 1971; Thompson, 1980: 909; Bovens, 1998: 30), although it is difficult to say in general terms which do so and to what extent. Here, we need only note the general principle that some forms of influence lessen the extent to which we can be held morally responsible, and liable for praise or blame. (This is something to be borne in mind when we later note some specific types of influence such as social conformity pressures and group identification that are especially salient in the context of social obligation.)

A third secondary principle of 'help and hindrance' will be even more prominent in our discussion of social obligation and group allegiance. It identifies factors we would not refer to as mitigating factors, but they do have application only in conjunction with primary factors like effects on well-being, honesty, fidelity and so on. That is, if you aim to do something blameworthy, then other things being equal I am blameworthy if I help you and praiseworthy if I hinder you; if you aim to do something praise-worthy, then other things being equal I am praiseworthy if I help you and blameworthy if I hinder you.

Here, 'helping' and 'hindering' are shorthand ways of referring to a wide range of possibilities. There is a wide range of ways in which I can be related to actions of yours. At one extreme, I may be a mere observer. At the other extreme, I can so completely influence you – by hypnosis or physical force, perhaps – that the action is more correctly said to be mine than yours. In between, there are various possibilities. I may be aware of your action and disapprove, but take no action. I may be not only aware of your action, but approve of it, without doing anything more than that. I may encourage you by showing my approval, but no more. I may assist, by providing you with advice or resources, or by removing hindrances. I may provide you with incentives to act, or threats about what I will do if you fail to. I may take an active part in the action, as an assistant or equal participant.

The general point is that often our relationships with others and our involvement in groups open us up to praise or blame, depending both on the nature of others' actions and our position with regard to them. This will be important in regard to many social obligations. If I am associated with an action by another individual, then in evaluating what I do we may take account of many of the same factors as would be relevant if I were performing the action myself.

It is not easy to say in more detail what implication is added by the fact that I am an assistant or supporter, rather than the primary agent. By and large, neither causation nor moral blame and credit are susceptible to arithmetic addition or subtraction. Blame is not like a cake, that is fixed in amount, with only the proportions for each recipient to be determined.[2] If you and I together do some evil, then each of us may be as fully to blame as I would be if I did it alone, and so also for creditable acts. If I benefit from an act, or lose by it, then neither the amount of the benefit or loss, nor the part I played in achieving it, are the only things relevant: also to be considered is the extent to which I understood what was at issue, for example.

For some cases we shall be concerned with, it is equally difficult to say how to regard people's approval of an action when they play no direct part in it. It often happens that we may approve or disapprove of someone else's action, but do not see any way to assist or hinder it. There are some cases when we can think that people are worthy of praise or blame when they have made unsuccessful efforts of one kind or another: for example, when I have unsuccessfully opposed my neighbour's maltreating his dog. It is harder to know what to say when people refrain from action because there is no reasonable prospect of success. In some cases individuals involved in groups may be confronted with a substantial issue, when they have to decide whether they ought to express approval or disapproval of some course of action even when there is no prospect of them affecting the outcome. Here, I shall take it that approval and disapproval are limiting cases of making efforts to help or hinder, and for simplicity shall refer most of the time just to helping and hindering. Then the general point is that opportunities to help or hinder create various obligations: for example, clear obligations not to help others do bad things.

Thus, we can see several principles that identify secondary factors relevant to ethical appraisal: factors like self-defence, influence or constraint, and helping or hindering action by another. The factors are secondary in the sense that they are relevant to ethical appraisal only when we are inclined toward appraisal of an act on the basis of other primary factors like effects on well-being, honesty, fidelity and so on.

To some extent the secondary and primary factors may be entwined. It ought to be emphasised again now that the principles identified here do not purport to be independent or exhaustive. Neither do I suggest that the ones mentioned in this chapter are all the moral principles there are, or that they cover all the ethical requirements we face in all different kinds of situations.

---

2 As noted by Thompson (1983: 554) and Wolgast (1992: 62).

On the surface, they may even run in different and contrary directions. Considerations of general well-being may conflict with fairness, and rights to privacy may run counter to obligations to be honest with others in our communications with them. In the following section, I make some general observations about the relationships amongst different principles. The purpose of drawing attention to the ones mentioned here is just that they will be important in some of our subsequent discussion, where we shall also consider some of them in a little more detail.

In this section, it is enough to conclude with just one more point, which is a little different from those that have been mentioned so far. We might refer to it as the 'moral discretion' principle. This refers to the fact that in very many situations we have some discretion about what to do, so far as ethical requirements are concerned. Here, there should be some emphasis on the word 'requirements'. There may well be things that it would be good to do, but which we are not ethically required to do. In the Gospel according to St Matthew, we read 'if any one strikes you on the right cheek, turn to him the other also' (Matthew 5:39 RSV). We may agree that that would be good to do, but still accept that it goes beyond what is ethically required. Even though it may be good for us to yield to an aggressor, it may still be that we have the right to defend ourselves. In that sense, ethics is a kind of bottom line. There are many things that it would be good to do, which nevertheless are not obligatory. We may contrast this with the situation described by T. H. White in *The Once and Future King*, when the boy Arthur is shown what it would be like to live in an ants' nest, and confronts a notice saying 'Everything Not Forbidden Is Compulsory'. The ants' nest is portrayed as leaving no room for discretion, and the result is a machine-like lack of autonomy, foreign to ideas of human choice and aspiration.

This principle reminds us that even if neoliberalism may have taken our attention away from ethics too much, it is also possible to put too much emphasis on obligations. Obligations are important, but it is natural that a book about ethics should attend to them more frequently than we have to as we go about our daily lives. Most of the time, we have some moral discretion about decision and action. In addition, however, I shall argue that although our obligations are often important in group contexts, there are also pressures on us that can present themselves as obligations, but which have no real moral force. In these situations, the main task of analysis is to make us aware of the extent to which these pressures are consistent with us having moral discretion in what we choose to do.

THE POSSIBILITY OF MORAL CONFLICT

This section deals with decision making about matters of obligation. In this book I tend to focus on cases where distinguishing our obligations is not straightforward. I shall discuss some cases where determining obligation is quite easy, so as to appeal to our shared intuitions about what is right or obligatory; but my intention in doing this will be to call on such shared intuitions about cases that are relatively clear and then to use those as a basis for argument about more difficult cases. Whether this strategy succeeds, the reader will have to judge. It would be nice to think that it is possible always to be clear about what we ought to do, and at least some writers would want to say that there is a general 'bright line' between what is ethical and what is not (Kiss, 2006). But there are examples to show that many statements about what we ought to do, and about what is the wrong thing to do, are more complex and difficult than we might like.

Consider the case of conscientious action, for example, which we shall come to again in Chapter 8. In general, we might want to say that people ought to act conscientiously, that is, in accordance with what their conscience dictates. However, their conscience might differ from ours on a range of issues. We may see things differently, or evaluate risk differently. Should I have my pet dog put to sleep, because she has a cancerous growth that is causing her distress? You may believe I ought to. But I think that at present still she has enough enjoyment from her little doggy life to outweigh the discomfort she suffers. That is my conscientious belief, and if you think I ought to act in accordance with my conscience then you think that I ought to have her put to sleep, because of her distress, but you also think that I ought to do what I think is right. The problem is not a merely academic paradox: you may feel genuine unease because you can see things from both points of view.

Or suppose that I invest money for you, and take reasonable care to ensure that the company I invest in is sound, with good prospects of providing you with a satisfactory return. The company fails, for reasons that with hindsight can be understood – say, unforeseen competitors emerged from abroad – but that I could not reasonably have anticipated. Did I do the wrong thing? In one way, yes. In another, no.

In that sort of case we may distinguish 'subjective' from 'objective' rightness.[3] For some purposes, we may wish to focus on subjective rightness; for others, on objective rightness. It seems as though the extent to which we can reasonably praise and blame people depends on what information they had at the time they acted. It is possible that we might blame them for not having obtained as much information as they ought to have. That is a sense of the term 'reckless': if we are reckless, we have not done the reckoning we ought to have done. But if people have done what they reasonably could be expected to by way of obtaining relevant information, it does not seem as though they ought to be blamed if their actions go awry, even if we see more clearly as further information becomes available.

3 E.g. Jackson (1987: 92) and Brandt (1959: 360–67); this is partly the problem analysed by philosophers as the problem of internal vs external reasons: see e.g. Williams (1979).

Philosophers can deal with that problem by the simple device of avoiding the blanket terms 'right' and 'wrong', and instead considering whether actions are 'blameworthy', and in what follows I shall sometimes avail myself of that device. Here, though, the point shows different approaches we can take to ethical issues. One approach is quite plain: we want to decide what to do. The other is that we want to work out after actions have been performed whether they were ethical or not, because we want to work out whether the people who performed them are to be praised or blamed for what they did. More generally, we can distinguish between the standpoint of an agent who is trying to work out what to do, and the standpoint of an observer who is evaluating the agent's action.

So far, we have freely mingled these two standpoints, and they cannot be completely separated. On the one hand, in deciding what to do I may consider how different choices might be viewed by others. This is a well-established way to approach ethical problems.[4] On the other hand, in evaluating an action as observers, we often ought to consider how the choice presented itself to the agent. Because they are so intermingled, we shall continue to use both standpoints in our subsequent discussion, sometimes trying to decide what an agent ought to do by considering whether it would be blameworthy, or trying to decide how others ought to appraise it by considering how it presented itself to the agent.

Nevertheless, our primary interest will be the point of view of the individual agent who has to decide what to do. As well as sometimes setting aside questions of 'objective' rightness, this approach will also be different from the approach taken in some writing on applied ethics, which is concerned with systems of governance and accountability rather than individuals' decisions (e.g. Donaldson, 1982: ch. 3; Bovens, 1998: ch. 1). In later chapters, we shall sometimes be drawn towards questions about what organisational arrangements best support ethical decision making, but we shall not approach those as our primary concern.

In approaching ethical issues from the point of view of decision-making agents, we are concerned with problems of identification, rather than problems of compliance (Jackson, 1996: ch. 1): that is, we are concentrating on what ought to be done, not how to ensure that people do what ought to be done. We know that sometimes we let ourselves down, not doing what we know we ought to do. Sometimes, it seems like too much effort, sometimes we are greedy, or lustful, or prey to other shortcomings of character. Quite often, we fail in compassion, elevating our own concerns above others'. Those are

---

4 Thus the advice of St Ignatius Loyola: 'Let me picture and consider myself as standing in the presence of my judge on the last day, and reflect what decision in the present matter I would then wish to have made' (1951: 77). More recently, Treviño and Nelson have referred to the 'disclosure rule': 'It asks whether you would feel comfortable if your activities were disclosed in the light of day in a public forum like the *New York Times* or some other medium' (2007: 108).

real and important problems. We need to give them attention, to avoid or mitigate their effects, in ourselves and others. But they are not the problems this book is primarily concerned with. Our concern is primarily to identify what ethics actually requires, partly because confusion is a challenge in itself, but also because clarifying ethical demands will make it easier to comply with them.

Problems of identification arise partly because the principles identified in the previous section that guide us in ethical decision making may pull us in conflicting directions. Sometimes, moral requirements to be honest may not be fair to everyone involved, or produce the best consequences, for example. One of the merits attributed to utilitarianism by its proponents has been its potential to overcome such problems: Mill said 'difference of opinion on moral questions was not first introduced into the world by utilitarianism, while that doctrine does supply, if not always an easy, at all events a tangible and intelligible mode of deciding such differences' (1968: 19). However, there are some well-known problems that utilitarians have to put up with to get that benefit, and it may be that often we shall do best to accept that moral decision making confronts us with problems and tensions.

In fact, we may find that from time to time we shall inevitably be involved in what has come to be known as the 'problem of dirty hands'. The issue has been raised especially in regard to politics, as the idea that effective politicians have to get their hands dirty in order to achieve anything at all, the idea that 'the vocation of politics somehow rightly requires its practitioners to violate important moral standards which prevail outside politics' (Coady, 1991: 373).

The critical point about the problem of dirty hands is the idea that it is not just evil and unscrupulous politicians who may need to do bad things to achieve results, but even politicians who are motivated by good intent, acting not for reasons of self-aggrandisement but for worthy ideals and the ultimate benefit of others. The general problem is not one that confronts only politicians. The vexed and complex nature of life in politics can make the problem especially likely to occur there, but it is part of human life more generally. It may occur in any situation where we are caught in a conflict between different ethical demands. As Michael Stocker has noted, what creates the problem of dirty hands is that the best course of action requires 'a violation and a betrayal of a person, value, or principle' (1990: 18), and this can happen to any of us, in ordinary life. At the simplest level, perhaps I make a promise to you, and then discover that to keep it I shall have to disappoint a friend who expected me to meet him, or forsake some other commitment. Sometimes, such problems are of little weight, but sometimes they are very weighty indeed. In Chapter 6 we consider some of them in more detail.

The dirty hands problem highlights the fact that we can be faced with moral conflicts, and that is an uncomfortable fact. Often, the point about duty or obligation is that it overrides other considerations. When Nelson signalled 'England expects that every man will do his duty', the point is that we must put aside our inclinations and fears: this duty takes priority. At least, then, we know what to do, however hard it may be to summon up the determination and courage required. Terms like 'required' and 'must' go along with duty and obligation. One of the principles mentioned in the previous section is the 'moral discretion' principle, that in very many situations we have some discretion about what to do, so far as ethical requirements are concerned. When we are confronted with duties and obligations, then in some sense or other that discretion is taken away. Duty is an effective guide to decision, a moral signpost. When we are faced with conflicting duties, it is as though signposts give us opposing directions.

It has therefore been no small attraction of utilitarianism that it offers a way out of such dilemmas. It suggests that one only ever has one duty: to maximise utility. What is more, we can ascertain the duty by the familiar processes of measurement and comparison: first, we measure or calculate the utilities to be achieved through different possible actions, and then compare them, to determine our duty, which then we do.

This general approach to decision making is hypnotically attractive, because it is so often effective and successful. If you and I are in conflict about how many oxen I still owe you, the way forward is simple. Count how many I have brought to you, and subtract that number from the total I owe. If oxen are problematic, because of their varying size and health, calculate the debt in gold pieces, of standard size and weight. Measurement, counting and comparison can overcome problems of conflicting subjective judgment. Mill's 'tangible and intelligible mode of deciding such differences', they are very basic reasoning processes, and they can be very useful.

Nevertheless, such approaches to moral decision making have many problems.[5] Utilitarians and other consequentialists have sometimes disclaimed too great a penchant for a calculative approach to decision making: 'actuarialism', as Pettit has called it (1997: 99–102). Is there any other way for us to try to approach problematic cases of moral conflict? In Chapter 6 we shall look in more detail at some of the sorts of moral conflicts that arise in group contexts, and especially in organisations, where people's roles may create obligations for them that conflict with requirements of other roles they have, or with other moral requirements. In Chapter 8, I shall criticise some approaches like 'rational choice theory', which downplay the importance of reflection and dialogue about ethical problems. In the remainder of the present chapter, I note some general points about ethical decision making. Dealing with problems of moral conflict requires some overall understanding that there are approaches to reasoning and decision other than rule-based, step-by-step reasoning.

---

5   And often for other decision making, if carried too far: see Power (2004).

ETHICAL DECISION MAKING

Modern work in logic and cognitive processes suggests that much of our reasoning is a process of pattern recognition rather than rule following. For example, it seems that a good deal of our reasoning in many circumstances is based on 'prototypes' or 'exemplars', rather than on rules. Prototypes and exemplars in this sense are typical or important or salient examples that we compare with a present instance in determining how to classify it and how to act with regard to it.[6] Churchland has discussed the way in which our understanding and use of concepts surpass what can be embodied in the measurement-oriented, step-by-step reasoning that is reflected in statements of rules and definitions:

> Consider the humdrum category, 'Cat', for example. A reasonable commonsense definition of this category might go, 'Cat: a smallish, furry, four-legged predatory mammal with small, sharp teeth, a serpentine tail, a fondness for chasing mice, and a "meow"-like cry.' To be sure, a biologist could give a more penetrating definition, but that is here beside the point: children and ordinary folks neither know nor depend on a biologist's scientific definition. Human familiarity with cats antedates modern biology by thousands of years. But neither, it turns out, do we depend on any commonsense definition in order to recognise cats. A mute, three-legged feline amputee with a bobbed tail, dull teeth, and all the predatory instincts of a couch pillow will still be quickly and reliably identified as a cat by any normal person, even by a child. Plainly, our commonsense grasp of cathood must outstrip, and by some margin, the commonsense 'definition' at issue, if we can still make such identifications, effortlessly, in the face of outright violations of almost every one of its conditions.
> (Churchland, 1995: 144–45)

In fact, there is evidence that encouraging people to categorise things on the basis of clear, stated criteria before ranking them actually leads to worse choices than allowing use of this sort of unanalysed intuition (Lehrer, 2009: 141–45). We may indeed use rules in reasoning to some extent (Smith et al., 1992), but often good reasoning does not classify things by working out whether they conform to some definition or rule, and this is as true in ethical matters as elsewhere.[7]

This is not to say that it is wrong to use step-by-step reasoning that is based on the comparison of a current instance with a general rule, only that

---

6 Psychological theorists make a significant distinction between 'prototypes', which are ideal instances mentally constructed from experience, and 'exemplars', which are actual examples held in memory: see e.g. Moskowitz (2005: 164–65). However, for our purposes the essential point is the same.

7 Luban comments that 'deliberating-by-number bears precisely the same relation to genuine practical reasoning that painting-by-number bears to art' (1989: 136).

this is by no means the only sort of reasoning that is possible and common, and there is no presumption that moral conflicts have to be resolvable by step-by-step, rule-based reasoning. Often, it may be possible to arrive at similar conclusions by more than one mode of reasoning. Prototype-based reasoning involves comparison of the present instance with others in memory, looking for similarities, proceeding by pattern recognition, rather than comparison of the present instance one by one with others until an exact match is found. In ethics, rather than trying to work out whether the present situation falls under some moral rule – 'maximise utility', say, or 'treat everyone equally', or 'never tell lies' – we often compare it with other situations we have encountered, where we have an understanding of what was to be done.

Churchland points out the similarity between prototypes and legal precedents: cases that are subsequently used as a basis for deciding what is legally right and wrong in other instances (Churchland, 1995: 289). Taking Churchland's cue, we might expand on the similarities between legal and ethical reasoning. The significance of precedent varies from one jurisdiction to another, although it has some force almost everywhere (Cross and Harris, 1991: 3). In the English system and others based on it, there is an especially strong requirement to conform to precedent. The idea of a *ratio decidendi* is the idea of a rule on which a case was decided, which must be followed in later cases, and to that extent it seems as though legal decisions emerge from rule-based reasoning. However, even in the English system, 'the perception of relevant resemblances or distinctions between the previous case and the one before the court is largely dependent on the context', and 'the discovery of the *ratio decidendi* of the previous case is primarily a psychological problem' (Cross and Harris, 1991: 195). We can state rules, and try to ensure that there are rules that can be stated to explain a decision, but often the decision is not arrived at initially by deductive application of a rule. Once again, it seems to rely on recognition of a pattern-like similarity, rather than a routine, step-by-step process. Karyn Lai has suggested a similar approach as being dominant in the Confucian ethical tradition: 'Within the Confucian ethical tradition, validity in moral reasoning may include appeals to tradition and precedents, as well as consideration of contextual, personal and circumstantial factors' (Lai, 2006: 109–10).

Decision making based on pattern recognition is still a matter of research by cognitive scientists, but it is clear that development of expertise in many fields goes along with development of a greater variety and depth of mental patterns (Solso, 1995: 274–77; Klein, 1998). Developing such patterns is associated with 'intuition' as a form of cognition that may be different from step-by-step deliberation (Klein, 1998; Plessner et al., 2008; Lehrer, 2009). The idea of intuition is not a new one, but advocating it as the basis of ethical judgment is potentially hazardous. After being supported in philosophical ethics during the first half of the twentieth century, the idea of 'intuition' as a basis for ethical judgment fell into discredit (see e.g. Frankena, 1963: 86–87).

It seemed as though basing ethical judgments on intuition implied some esoteric mental faculty and some unexplained properties of events and actions that such a faculty somehow apprehended. However, these hazards are avoided by ideas of intuition in modern research. Those ideas have been taken forward by recent work in modern cognitive science, which has drawn together ideas from psychology, biology, computing and elsewhere to advance our understanding of decision making (see e.g. Clark, 2000 and references therein). One definition is that:

> Intuition is a process of thinking. The input to this process is mostly provided by knowledge stored in long-term memory that has been primarily acquired via associative learning. The input is processed automatically and without conscious awareness. The output of the process is a feeling that can serve as a basis for judgments and decisions.
> (Betsch, 2008: 4; see also Kahneman and Klein, 2009: 520; Lehrer, 2009)

Another way to put the point is to say that such intuition is a process of pattern recognition. Such patterns may not be well-defined categories with clear boundaries. They may be much more like the family resemblances referred to by Wittgenstein (Edelman, 1992: 234–35; see Wittgenstein, 1958: 32). However, the main point here is that through repeated exposure to a variety of examples we may develop ability to recognise patterns, without necessarily learning a rule of any traditional form, or acquiring any ability to measure and calculate.

Some modern literature on management decision making emphasises that good decisions are often arrived by intuition rather than calculation (e.g. Dane and Pratt, 2007; Sadler-Smith and Sparrow, 2008). In an ethical context, such intuition resembles Aristotle's ancient idea of *phronēsis*, translated sometimes as 'practical wisdom', sometimes as 'moral wisdom'. In modern times, the fact that good judgment is often pattern-based and intuitive has been developed in various areas. In social contexts, the patterns we learn to recognise have been described by sociologists like Erving Goffman (e.g. Goffman, 1971), who referred to such social patterns as 'scripts'. Social skill is partly a matter of learning to recognise such patterns. In Chapter 3, I shall argue that patterns like social scripts are fundamental in determining role-based obligations. In some other chapters I shall note specific social contexts in which intuition can help to explain how we come to good decisions. In Chapter 8, I shall try to add ideas about how moral intuition can be developed and improved in social contexts.

The general point is that good ethical decision making does not necessarily require us to identify moral rules that apply to every situation we encounter, which we can use as a basis for reasoning. We can proceed by recognising patterns, seeing ways in which current situations resemble others where we feel clear about what was right. Sometimes we shall see only one line of action that we perceive as obligatory, and then, to proceed in an ethical way, we act along that line. In other cases, we see conflicting obligations. Then we have to consider the various ways to act by comparison with other examples we understand better in ethical terms, and look for the way that fits best. Whatever we do, our course of action may involve regret or remorse, even though we may still be able to see that one course is better than another. Sometimes, we may be morally insensitive, if we do not feel some such emotion (Stocker, 1990: 115). Sometimes, we may reproach ourselves for ever having allowed ourselves to be drawn into such a situation, and later we shall consider the need to avoid such situations so far as possible, but there is no reason to believe that we can always avoid them, or that in them we have no way of making an ethical decision. In various ways, the complexity of our obligations in group situations leads to some great difficulties for ethical decision making. In our later discussion it will be important that we can make ethical decisions through recognition of patterns in events, even though we cannot calculate outcomes or articulate clear, precise rules.

The fact that we often make ethical decisions through pattern recognition does not mean that there is no place for moral principles. Even if we expect that often our ethical decisions have to be arrived at through processes of pattern recognition, rather than by routine application of moral rules, argument and dialogue are still important (see further Chapter 8 below). They allow us to improve the intuitive pattern recognition we have to use to make decisions in complex real situations. The principles mentioned in the previous section identify the sorts of considerations that are often likely to be relevant. Problems will occur only when we start to misuse them, treating them as intractable moral rules or using them for ratiocinative calculation. Then we shall face problems, especially in social situations:

> An exclusive focus on moral laws and rational principles is a threat to human well-being because it blinds us to the cultivation of moral imagination that is necessary if we are to be morally sensitive and fully responsible to other people.
>
> (Johnson, 1993: 5)

SUMMARY

This scene-setting chapter has identified the sorts of ethical principles that will be assumed in subsequent discussions of more specific issues to do with individuals' obligations in group contexts. They have included a variety of principles, both basic ones like beneficence and fairness, and secondary ones like the 'help and hindrance' principle. I gave some particular attention to the fact that others' expectations may create obligations for us, sometimes readily identifiable obligations to do with telling the truth or keeping promises, but sometimes other obligations less easily labelled. Finally, we have considered some issues about ethical decision making, including the sort of situation typified by the 'dirty hands' problem, where one faces a conflict between different moral requirements, and the idea that we can best account for moral choice in these and many other situations as a process of pattern recognition rather than step-by-step rule following.

The general picture that I draw in this chapter is of agents who are pressed by normative considerations, considerations to do with right and wrong, who can do better than just blindly accept the common standards or beliefs of those around them, through reflecting on the basic sorts of principles and considerations that are important to them and to others whom they respect, and coming to decisions not by a routine or mechanical process, but through a process of recognising what factors are important, and how they relate to one another, which is a kind of 'practical wisdom'. That is the widely accepted translation of Aristotle's term *phronēsis*, and it serves very well to conjure up what is required of agents who wish to act well in group contexts. In the following chapters the aim is not to set out guidelines to replace practical wisdom so much as to cast light on the logic of our obligations in such group contexts, in a way that may aid reflection and support the use of practical judgment.

2 Ethics, society and individuals

> If I had to choose between betraying my country and betraying my friend,
> I hope I should have the guts to betray my country.
>
> (Forster, 1965: 76)

In the first chapter I noted some generally accepted ethical principles. In sound ethical decision making, such principles figure as guidelines rather than as prescriptive rules. I have also noted that the present study is primarily focussed on ethical decision making, but this is often bound up with a second standpoint, when we evaluate actions as observers, partly to assign praise or blame.

Whether we are deciding on actions or evaluating them, the question arises how groups may figure along with individuals when we evaluate actions in terms of principles like beneficence or respect for persons. Is there some moral requirement on us to enhance the well-being of groups, as well as of individuals? Is there some requirement on us to respect groups, as well as respecting the individuals who make them up?

The conceptual relationship between groups and individuals is difficult and controversial. 'Society? There is no such thing!' said Margaret Thatcher, famously. 'There are individual men and women, and there are families' (quoted in Keay, 1987: 10). Like so many memorable comments, it has an air of paradox. Of course there is such a thing as society: it is made up of men, women, families and perhaps some other things. The point that Thatcher was aiming at may perhaps have been that there is no such thing as society over and above individuals and their families. If we eliminate the people, there is nothing left of the society: in some way or other, society consists of people. More especially, she was cautioning against a tendency to ascribe responsibility to society, to blame society for our ills and short-comings, and to decline to take responsibility as individuals for things we can do something about.

The rhetorical force of her statement is very strong, for indeed we have to agree that society is made up of people. But the moral and ethical implications of that fact are not straightforward. Many of us would agree that often we as individuals ought to accept responsibilities rather than push them aside on to some abstraction called 'society'. However, what that means in practice is not clear.

On an opposite tack, almost thirty years before Margaret Thatcher's interview with *Woman's Own*, John F. Kennedy said in his inaugural address 'ask not what your country can do for you – ask what you can do for your country'.[1] While Thatcher was aiming at the issue of to what extent society can be the source of benefit, Kennedy was enjoining his audience to turn away from that question to consider society – or country – as receiver of benefit. This view of one's country as worthy of support and benefit is tied to ideas of patriotism and loyalty, but like Thatcher's those ideas also arc contested, for example by E. M. Forster in the quotation at the beginning of the chapter.

Forster's emphatic statement lies at the heart of this discussion. How do our obligations to groups compare with our obligations to other individuals? Even stating the question is difficult. Is there a difference between having an obligation towards a group, and having obligations towards the individuals who make it up? In this chapter, that sort of question will be our primary focus, rather than the question of whether groups themselves have obligations and responsibilities. We will be looking here at the relationship of the individual agent to the group, rather than looking at ways in which groups themselves figure as agents. The two sorts of questions cannot be completely separated, but I shall try as much as possible to push aside most questions about group action. For the time being I shall also leave aside more complex questions about the creation of obligation for an individual by his or her membership in a group: for example, the ways that relationships within groups can affect personal responsibility. These issues will be dealt with in later chapters, but for now I will be focussing on questions about the extent to which we have obligations of beneficence, justice, respect and so on toward groups, as we do toward individuals.

There is novelty and value in this approach. Very often, when we evaluate actions from an ethical point of view, we consider things to do with people: their well-being, their expectations, what we have promised them, and so on. While it is appropriate to consider the well-being and expectations of individuals, it is not so clear that there is a separate place for consideration of the well-being or expectations of groups, whether they are small groups or large corporations or even whole communities. Is a group's welfare a consideration, separate from the welfare of the individuals in it? Do we have an obligation to keep faith with the group, separate from our obligation to keep faith with the individuals in it? This is the sort of issue that we attend to for the time being.

Such issues are potentially affected by the logical relationships that exist amongst individuals who are group members, and between the individuals

1   20 January 1961.

and the group itself. Early in this chapter, I note a basic but important point when considering the logic of individuals' relationships with one another: for purposes of ethical analysis, it is hard to say where a person's 'self' begins and ends. This point about individuals' ego boundaries leads us on to other points about how individuals may identify with one another and regard one another's welfare as their own, and this leads us to a discussion of the ways in which they may construct social identities for themselves. On the surface, this seems to involve some relationship between an individual and a group, but such a relationship is unlike personal relationships amongst individuals.

In the next chapter, we shall notice institutionalised role relationships as another different sort of relationship amongst individuals and groups, and examine those relationships more closely. The overall effect of the discussion in the present chapter and the next is to distinguish three different sorts of groups: 'common-bond' groups, which emerge from members' personal relationships with one another; 'common-identity' groups, where individuals share some social identity through categorising themselves as members of that group; and institutionalised groups, made up of individuals with inter-mingled roles. Distinguishing these three types of groups allows us to draw some immediate conclusions about the moral worth of some different sorts of group arrangements, and paves the way for further ethical analysis in later chapters.

INDIVIDUALS, GROUPS AND SOCIETY

The relationship between individuals and society has been a matter of analysis and debate in philosophy of social science, with some notable figures contending that sound explanations of social phenomena must be reducible to statements about things done or experienced by individual persons. This view, 'methodological individualism', is traceable to Max Weber (1968: 13), but has also been propounded by many others, most notably Karl Popper (1957; for comprehensive discussion see Udehn, 2001). To some extent, the position reflects a general approach to philosophy of science that was popular in part of the twentieth century: the 'reductionist' approach that sought to reduce explanations of phenomena at higher levels of complexity to lower levels, in the way that explanations of chemical phenomena were reducible to the physics of atoms and molecules, and the way that explanations of many biological phenomena were reducible to the chemistry of complex molecules like DNA.

By this reductive approach it was possible to show respect for Ockham's razor, interpreted as the principle that we ought to give explanations in the simplest possible terms. Through so doing we can eliminate assumptions about mysterious entities such as 'life force', 'chemical affinity' or the like. In the social sciences, methodological individualism opposes explanation in terms of 'historical forces', or 'civilisations', and contends that good explanations can only be found in terms of the myriad actions of separate individuals. Methodological individualism appeals to the same intuition as Margaret Thatcher does. Society does not exist over and above individual persons, and so how can good explanations refer to the idea of society, or other social entities like nations or civilisations?

'Methodological individualism' is linked with the idea of individualism more generally (Udehn, 2001: 336–45), which is important for us in regard to ethics, and which is the more general idea raised by both Kennedy and Thatcher. Individualism, according to the dictionary, is 'self-centred feeling or conduct, egoism; self-reliant individual action; social theory favouring free action of individuals'.[2] It raises a series of ethical questions. One, which we might label 'Thatcher's issue', concerns whether we can ascribe ethical responsibility to society and social groups, or if it should be attributed primarily or exclusively to 'self-reliant individual action'. Another, which we might label 'Kennedy's issue', is whether we have moral obligations to groups, contrary to our 'self-centred feeling or conduct'. We accept some obligations to other individuals. Do we also have separate obligations to society and social groups? How do our concerns for other individuals relate to our concerns for our country?

Methodological individualism is a theory about metaphysics, about what really exists, and about social explanation. From a view that societies and social groups consist of individual persons, it draws the idea that good social explanations have to be in terms of individual persons. So far as we can, we shall avoid the issues about explanation and metaphysics, but in ethics, from a view that societies and social groups consist of the individual persons, the idea may be drawn that good decisions have to aim at benefits to individuals, and that is an idea we do have to consider.

Most of us, certainly most of us in modern Western communities, will probably be quite comfortable with that idea in general terms. It reflects 'the ultimate moral principle of *the supreme and intrinsic value, or dignity, of the individual human being*' (Lukes, 1973: 45, italics in original). However, alternative conceptions are certainly to be found. If we go back in time, we find less emphasis on the significance of the individual. Morris has said that

> It is at once obvious that the Western view of the value of the individual owes a great deal to Christianity. A sense of individual identity and value is implicit in belief in a God who has called each man by name, who has sought him out as a shepherd seeks his lost sheep.
>
> (Morris, 1972: 10; cf. Lukes, 1973: 45–46)

Even during the modern history of Christian Europe, there has been change. There has been a move away from the feudal emphasis on individuals'

2 *The Concise Oxford Dictionary of Current English*, seventh edition.

interconnections through mutual allegiance and traditional roles (Bloch, 1965), perhaps associated with the Reformation's renewed emphasis on the relationship of the individual directly with God rather than through the mediation of the church community (Weber, 1930; Tawney, 1938). In our own time, across the world, there is not everywhere the same emphasis on individuals. For example,

> Because of the heavy influence of Confucianism, Chinese often view themselves as interdependent with the surrounding social context. The self in relation to the other becomes the focus of individual experience. This view of an interdependent self is in sharp contrast to the Western view of an independent self ... In a relation-centered world, social relations are accorded much greater significance. Relationships are often seen as ends in and of themselves rather than as means for realizing various individual goals.
>
> (Luo, 2000: 8)

To that extent, Margaret Thatcher's comment seems very much in keeping with the modern Western view of things, and sharply distinct from earlier views or those of other communities even today.

However, on reflection we may start to ask how clear the distinction really is. Is it not the case that even in our modern Western communities 'relationships are often seen as ends in and of themselves rather than as means for realizing various individual goals'? Suppose that you and I are friends. Is there not something mildly problematic in the idea that we should treat our friendship just as a means for realising our own separate individual goals, even in our modern Western eyes? Wouldn't that suggest that there was something artificial, or contrived, or inauthentic about it? Perhaps we may agree with Aristotle that there is such a thing as 'useful friendship' (Aristotle, 1934: VIII, iii), the sort of relationship based on the understanding that 'you scratch my back, and I'll scratch yours', but it seems likely that we shall also agree with him that this is not the only sort of friendship that there is, or that is worthwhile. Sometimes, friendship is based on mutual regard, where people are concerned about one another, as well as about themselves. In that sort of case, may not the relationship emerge as an end in itself?

It may be said that friendships based on mutual regard are still consistent with individualism. Friends may be concerned about one another, as well as about themselves, but the emphasis is still on their well-being as individuals. Is that correct?

It is not quite so clear-cut as that, at least. If you and I are friends, we may have regard for one another as well as for ourselves, and we may certainly seek to further the ends we have as individuals, one another's as well as our own, but that is not all. In all likelihood there will be things we do together, which we enjoy because we do them together, partly because they enhance our friendship: they draw us closer together, help us to understand one another better, and to relate more closely. In doing so, certainly, they may be good for us as individuals, but does that exhaust the story? Should we consider our friendship itself as something that is enhanced in a worthwhile way?

To some extent, the answer lies in considering how individuals may extend their sense of self. When the dictionary definition of individualism refers to 'self-centred feeling or conduct', it presupposes understanding of what is meant by 'self-centred', but what does that mean? There has been a good deal of critical writing about the idea that we are only ever motivated by self-interest (see e.g. Elster, 1989: ch. 6; Rachels, 1995: ch. 5; Schroeder et al., 1995: ch. 1; Frank, 2004: ch. 7), and the idea embodies a number of confusions and difficulties. For our purposes, the most significant difficulty is that it is not always clear where one's 'self' begins and ends.[3] Two or more friends might in some sense identify with one another, considering harm or benefit to the other as harm or benefit of their own. They may cease to distinguish their own interests from their friends' interests. But if they can identify with one another as individuals, can they also identify with themselves as a couple, or a group? In a more general form, this question leads us to fundamental issues for ethical analysis of groups, individuals and their relationships.

Ego boundaries

What is my 'self'? 'Some thirty inches from my nose the frontier of my Person goes', wrote W. H. Auden.[4] Certainly, I feel some proprietary rights over my 'personal space', and intruders in that space are to some extent intruding on my 'self'. Or again, consider parts of my body. Physically, my tooth is part of me. Presumably, it ceases to be so when it is extracted. What, then, if the dentist re-implants it? Does it become part of me again? At what moment?

Psychologically, what I conceive of as my self is even more complex. Scott Peck has given the case of a man who loves gardening, using the psychiatric term 'cathexis' to refer to the extent to which the man's ego, his self-concept, may go beyond his physical body:

> Despite the fact that the garden exists outside of him, through his cathexis it has also come to exist within him. His knowledge of it and the meaning it has for him are part of him, part of his identity, part of his history, part of his wisdom. By loving and cathecting his garden he has in quite a

---

3 Batson has commented that psychological study in the area 'begs for a better understanding of cognitive representation of the self-other relationship' (1998: 306). This issue can be distinguished from the questions considered by various authors about where one's self begins and ends in time (see especially Parfit, 1984). It is closer to questions about Singer's (1981) 'expanding circle' of altruistic concern, but distinguished by being the question of where the self ends and the other begins, rather than the question of what others the self may care about.

4 *Oxford Dictionary of Quotations*, from 'Prologue: The Birth of Architecture' (1966) postscript.

real way incorporated the garden within him, and by this incorporation his self has become enlarged and his ego boundaries extended.

(Peck, 1990: 100)

From some points of view, at least, it seems reasonable to say that this man suffers harm or benefit if his garden does. To that extent, issues of ethical significance go along with such extension of his ego boundaries (cf. Bok, 1984: 11–12).

What we conceive of as part of ourselves, the limits to what we conceive as self, are elastic, and can vary with a person's experience and development. If so, it is unsurprising that what we conceive of as benefiting or harming us is also elastic, and the idea of 'self-interest' is not firmly defined. Very often, it will be taken as including more than benefit to a single physical individual.[5]

We referred to friendship, and this may also be a case where individuals identify with one another and the boundaries start to break down between the welfare of one individual and the welfare of another. There are other sorts of relationships, like parent–child relationships, where individuals in some way merge their identities with others', in the sense that they do not themselves make a clear distinction between what is good or bad for them and what is good or bad for another, and as observers we cannot make a useful distinction either.

This is at least one way in which the idea breaks down that individuals are always motivated by self-interest. The fact that individuals can vary in the boundaries they conceive for their 'self' means that the idea that individuals are always motivated by self-interest ceases to be as significant as it may have seemed at first. If I identify your welfare as part of my own, and pursuing it then is pursuit of self-interest, then the idea that I am motivated by self-interest ceases to be distinguishable from the idea that I am motivated by regard for your welfare.

At present, though, the reason for being interested in the permeability of ego boundaries is its bearing on individualism. If we accept that individuals' sense of self is elastic and changeable, we also need to reconsider what may be meant by 'individualism'. In a family, it is possible that a parent may so strongly identify with a child that it is problematic to say that there are only the two separate individuals who are the bearers of moral value and the basis for ethical thought. If the child identifies her welfare with the parent's, and the parent identifies his welfare with the child's, how many distinct sets of interests do we have? Should we perhaps conceive the family as a separate and distinct entity, of moral worth in its own right, because of the ways in which the identities of its members may intermingle?

---

5 This can be seen in the notion of a conflict of interest, which can occur not only when an official stands to benefit by a decision, but also when a family member does (see also Chapter 6 below).

INDIVIDUALS, GROUPS AND RELATIONSHIPS

People can regard one another's interests as their own: we may say that they identify with one another. They may also see their relationships as important. We often think of friendships as two-person relationships, but they may be multi-person as well. Does a two-person or multi-person group of friends gain some importance in its own right, beyond the individual friends comprising it? We can phrase the point about importance in terms of interests: Does the group have interests of its own? Then, more generally, we may ask if groups have interests separate from the interests of their individual members. If they do, then we may ask a further question about whether individuals may regard these group interests as their own. In formulating the questions, we come to see complexities in ideas of self-interest and individualism.

We can separate at least two ideas in the notion of individualism. One is about people acting from self-interest, maximising satisfaction of their own individual interests rather than the interests of other individuals or the community in general. The other is tied to Kennedy's issue: opposing the sort of call he was making, it denies that countries or groups have claims on us in their own right. It is the idea that only the individuals in a community have interests, and the community does not have separate interests of its own. This second idea of individualism is tied to application of some of the ethical principles we identified in Chapter 1. The idea that only individuals are ultimately important implies that ultimately the principle of beneficence has to be applied in terms of harm or benefit to individuals, and that harm or benefit to groups or organisations do not have any weight over and above harm or benefit to individuals. Similarly for principles of justice, respect and so on. We might put this by saying that ultimately it is only individuals who are bearers of value, or ethical worth.[6] If this is so, then the other meaning we give individualism is that it is individual human beings rather than groups who are the bearers of value, and the basis for ethical demands. Even if in cases like friendship we find people concerned with welfare of a group of others, that is consistent with the possibility that only individuals in that group are important, either as agents or objects of action.

The extent to which we think that individual persons and not groups are the basic bearers of value may depend in part on what comes to mind as an alternative possibility. If, for example, we think of 'the state' as the alternative, we may shudder at the idea of a faceless bureaucracy subsuming the rights to individual choice and claiming moral worth independent of its citizens. We may be reminded of collectivism as seen in its worst excesses in Stalinist Russia, or fascism as seen in Hitler's Germany. Or we may even

6 We can set aside questions about the value or ethical worth of animals or natural objects: here, the issue is whether individuals are the only human objects of value, or whether human groups are also of value in their own right.

think of 'the economy' as we often hear it referred to in news programmes and government press releases, which tell us that some measure is necessary for the good of the economy, or that the economy is improving, like a patient who has received some stern medicine, and has now started to recover from some fearful sickness. In each case, we may think, we ought not lose sight of the individual beings who make up the state, or the experiences of individuals whose transactions make up the economy.

However, our thoughts in that case may be affected by the extent to which we are contrasting individual human beings, who have thoughts and feelings and intentions we can relate to, with distant impersonal abstractions. There are other possibilities we might contrast with individual human persons: families, for example. Margaret Thatcher said 'There are individual men and women, and there are families.' We might say the same sort of thing about families as about society, if we want to be consistent: 'There is no such things as a family; there are only individual men and women, and, perhaps, children.' If we want to say there are families, and give them some importance, why not also all kinds of other groups and associations, from the local tennis club, to society as a whole?

Families are more intimate and familiar, less threatening than 'the state', or even 'society'. Perhaps there will be something we can say about families that we cannot say about societies and states. To begin with, though, do families really give us an example of bearers of value that are somehow different from the individuals who make them up? We might want to say that a family is just the collection of individuals who make it up, like a pair of friends. But then why did Margaret Thatcher set families alongside men and women, in contrast with 'society'? Was it merely political rhetoric?

Clearly, in some ways a family is more than merely a collection of individuals. The details can vary a lot. There do not have to be two adults, or there can be more than two, with all kinds of relationships, from those of a conventional extended family to the multi-partner arrangements common in some societies. The children's relationships to the adults, and to one another, can also vary widely. But some such relationships there must be. Often, the relationships are so close that the individuals identify their own welfare with that of the others.

To that extent, the family group is constituted out of the individuals' relationships with one another. In addition, though, family members may develop a shared 'social identity'. These two cases correspond to social psychologists' distinction between 'common-bond' groups, on the one hand, and 'common-identity' groups, on the other (e.g. Prentice et al., 1994), and the distinction is important for ethical analysis. Each reflects a different sort of arrangement of individuals into a group. In what follows, I will consider that distinction further. Then, in the next chapter, I will turn to another sort of arrangement that will prove even more important for our subsequent discussion: the case where individuals have intermingled role relationships in an institutionalised group.

Personal relationships and common-bond groups

To begin with let us consider 'common-bond' groups, and the kinds of relationships that create them. They revolve around the sorts of personal relationships of regard and affection that are to be found amongst friends and often amongst members of a family.

The extent to which such personal relationships have a special importance in ethical deliberation has been the focus of increasing attention over the past twenty years or so. Since at least the late eighteenth century, the focus of Western ethics has been on making decisions in abstraction from the concrete individuality of the people involved. As we saw, Kant espoused the idea of 'respect for persons', but he considered that 'the good will' that lies at the heart of ethics must eschew any laws which are 'merely empirical' (Kant, 1964: ch. II, p. 76). The implication for Kant seems to have been that 'respect for persons' consists of respect for them as abstract, rational beings, not as specific concrete individuals whose personal identity makes a difference to what ethics requires and allows. From this perspective, duty is derived from universal reason, not from any accidents of an individual's own identity. Equally, for utilitarians who followed in Bentham's tradition, our duty is to achieve the greatest happiness for all; each person's happiness is to count with equal weight (see e.g. Sidgwick, 1907: 382, 385–86). It has been a problem for utilitarians to account for the feelings of special obligation we have to family members, friends and others with whom we have personal relationships. They have sought factors that justify feelings of special obligation, since, on their view, we ought to be quite impartial in counting the worth of different people's happiness.[7]

Questions about this approach have come from several different directions. One is the 'philosophy of care' that has grown up in nursing literature (e.g. Watson, 1988) and elsewhere (e.g. Noddings, 1984), and out of work done by Carol Gilligan on moral development, which suggested that women's moral development may not follow the same course as that identified by Lawrence Kohlberg in the studies he did on male subjects. His work found that higher levels of moral development oriented subjects toward abstract values and rights, and toward universal ethical principles (Kohlberg, 1976). Gilligan suggested that while boys' development increases differentiation of self, emphasising rules and fairness, girls' development rather accepts connectedness, emphasising relationships and responsibilities (Gilligan, 1982). Writers on the ideas of loyalty and friendship (Blum, 1980; Fletcher, 1993) have also suggested that specific individuals and concrete relationships with them may be ethically important in a way that escapes orthodox Western moral philosophy. The differences between Western and Eastern thought

---

7 For example, there may be obligations that stem from undertakings we have given to those close to us, or we may have better opportunities for enhancing their happiness: e.g. Sidgwick (1907: 257–59, 437).

have already been mentioned above, and ethical writers have turned increasing attention to their significance. For example, a number of authors have considered ethical implications of the Chinese concept of *guanxi*, the network of personal relationships that a Chinese individual may use to facilitate all kinds of business dealings and other arrangements (see e.g. Dunfee and Warren, 2001; Leung and Wong, 2001; Tan and Snell, 2002).

Many of these approaches highlight the kinds of relationships based on care and affection that are common amongst friends. When they hold amongst several people, the outcome of such relationships can be a group with some continuing existence, where the people who make it up see one another regularly, and meet to enjoy one another's company, engaging perhaps in some shared pursuits, like card games or fishing or other pastimes, but where it is important for them that they engage in the activities together, in one another's company. We can see them as a group, but they may or may not see themselves as a distinct group: what is most salient for them are the other individuals, and the things they share.

In this sort of 'common-bond' group we may see the sorts of relationships that some recent moral theory has emphasised. The logical issues that arise in the theory are complex (see e.g. Nagel, 1986; Stocker, 1987; Pettit, 1988; Scheffler, 1997), but it seems to be on quite firm ground in emphasising the moral significance of close personal relationships. The importance of personal relationships for individuals' well-being is documented in social psychology (e.g. Buunk, 2001). Such relationships are sources of happiness, but their importance goes further than that. Close relationships are 'the crucibles of inwardly generated identity', to use Charles Taylor's words (1991: 49), in the sense that a person's self-conception and self-understanding are shaped by recognition and responses received from others, and such recognition or responses have their greatest effects when the individual has intimate personal relationships with those others. Thus, for example, little Johnny may to some extent see himself as the boy who is most loved by Betty, but identifies Betty as the woman who specially loves him. Betty's own identity may grow partly from her relationships with Geoff and little John and Marsha. The individuals in such relationships are involved in reciprocal interaction that grows out of their entwined identities but also modifies them. Geoff tells little Marsha that she is just like Betty in some way or other, or that she can be happily assured of his own regard for her. The identities of the family members are both logically and causally entwined.

These are mutual, interdependent relationships, and this implication may take us beyond separate individuals as a foundation for ethics. It is simply not clear how we can account for requirements of principles like beneficence and respect only in terms of discrete, separate individuals. The character of close personal relationships may imply that we have to go beyond individuals in setting ethical analysis on a sound footing. Close personal relationships bind people together in groups: as groups of friends, as families and so on. It is possible that these 'common-bond' groups have some ethical importance in their own right, beyond the importance of the individuals who make them up. However, we need to contrast 'common-bond' groups with 'common-identity' groups, and the shared social identity that individuals may have that creates such a group.

Social identity and common-identity groups

Some friends may appear to outsiders as a group, but not think of themselves in that way, focussing attention on one another as individuals. But very often members of a group are conscious of themselves as a group. They may give themselves a collective nickname, they may establish regular meeting times and places, and so on. Whatever the details, to the extent that they conceive of themselves as members of a specific group, the group is to that extent not only a common-bond group, but a common-identity group: one where individuals share an identity as group members, which differentiates them from outsiders.

It is hard to overestimate the significance of identity groups and their dynamics for ethical discussion. The ideas of 'ingroup' and 'outgroup' nowadays are familiar to us all, and group rivalries are also well-known to us, many of them enormously problematic in the hostility and violence they generate.[8] In some cases, the reasons for conflict are clear, as groups compete for resources. However, it came as something of a surprise to researchers some years ago to discover that inter-group rivalry and hostility did not arise only from competition for scarce resources or from incompatible goals. In 'minimal group' studies they found clear tendencies for people to favour members of their own groups in matters of resource allocation, even when the 'group' in question was essentially a fictional construct, identified only by some minor difference in description. Forsyth has given a striking description of some of the early research by Tajfel and his colleagues:

> First, researchers randomly assign participants to one of two groups, although the participants themselves are told that the division is based on some irrelevant characteristic such as art preference. Next, the subjects read over a series of booklets asking them to decide how a certain amount of money is to be allocated to other participants in the experiment. The names of the individuals are not given in the booklets, but the subject can tell which group a person belongs to by looking at his or her code number. Tajfel calls the result a minimal group because (1) members of the same group never interact in a face-to-face situation, (2) the identities of in-group and out-group members remain unknown, and (3) no one

8 See, for example, Roger Brown (1986: ch. 15), 'Ethnocentrism and Hostility'. For some more recent discussion about ways that group-based social identity impacts on individuals, see Postmes and Jetten (2006).

gains personally by granting more or less money to any particular person. In essence, the groups are 'purely cognitive'; they exist only in the minds of the subjects themselves.

Tajfel's research revealed a systematic in-group bias even in this minimal-group situation. Participants did not know one another, they would not be working together in the future, and their membership in the so-called group had absolutely no personal or interpersonal implications. Yet the subjects not only awarded more money to members of their own group, but they seemed to try actively to keep money from members of the other group. Indeed, the in-group bias persisted even when the researcher went to great lengths to make it clear that assignment to a group was being done on a random basis and that giving money to the out-group would not cause any monetary loss for any in-group member.

(Forsyth, 1990: 396; see also Brown, 1988: 223–24)

The research is worth such a detailed account here because the result is so important to our study of individual behaviour within groups. In some ways it is related to material in the previous chapter about ethical decision making, and in particular the way that such decision making often involves processes of pattern recognition rather than rule-governed, step-by-step calculation. The way in which we categorise ourselves as members of one group rather than another may also be a process of pattern recognition. There are a number of mechanisms that seem to play a part in our tendency to favour members of our own group both in our evaluations and in our actions, but an especially significant set of ideas comes together in 'social identity theory'. This is tied to ideas about categorisation: we see ourselves as part of one group rather than another, and that then affects our evaluation of the group, including its merits and what its members deserve. Our tendency to believe that we and other members of our own group are better than others is 'a powerful means of establishing or maintaining an adequate "social" identity for group members' (Baron et al., 1992: 142), including enhanced self-esteem.

We all know that we tend to identify ourselves with groups, whether they be Bolton Wanderers supporters, citizens of our own country rather than another, as men rather than women, or vice versa, and so on. However, the fact that we can identify ourselves even with groups that are essentially fictional brings out most forcefully a question about the idea that we can extend our ego boundaries beyond ourselves as separate physical human creatures. It seems that as well as extending my sense of self to other family members and friends, I may be able to extend it to wider, abstract groups, most of whose other members I do not even know, and even to groups that have no substantial existence at all. In some ways, it is as though I extend my sense of self to a fictional character like Sherlock Holmes or Superman.

When we were considering the ethical importance of individuals as opposed to groups, it seemed as though we might want to take account of the fact that individuals can extend their sense of self beyond themselves as specific human creatures, to include others who are family members and friends. The personal relationships found in common-bond groups involve people intermingling their perceived interests and sense of self. Perhaps, as a result, we might want to consider a group like a family to be of separate worth, since it is the intermingling of separate individuals to an extent that could make it hard in some terms to separate one from another.

But now we have to ask whether all 'extensions of self' have genuine ethical implications. We may now have just seen some that do not. If individuals can extend their sense of self not only to their friends and family members, but beyond that to other Bolton Wanderers supporters or to compatriots whom they have never met, and even identify themselves with others who are members of a group that is essentially a fictional construct, then we begin to realise that such extensions of self are only of ethical relevance when they involve genuine personal relationships, as opposed to relationships that are essentially just cognitive constructs.

GROUPS, RELATIONSHIPS AND IDENTITY

If we look back at the case of family members' identification with one another, we can now see distinct sorts of cases. One is where individuals identify themselves and their welfare with others' in a mutual process of reciprocal interaction. Another is where people simply categorise themselves as linked with something beyond their own physical individual person, perhaps a garden, perhaps a stamp collection, perhaps another individual person, whether an acquaintance or a film star known only from afar, or perhaps an abstract group like Bolton Wanderers supporters. In this sort of case, an individual identifies with some object or group, but there is no reciprocal attachment or identification, and no back-and-forth interaction.

Whether there is back-and-forth interaction is important for a number of reasons. For example, it may confirm and deepen the perceptions and mutual understanding of those involved. As in the family processes of Betty and Geoff and John and Marsha, people's identities become both logically and causally entwined. Without mutual interactions, the significance of identification is doubtful, a point that emerges most clearly where the object of identification is essentially fictional or imaginary. Identification with fictional characters or groups can clearly be important in a number of respects; it can make people happy or sad, as they follow the fictional adventures and fortunes of the characters or groups, and it may prompt them to some actions rather than others. However, that does not imply that there is a genuine relationship that is important. The same is generally true of identification with abstract groups. Identifying myself as a Bolton Wanderers supporter, I am buoyed up by their victories and saddened by their defeats. However, my relationship with the abstract group of Bolton Wanderers supporters does not bear in any substantial way on my welfare or identity, and that abstract group itself has no moral call on my loyalty or commitment.

There is a strong tradition that sees individuals as contracting obligations equally through a wide variety of different sorts of relationships they have, from family relationships through relationships with friends and colleagues to relationships with other members of social groups like trade unions or nation-states (for references and discussion, see Scheffler, 1995: 224). However, there are ethically relevant differences between relationships we have with individuals like family members and friends, on the one hand, and relationships we have with other individuals we have never met who just happen to be members of the same abstract social group. The former sorts of relationships have an ethical importance that the latter do not, and so do the groups they make up.

Ethical principles that I identified in the previous chapter identify various factors that are relevant to ethical decision making, like beneficence, and fairness, and respect. We may consider how any of these factors is relevant when we are making a decision about a group of one sort or another. We might assess outcomes for a family, or a community of friends, in evaluating the outcomes; we might consider whether such families or communities were treated fairly, equally with others or in accordance with their merits; we might even consider there to be some obligation to respect such groups for their own sake, and not just as means to ends. If we consider factors like those, it is plausible to suggest that we should treat groups differently if they embody close personal relationships, compared with abstract identity groups. We can see reasons to take account of a face-to-face group, in regard to factors like those, which are more problematic in the case of an abstract group like Bolton Wanderers supporters, and very much more problematic in the case of a group that is a fictional construct.

It may still be true that members of an abstract identity group can have reason to value their membership of the group. It might be that one's self-perception as a member of the club, in company with others, gives one some sense of satisfaction (cf. Scheffler, 1997: 198). But so, too, might one gain some sense of satisfaction from fantasy and imagination. Such satisfaction does not have much to do with the reality of the relationship. On the other hand, when we have relationships with other known individuals, the reality of the relationship can be very important in determining what we think and feel.

Within and between face-to-face groups, it is possible to distinguish a number of separate dimensions that relationships may have, including their varying content, quality and patterning, the difference between reciprocal vs complementary relationships, the degrees of intimacy and commitment they involve, and others (Hinde, 1987: 34–39). By and large, these are characteristics of personal relationships that often pertain within face-to-face groups, and may pertain to relationships with such groups. This makes such relationships quite different from the relationship I have with an abstract social group that sustains my social identity. Most especially, such personal relationships can involve mutual awareness of one another as participants in the relationship. Such differences allow us to draw a line between close personal relationships and participation in an abstract social group.

Not all close personal relationships are mutual ones, of course. I may care for someone who for some reason or other is unable to respond: perhaps through illness or some other condition that inhibits awareness, understanding or emotion. But usually close relationships are mutual at least to the extent that each individual is aware of the other. Beyond that, each is often aware of the two of them as being aware of one another. Lovers, for example, often understand themselves as a couple, and think of the couple they are as having some worth in its own right. It is plausible to think that something similar can occur with families, also, and with friends, and perhaps also in other contexts, in sport and in business, wherever endeavours bring people close to one another in ways that involve them in processes of extended mutual response that includes a shared awareness of their relationship.

This is a major difference from the sort of way in which I may extend my sense of self to identify with a particular football club, or nation, or the like. The implication is a significant ethical difference between common-bond groups and common-identity groups. In the case of the latter, there is no necessary mutual relationship with others who are part of that group or association. The first is a process of interaction; the second a process of self-classification.

Common-bond groups, common-identity groups and individualism

The fact that we can distinguish these processes and groups does not mean they are always separated in practice. In many cases, a process of interaction will go together with a process of self-classification, and a common-bond group will at the same time be a common-identity group. There is more than one way for this to happen. Sometimes, a common-bond group may grow to be also a common-identity group. Sometimes, on the other hand, sharing an identification with an abstract group may provide a basis for individuals to form a common-bond group. Then the fact that they share a particular social identity provides a basis for them to establish or maintain interpersonal bonds, as compatriots abroad may strike up a relationship or part of some people's personal relationships may turn on our shared support for Bolton Wanderers. In a group where individuals share both personal relationships and a social identity, it may sometimes be one, sometimes the other that is the focus of their attention. Brown has noted evidence for a 'switching' process that might take us in a relatively discontinuous way from seeing ourselves as individuals to instead focussing on our social identity (Brown, 1988: 6, 226–28). It may need close study of a particular episode to see whether participants orient towards one another primarily on the basis of individual or group characteristics: 'most social situations will contain elements of both interpersonal and group behaviours' (Brown, 1988: 8).

Both sorts of things can occur within families. One can participate in close personal relationships with other family members, mutually aware of doing so, and simultaneously have an important social identity as a member of this family, the Johnson family, perhaps, or a Hatfield or a McCoy. One effect can be development of 'ingroup–outgroup' dynamics, where the social identity shared by members of a common-bond group sustains a sense of legitimacy and self-righteousness that is tied to a shared sense of superiority compared with others who are not members of this group. As noted above, the tendency to favour members of the same common-identity group is directly evidenced by research. Interpersonal bonds seem likely to strengthen it. The tendency to favour ingroup members may be further strengthened if the group has or gains the sort of institutional structure that we shall consider further below. Clearly, there are some ethical implications from what we know about ingroup favouritism: most obviously, we need to be aware of such factors if we are to act fairly towards others who may or may not be members of our own ingroup. Here, though, the main point is how the dual nature of many groups fits into our discussion of individualism.

In practice, in families and elsewhere, many common-bond groups are also common-identity groups, involving processes of group identification as well as interaction amongst members. Nevertheless, the major implications for individualism still revolve around the groups' character as common-bond groups, not as common-identity groups. It is the interaction involved in personal relationships that suggests that in some ways we need to go beyond individuals as a basis for ethics.

In regard to what is good and valuable, it may be that there are some situations where a couple or a group merit consideration as a couple or a group: not just as an aggregation of individuals. In choosing a wedding present for a couple, it would be misguided to buy one gift for the bride, another for the groom, and wrap them together as a gift for the couple. We seek things that will be appropriate for them as a couple, and will enter into their life as a couple. It may be banal enough: a toaster they will share at breakfast, or a pair of theatre tickets. But it would be gauche to offer them tickets in separated seats, because we have in mind not only the pleasure they will receive from seeing the show, but the pleasure they will receive from seeing it together, in one another's close company, responding to one another's reactions to it and feelings about it.

Equally, in regard to actions that are right or obligatory, there are situations where we have to make judgments about a couple or a group as a couple or a group. If my family seek permission from neighbours to cut down a tree on our boundary, the permission and corresponding right may be given to the family as a whole. If the neighbouring family have discussed the matter, or even if they just have customary family processes about how decisions are made, and all the members of the family have over time participated in the establishment of those processes, then it seems that they have an obligation as a family to abide by their word.

In these sorts of situations, and many others, we would have difficulty in trying to give an account of people's duties, rights and deserts without letting couples and groups figure in the account. To that extent, ethical analysis and judgment cannot be carried out solely in terms of individuals. What remains unclear for the present is how far the analysis in terms of groups and multiples of persons should be taken. The issue of 'collective responsibility' has been addressed by a number of writers, in a number of different contexts, from the Nazi Holocaust to mob violence and corporate social responsibility (see e.g. May, 1987; Bovens, 1998: 94–96; Kutz, 2000; Shaw, 2005: 152–67; Smiley, 2005). Some of the issues are very important in practice, such as the extent to which one can hold individuals responsible for atrocities committed in the name of their country, or hold directors or shareholders responsible for deaths of employees or consumers when they are victims of unsafe machines or products.

We shall come later to some aspects of those issues, so far as they bear on individual decision making. For now, we focus on the difference between cases like those of couples who are involved in close personal relationships, on the one hand, and cases where individuals identify with abstract collectives or institutions like football clubs or countries. The cases are intermingled in practice, but can be separated conceptually, and the distinction has significant implications. Even if we accept that it would be very difficult to conduct ethical appraisal and decision making without giving a significant place to couples and many small groups, it may still be that abstract groups like nations and societies and so on do not have the same ethical importance as groups whose members participate in personal relationships with one another.

One conclusion is that we cannot conduct ethical discussion solely in terms of individuals. Another conclusion is that abstract groups like nations and societies and so on do not necessarily have the same ethical importance as groups whose members participate in personal relationships with one another and have mutual awareness of themselves as doing so. In particular, they do not create moral calls on the basis of principles like beneficence and respect.

To the extent that individuals develop their sense of identity by reference to some abstract social group, their relationship with it may certainly have some ethical significance. It may enhance or detract from their self-understanding, it may make them happy or sad, it may prompt them to good or bad behaviour.[9] But in those respects such a relationship has no distinctive ethical significance, any more than reading a book may enhance or detract from my self-understanding, than drinking a glass of beer may make me happy or sad, than watching a movie may prompt me to good or bad behaviour. On the other hand, participation in personal relationships is both good for

---

9 In particular, such identification may prompt them to some actions that when performed in conjunction with the actions of others have some good or bad effects, and so may give room for some further analysis of collective responsibility: see e.g. Kutz (2000: ch. 3).

individuals and can make them into couples and groups that have ethical importance in their own right.

In thinking about individualism, and the possibility that people's involvement in groups may provide a different approach to ethics than an individualistic approach, common-bond groups and common-identity groups appear to provide two different alternatives. They are salient options in political terms, with discussion and debate occurring in social democratic parties about the extent to which it is better to seek improvement through centralised groups and organisations like large trade unions and government departments, rather than by devolving power and development initiatives to small-scale groups and associations based on local communities (e.g. Latham, 1998: 295–99). The former approach is explicitly opposed to Margaret Thatcher's political position (Latham, 1998: xxxii). From an ethical point of view, considering some of the ethical principles mentioned in the first chapter, forms of respect for persons may be more likely to find fulfilment in smaller groups like families and communities that embody 'face-to-face' relationships (Laslett, 1956).

Overall, I am arguing that individualism is too restrictive if it denies ethical status to common-bond groups, but correct in denying separate moral weight to common-identity groups. In so far as a country is a common-identity group, the argument supports Forster's emphasis on the importance of one's friend compared to one's country. I shall return to the point later in the book. So far, though, we have not considered a third case: institutionalised groups. Many large identity groups like countries and corporations are not just identity groups but complex arrangements of relationships and roles. Such large-scale, centralised organisations are often ethically important. Many beneficial outcomes can best be achieved through large-scale organisations that offer economies of scale and centralised concentration of resources, to improve economic results and material well-being. In terms of economic justice, it is also possible that focussed central attention to issues of equality and equity may do better than devolved activity that may give different outcomes to people in different areas or communities, or which might see different levels of commitment to principles of equity, or different interpretations of what they mean. All these sorts of achievements by large groups revolve around their institutionalisation. A football crowd is a large group, and it may share some feelings and attitudes that make it more than merely fictional, but it lacks the internal structure and role differentiation that allow organised groups to achieve complex outcomes. That internal structure and role differentiation is to be found in groups that are institutionalised, in ways considered in the next chapter.

SUMMARY

In this chapter we have seen some initial complexities in ethical analysis of individual obligations in group contexts. To begin with, we noticed Thatcher's issue, how far a collective like 'society' can be considered in separation from the individuals who make it up. That prompts us to consider the extent to which groups are like individuals in having interests or rights. This – Kennedy's issue – has been our main focus so far. We have approached both of the issues by considering the notion of individualism, and noting that it is a problem for individualism to say where individuals and their interests start or end. Individuals' interests and identities are established in relationships, and in relationships they begin to constitute groups. However, in thinking about how individuals come together to make groups, we can distinguish different types of groups. Some – common-bond groups – are held together by close personal relationships usually involving reciprocal interaction and linked individual identities. Others – common-identity groups – are constituted out of individuals' shared social identity but may involve no mutual acquaintanceship.

I have argued that we can see ways in which common-bond groups may have interests or rights that can impact on individuals' obligations, but it is harder to see how common-identity groups do so. An implication is that calls for loyalty to abstract identity groups like nation-states may have doubtful ethical force.

In the next chapter, we move to consider a third sort of group to set beside common-bond groups and common-identity groups: institutionalised groups, where individuals' mingled roles add a new dimension to ethical analysis, and further complexity to ethical appraisal or decision in concrete situations.

3   Individuals, expectations and groups

Individuals sometimes identify with one another in personal relationships that involve mutual awareness and response. Such relationships can be important goods for human beings, and such relationships also construct couples and small groups, which can play significant roles in ethical discussion and analysis. I have argued that the personal relationships embodied in these common-bond groups are not matched in their moral importance by the shared social identity that creates a common-identity group. A group that is defined by such a shared social identity does not seem in itself to have the same moral significance as a group that is constituted out of interactive personal relationships.

However, large, abstract groups can have an instrumental role in achieving many goods. Large corporations may be important because of the extent to which they effectively organise production, and thereby improve people's well-being. Nations and state institutions may be important because they facilitate production and defend their members against harm, and because they administer justice, both through courts and through taxation and welfare systems. Companies, nations, trade unions and many other institutionalised groups and organisations have significant parts to play in social life. If my argument is correct then common-bond groups may have inherent worth that calls for loyalty, in a way that an abstract identity group does not. But it may still be that large, organised groups have instrumental worth.

If so, what resulting obligations do we as individuals have towards large, organised groups? This is not an easy question. With any group, it can be hard to say how the obligations of individual members of the group are linked to the obligations and responsibilities of the group itself. If, as a family, we have given an undertaking to do something – visit the neighbours for afternoon tea, say – it is unclear where your individual obligations start and end. If you are unavoidably detained, the rest of us may meet the family obligation even in your absence. You seem obliged to do the best you can to join us, and to let us know when and why you cannot, but your obligations are not clearly defined.

The problem arises more forcefully when we are considering large, abstract groups. If we accept in principle that such groups may have obligations and responsibilities, it is even more problematic than in the case of small, common-bond groups to say how those group obligations are related to the obligations of individual group members. I want to suggest that we can approach this general question through the principle that we have obligations not to help others do bad things and may have obligations to help them do good things. If groups are agents and can be said to perform actions, then we have obligations not to help them do bad things, and may have obligations to help them do good things. That will apply just as much when we are members of the groups as it would otherwise.

INDIVIDUALS AND INSTITUTIONALISED GROUPS

Consider examples where a group like a corporation or a nation-state or a trade union is said to perform an action. We can say that a company ought not to do things that pollute the atmosphere, that rich nations ought to provide aid to poor nations, that unions should treat all their members equally, and so on. There certainly are links between actions of some individual members and actions of the groups. When a company officer orders chemicals to be dumped into a river, when a foreign minister signs an agreement to provide aid to another country, when a union secretary denies assistance to a group of members who are seeking it, these are cases where moral praise or blame may then be due to the company, the nation or the union on account of actions then attributed to the group.

However, some kind of ambiguity or fiction seems to be involved in these attributions. When we praise or blame a company on account of things that are done by its officers, nevertheless there may be members of the company, whether managers, employees, directors or shareholders, who do not approve of those things, who do not agree with their being done, and who do not themselves perform those actions in any overt way. The attribution is different from cases where saying something about a group says something about each of its members. If I mention to you that the Smith family drink beer rather than wine, the implication seems to be that the separate individuals do, but if I say that the firm of W. H. Smith have opened a new store in Slough, the attribution is not to all the separate individuals associated with the company W. H. Smith. It is about certain transactions entered into by some authorised company officers.

There has been extended debate regarding the extent to which corporations may reasonably be construed as agents, particularly in connection with the idea of 'corporate social responsibility'. The most prominent question has been whether corporations can be held morally responsible for actions. Tied to that issue are questions about the nature and extent of their duties, how such duties may be the subject of regulation, and what sanctions may appropriately be used against corporations (some prominent examples of the literature are Ladd, 1970, 1984; French, 1979, 1984, 1995; Donaldson, 1982; Pettit, 2007).

For some purposes, at least, it is widely accepted that groups may sometimes be said to perform actions when specific individuals do. In tort law, for example,

> there are some servants or agents of a corporation who can be treated as the 'directing mind and will of the corporation, the very ego and centre of the personality of the corporation', whose acts will be attributed to the corporation, not by way of vicarious liability, but on the footing that their acts are those of the company itself.
>
> (Atiyah, 1967: 382; quoting Lord Haldane in *Lennard's Carrying Co., Ltd. v. Asiatic Petroleum Co., Ltd.* [1915] AC 705, HL at 713; cf. May, 1987: 42)

An action by company officer Jones may constitute an action by the company, to which some ethical principles can be applied. But what makes it the case that Jones' action constitutes an action by the company? Typically, it is that other members of the company who are in a position to do so have given Jones some authorisation for such action. The authorisation might be specific, such as a resolution at a meeting, or it may be more general, like appointing Jones to that office, which has attached to it the rights and duties to perform actions of a certain sort. In either case, it has become part of Jones' role to carry out such actions. Then, when he acts in that role, we can say that the company does something.[1]

It is at this point that we see 'institutionalisation' of the group. Jones has acquired his role because it is part of the role of those other people to authorise Jones to carry out this role. This intermingling of roles is characteristic of an institutionalised group, as individuals with some roles have power to assign roles to others, who then themselves have power to assign further roles, and so on. Such institutionalisation allows legal evaluation in areas like tort law, and may allow us to attribute actions to groups for purposes of moral evaluation in a similar way. Through role assignments we can identify some individuals' actions as constituting actions by institutionalised groups, and it is in this way that we can apply to the groups many of the ethical principles we can apply to individuals.

However, even if we accept that corporations and other institutionalised groups can be moral agents with obligations and responsibilities, it is not immediately apparent what implications this has for individuals within those groups. Sometimes, there will be a person who can be treated as 'the very ego and centre of the personality of the corporation'. Then we might consider that individual to bear responsibility for actions of the group. Most often, though, that will still only be a convenient fiction. Often, at least, we shall need to look more carefully at the details of what occurs in order to work out where moral praise or blame are due. When Germany invaded Poland in 1939, we might say that Hitler was 'the very ego and centre of

---

1 In French's terms, we can identify the Corporation's Internal Decision Structure (1979: 211).

the personality' of the country, but moral responsibility is attributable more widely, from other senior members of the Nazi regime back perhaps to the world leaders who signed the Treaty of Versailles.

In many cases, it is not even easy to find a single prominent individual like Hitler who seems to be the central focus for attributions of responsibility. Here we owe to Dennis Thompson (1980) the phrase 'the many hands problem' as a shorthand way of describing the lack of a single accountable individual. Reminiscent of the problem of 'dirty hands', where an individual has clearly delineated obligations that are horribly in conflict with one another, the problem of 'many hands' occurs in organisations where it is hard to find any single individual who has clearly delineated responsibility for corporate behaviour. Thompson's concern is with public officials and government action, but the point is applicable more widely, to any context where the behaviour of an institutionalised group emerges from intermingled actions of various group members (Wolgast, 1992: 34–35; Bovens, 1998: ch. 4). Theoretically, the point is related to sociological debates about the weight that ought to be given to institutions rather than individuals in accounts of social life (see e.g. Homans, 1964; Goodin, 1996: 5–6). For practical ethics, the point is more concrete, as most of us know from experiences with 'faceless bureaucracy', as one member of an organisation after another points elsewhere to responsibility for an action or outcome.

Even when legal responsibility resides with a single individual such as the CEO, it is not necessarily clear where moral responsibility lies. Thompson has observed that it may sometimes be appropriate to hold a particular individual accountable for corporate action, 'but these considerations show only that strict liability in politics may be morally justifiable; they do not establish that such liability is equivalent to moral responsibility' (1980: 906). Again, however, the point is not just true of politics and government. For corporations and other institutionalised groups it may sometimes be appropriate to hold an individual strictly liable for corporate actions, as 'the directing mind and will of the corporation', but that does not establish moral responsibility. In considering the relationship between what individual members of groups and organisations do, and what those groups and organisations are held to do, we need to look more closely at relationships established amongst individuals who play intermingled roles. As we proceed, we shall see how role relationships have ethical implications for the individuals involved in them.

Relationships, roles and institutionalised groups

We have already noted that a family may both be a location for close personal relationships and a focus of social identity for family members. This distinction cuts across other ways of conceiving families. For example, Weber identified the difference between a family conceived as a household or domestic group, and the family conceived as a kinship group (Weber, 1968: 356–60). In most societies, families are also given some institutionalised status. Schaefer and Lamm have suggested that the family may be taken as a leading instance of a social institution (1995: 357–59), where the basic definitional requirement for social institutions is that they are 'organized patterns of beliefs and behavior' (Schaefer and Lamm, 1995: 130).[2]

It is this idea of organisation that is central for our purposes. It embodies most especially the idea of sorting people according to descriptions, roles and activities. So far as families go, relevant sorts of descriptions and roles include parent and child, with the more precise categories of father, mother, son and daughter, and then the further categories of husband, wife, or partner, brother and sister, and then, building on these, the still further categories of uncle, aunt, niece, nephew, brother-in-law, grandmother and so on. There may be others. For example, 'breadwinner' or 'paterfamilias' may figure in some social contexts, but those to do with kinship relations seem basic. The organised patterns of belief that use these categories involve both descriptive and normative elements. The descriptive beliefs include beliefs about conception and birth, but also other beliefs about adoption, marriage and divorce that probably also have normative elements. The normative beliefs can vary widely. They may include beliefs about monogamy, about responsibility for provision of food and resources and for domestic work, for care of other family members, and many others. These may be tied to other role categories like breadwinner and housekeeper.

In the present context, the picture is made more complex because such normative beliefs may also prescribe behaviour that is a natural part of the sorts of close personal relationships we considered in the previous chapter, which are especially characteristic of common-bond groups. Thus, for example, Barrett has noted that

> wherever men and women are organized in society we find that they must play a series of highly differentiated social roles, each of which makes different demands on behavior. This is as true of simpler societies as it is in our own Western culture. In tribal communities these roles are typically allocated according to an elaborate system of kinship, so that appropriate conduct is specified for each role relationship. The individual must behave in a carefully circumspect manner with a mother-in-law, for example, being unable to speak to her or even to meet face-to-face. With a particular aunt it is necessary to joke, snatch at her breasts, and be intentionally flippant. With another relative one must be cool and reserved.
>
> (Barrett, 1984: 172)

2 Schaefer and Lamm add as part of the definition that social institutions are 'centered on basic social needs', but it seems questionable whether that is a necessary part of the definition: for many purposes, the local stamp-collectors' club may be considered an institution, and if we want to contend that it must then cater for some such basic social need as a need for affiliation, it is hard to envisage cases that sustain organised patterns of beliefs and behaviour without being centred on basic social needs.

Barrett observes that one implication is the need for individuals to be sensitive to the different requirements made by roles in different circumstances, which is a point we shall return to. Here, what is significant is that such role-governed behaviour may clearly overlap with behaviour that is a spontaneous part of a personal relationship. Personal relationships tend to draw forth certain sorts of behaviour: smiles, backslapping, banter, sympathy in time of trouble, shared jokes that rely on special background knowledge, and many others. Some of these behaviours can also be prescribed as role requirements.

That point can be of ethical significance, because our moral evaluation of an action can be very much affected by the agent's motives (Stocker, 1976). The good things that we can find in close personal relationships may partly be tied to the spontaneity of the behaviour they call forth. In some way or other, relationships and actions seem less worthwhile, less fulfilling, less meaningful, if they are matters of duty rather than inclination. However, we are all familiar with circumstances where it is hard to say to what extent behaviour is spontaneous, as opposed to the dutiful fulfilment of a role requirement. A manager's sympathetic attention to a worker's problem, a parent's accompaniment of a child to a movie, a football player's pass to a team-mate, all these may be spontaneous and still be in fulfilment of role requirements. Quite often, role-prescribed duties coincide with spontaneous inclination. A corollary is that role relationships may coincide with personal relationships of the sort we have discussed as the basis for common-bond groups. It is therefore no surprise that institutionalised groups can also be common-bond groups, just as common-bond groups can also be common-identity groups.

Also unsurprising is that we can find a basis for some role-related obligations in personal relationships amongst role occupants. For our discussion, a key question is: Where do role requirements derive their genuine ethical force? As we examine the nature of role relationships, I shall argue that obligations emerge from role requirements largely because role-related obligations are tied to interpersonal expectations. There are many situations in which we have obligations to do what others expect us to. Certainly, we do not always have a duty to act as others expect, but I shall argue that on many occasions we do. In some such cases, our role-based obligations merge with obligations based on interpersonal relationships, and it is not easy to make a distinction between a motive to act out of a sense of obligation, and a motive to act out of concern for another's expectations.

ROLES, SCRIPTS, PREDICTION AND PRESCRIPTION

In 1986, Biddle wrote:

> Role theory poses an intriguing dilemma. On the one hand, the concept
> of *role* is one of the most popular ideas in the social sciences. At least
> 10% of all articles currently published in sociological journals use the

term role in a technical sense, chapters on role theory appear in authoritative reviews of social psychology, essay volumes on role theory appear regularly, endless applications of role ideas may be found in basic texts for sociology and social psychology, and role theory provides a perspective for discussing or studying many social issues. On the other hand, confusion and malintegration persist in role theory. Authors continue to differ over definitions for the role concept, over assumptions they make about roles, and over explanations for role phenomena. And formal derivations for role propositions have been hard to find.

(Biddle, 1986: 67–68, italics in original)

Since Biddle wrote there has been significant work done since (in particular, see Montgomery, 2000, 2005). Certainly, we still need to be careful how we use the idea of role. Nevertheless, the extent to which it is used reflects its importance. It is related to a series of issues that have great ethical significance, and any account of the ethics of institutionalised groups needs to consider how roles function in such groups.

As Biddle pointed out, the idea of role is drawn from theatre (1986: 68). Theorists have drawn on the analogy between social behaviour and theatre in a number of ways. The theorist who developed the notion most fully in the context of a dramaturgical metaphor was Erving Goffman, using the idea of a 'performance', and other such theatrical notions as 'backstage', 'in character' and so on (see e.g. Goffman, 1971). On the other hand, Goffman made relatively little use of another theatrical term, 'script', but this has become especially important in some social psychology discussion. Schank and Abelson used the term in their account of our mental processing of social processes:

> How do people organize all the knowledge they must have in order to understand? How do people know what behavior is appropriate for a particular situation? To put it more concretely, how do you know that, in a restaurant, the waitress will get you the food you ask for whereas if you ask her for a pair of shoes, or you ask her for food on a bus she will react as if you had done something odd?
>
> People know how to act appropriately because they have knowledge about the world they live in. What is the nature and form of that knowledge?
>
> (1977: 36)

The answer Schank and Abelson gave in regard to knowledge about social processes includes this suggestion that we organise our knowledge by the use of 'scripts' about social situations, where 'a script is a structure that describes appropriate sequences of events in a particular context'; it is 'a predetermined, stereotyped sequence of actions that defines a well-known situation' (1977: 41). They examined situational scripts where: '1) the situation is specified; 2) the several players have interlocking roles to follow, and 3) the players share an understanding of what is supposed to happen' (1977: 61). The restaurant script with customer and waitress is one example. The situation conjures up familiar scripts in the minds of the participants, with interlocking, complementary roles, and then 'the waitress typically does what the customer expects, and the customer typically does what the waitress expects' (1977: 61).

From one point of view, then, scripts are familiar descriptions or recognisable patterns of social behaviour. Thus, a script can also be referred to as an 'event schema' (Fiske and Taylor, 1991: 119; Moskowitz, 2005: 162), where we classify sequences of behaviour in the same way that we classify events that involve inanimate objects or the objects themselves. We may utilise schemas when we recognise animals or pieces of furniture, or thunderstorms or nesting birds. A schema is a way of seeing things that organises data into a pattern: 'a cognitive structure that represents knowledge about a concept or type of stimulus, including its attributes and the relations among those attributes' (Fiske and Taylor, 1991: 98). For example, there are 'person schemas', when we use our data about people to classify them as 'extroverted' or 'religious', and there are 'role schemas', which give us expectations about how a particular person is likely to act, whether the role be 'doctor', 'woman', 'customer', 'waitress' or the like. From this point of view, a script comes after the fact: it is used as a way of organising information for the purpose of classifying and understanding it. When we see the customer order, the waitress bring an entrée, then subsequently other courses, the customer pay, and leave a tip on the table, we can classify each part of the interactive behavioural sequence by using the familiar restaurant script. For our purposes, such schemas and scripts are like the prototypes and exemplars that were referred to in discussion of ethical decision making in Chapter 1. They are a basis for us to simplify our cognitive processing by recognising patterns and then respond accordingly.

However, scripts have not only a descriptive element but a prescriptive element that underlies the obligations that are often associated with role requirements. They help us understand episodes, as observers, and help guide us, as participants. Thus Moskowitz's comment that 'the preconditions for scripted behavior are the attachment of an action rule to a script; a context that will trigger the script; and a mental representation that can be triggered in memory, given the appropriate context' (2005: 163). The prescriptive element is the action rule, which guides us regarding what to do in a situation of this type. The descriptive element corresponds to the mental representation triggered in an observer's memory. The observer perceives the situation to fall under a particular description, such as 'waitress serving customer'. The observer recalls this description in association with a specific pattern of behaviour: as I watch the restaurant episode, I call on a script that I have stored in memory, which allows me to interpret and understand the actions performed by the people I see. In addition, though, the understanding of events in the restaurant includes appreciation of what is appropriate and inappropriate in that situation, and that knowledge of an 'action rule' is also the basis for decision-making processes used by participants in the process. For the waitress and customer, it prescribes a range of actions that are appropriate for the situation.

Thus, Moskowitz has referred to scripts as 'schemas that dictate specific ways of behaving for specific situations' (2005: 162). In the original theatrical context from which the idea of a 'role' is derived, a script might be something we read to assist following a play, but its primary function is to tell the actors what to do and say. Once more, of course, it refers to interactive sequences of behaviour, but the interaction is prescribed: when the actor playing Macbeth has spoken the line 'If we should fail?', then Lady Macbeth should speak the lines 'We fail! But screw your courage to the sticking-place, and we'll not fail.' If she does not, then she has failed in something that in some sense or other she ought to have done. This is true also for the situational scripts that apply in everyday social life. In a situation where a script prescribes certain behaviour, we contravene that prescriptive force if we act otherwise.

This distinction between the descriptive and prescriptive functions of scripts is important for us, because there are some implications for ethical analysis that revolve around such dual functions. The distinction, and the potential for it to be blurred, is noted by Biddle in his discussion of role theory. Referring to scripts for behaviour as 'expectations', he commented that 'whereas many role theorists assume that expectations are *norms* (i.e. prescriptive in nature), others assume them to be *beliefs* (referring to subjective probability)' (Biddle, 1986: 69, italics in original).[3]

The ambiguity carries over to the idea of role itself. On the one hand, we can use the term 'role' to refer to parts that people play, without an assumption that they are normatively required to play them, or to perform any specific behaviour as part of them. If I am fishing, for example, I may be seen to play the role of angler without assuming that I am normatively required to do so, or that my role as angler requires any specific prescribed behaviour. (There may be legal, normative requirements not to take undersized fish, or not to fish in certain reserved areas, but these are requirements on persons in general, not requirements that apply to me just as role requirements.) In this case, the role of angler is one that you may call to mind to help you more readily understand some of the things I do (and other things also, perhaps, such as the way I smell). On the other hand, the term 'role' can be used to emphasise parts that people play as a normative requirement, or to sequences of behaviour that they are normatively required to play once they have taken on the role. If I have accepted a role

---

3 Indeed, he also identified a third possibility, that the term 'expectations' could refer to 'preferences', but for the purposes of our discussion we do not at present need to distinguish preferences from normative prescriptions.

as a soccer referee, I have to make an effort to follow the course of play, and if a player commits a foul then I am normatively required to take some appropriate action.

In many cases, the dual functions of scripts, expectations and roles go together. At the simplest level, consider Nelson's signal, mentioned earlier: 'England expects that every man will do his duty.' In this there is the ambiguity we have been examining. In one sense, it expresses a normative requirement: if you do not do your duty, England will be disappointed, let down, displeased, and you will have failed to do something that you ought to do. In another sense, it expresses a confident prediction: England knows you, and your fitness for this task, and is assured that you will perform it. This ambiguity gives the signal its rhetorical force: exhortatory and supportive, both at the same time. The same combined force often pertains also to scripts and role descriptions, and gives them force that they could not attain without the dual meaning. In the restaurant, when the waitress gives a menu to the customer, the normative prescription of the script is that the customer should examine it and consider what to order. He will be subject to disapproval and potentially to some degree of sanction if he does otherwise. If he ignores the menu and continues to read a book, or if he tries to engage the waitress in extended conversation, the waitress is likely to interrupt in an effort to bring his attention to the menu, and if he persists in ignoring it then she will take further action: call the manager, perhaps. It is always possible that some circumstance might allow another script to be called into play: if an acquaintance arrives unexpectedly, we might see a 'greeting' script override the standard requirement of the restaurant script (see e.g. Schank and Abelson, 1977: 53–61). But if no such circumstances intervene to call up another script, then the expectations aroused by the standard script have peremptory impact.

So the script has normative force. But like scripts in general it also has predictive force. The waitress anticipates that the customer will read the menu and consider what to order, and organises her own activities on the basis of that assumption. She allows a certain amount of time for the customer to read the menu and consider it, and performs other tasks during that period, making a forecast both about how long the customer will take, and how long the other tasks will take. She goes to the kitchen, perhaps, knowing an order for the next table will probably be ready by now, and expecting that the time to get it and present it will take about the amount of time needed for a customer to reflect on the menu.

The normative force of the script is related to the predictive force, because the prediction enabled by the script is used as a basis for planning and decision by the waitress. If the customer has ignored the menu, then the waitress is inconvenienced when she returns and finds that the customer is not ready with an order. Instead of returning, she could have gone to a third table, to attend to another customer, and will now have to return here once more. To begin with, it is minor inconvenience, and waitresses are undoubtedly familiar with it. But it is inconvenience that will increase if the customer persists in ignoring the menu. It is at least enough to make the general point. Often, when we interpret events according to a known script, we make plans and decisions on the basis of the predictions it embodies about what others will do. More often than not, we are likely to suffer some cost if others depart from it. Often, the cost will be minor, but still enough to annoy us and elicit some unfavourable attitude toward them. Sometimes, the cost will be major: if a motorist fails to act as expected a serious accident can result.

That is one reason why scripts create obligations. In failing to adhere to them, we tend to inconvenience others and sometimes harm them. These can be important considerations, which draw moral force from the principle of beneficence. Sometimes, of course, they may clearly be outweighed by other factors. However, they are not the only reason why roles have prescriptive force. Another type of consideration adds to their force. The scripts we use to interpret events have an important role in allowing us to organise our understanding. When a script involves us as players, we derive some degree of self-understanding from participation in the script. This calls up all the points that philosophers and psychologists have made about the importance others have to our views of ourselves:

> In human society, at all its levels, persons confirm one another in a practical way, to some extent or other, in their personal qualities and capacities, and a society may be termed human in the measure to which its members confirm one another.
>
> (Buber, 1957: 101; cf. Laing, 1969: 98)

This can occur in a variety of ways: 'Confirmation could be through a responsive smile (visual), a handshake (tactile), an expression of sympathy (auditory)' (Laing, 1969: 99). A handshake has its function and significance as part of a common social script. A straightforward and innocuous gesture, it still figures importantly in our understanding of social situations we are engaged in. The point emerges vividly in the following passage from recollections by Milton Erickson, the noted hypnotist:

> When volunteers for a demonstration were requested, he came striding up and in a booming voice announced, 'Well, I'm going to show every-body that you can't hypnotize me.' As the man stepped up on the platform, the author slowly arose from his chair as if to greet him with a handshake. As the volunteer stretched forth his hand prepared to give the author another bone-crushing handshake, the author bent over and tied his own shoe strings slowly, elaborately and left the man standing helplessly with his arm outstretched. Bewildered, confused, completely taken aback at the author's nonpertinent behavior, at a total loss for something to do, the man was completely vulnerable to the first comprehensible communication *fitting to the situation* that was offered to him. As the

second shoe string was being tied, the author said, 'Just take a deep breath, sit down in that chair, close your eyes, and go deeply into a trance.'

(Erickson, 1967: 153, italics in original)

The effect of departing from a script will vary from case to case, but that example illustrates the potential depth of confusion that can result. Certainly, there are cases where we are justified in departing from a script. Erickson's may be one of them. In the restaurant case, a customer who persists in staring out the window rather than reading the menu will be forgiven when the waitress sees a carnival procession passing by. But without some such reason, the customer's behaviour has the potential to cause her discomfort and confusion, and other things being equal it also shows a lack of regard and respect for her. Scripts have normative force both because people plan their actions anticipating that others will conform to the script, and because their failure to do so has the potential to confuse and disorient observers and other participants in the scene.

Of course, it is not only normative considerations that motivate people to conform to scripts. People conform to scripts because doing so confirms not only others' understanding of the situation, but their own. In shaking hands with you, I confirm not only your perceptions of the situation, and your understanding of yourself as a civil participant in a friendly event, but my own similar understanding of myself. In many cases, such action will confirm my self-perceptions and my 'self-schemas' (Fiske and Taylor, 1991: 118; Moskowitz, 2005: 158–61). Self-schemas seem to be fundamental in cognitive processing (Rogers, 1981), and people act to confirm their self-perceptions (Swann and Ely, 1984). Recent literature has tended to focus on the fact that individuals' social identity is important in affecting their motivation and behaviour. Identity has come to be seen as emerging from roles people have (e.g. Golden-Biddle and Rao, 1997: 594; Weaver, 2006: 345–46), and ethical or unethical behaviour as being motivated by the emerging identity or identities (Treviño et al., 2006: 963). That sort of account is tied to views about primacy of some theoretical concepts rather than others: in particular, whether the concept of role or the concept of identity is theoretically more basic. Here, however, the point that matters is that if we accept that roles are associated with systems of interlocked social expectations, and that others' expectations are a comprehensible basis for moral obligations, then roles we have are tied to genuine obligations.

In short, roles and their associated scripts have dual predictive and prescriptive functions, which are interwoven. The predictive function sustains the prescriptive function because it creates others' expectations and understanding, and consequent disapproval if the expectations are not fulfilled. The prescriptive function then sustains the predictive function because both others' expectations and individuals' own self-understanding prompt them to conform to the role script. Most importantly, however, the role creates genuine obligations, because departure from the script may violate the principle of beneficence to the extent that it may harm or inconvenience others, and may violate principles of respect for others to the extent that it impairs their understanding of the world and their place in it. These obligations are not absolute: it is not very difficult to think of occasions where role obligations are outweighed by other considerations, but in the absence of other considerations they are important, genuine obligations. They emerge from some of the same basic ethical principles that are relevant to all our interactions with other people.

As a result of their dual predictive and prescriptive functions, it is not surprising that scripts and roles have major ethical significance. This is more salient as roles are intermingled with one another. In a stage play, scripts detail complementary lines and actions for different characters. Their roles are intermingled: each is effective and comprehensible only in the light of others. The same is true of roles in institutionalised groups. Roles are intermingled both in the way that individuals gain self-understanding from their complementary roles, and in the way that they plan their actions on the basis of what they expect of others. Within institutionalised groups like commercial organisations, government departments, and whole nations, people rely extensively on such expectations. Within a manufacturing organisation, failure of one person to purchase fuel for a forklift can result in another person being unable to move partly assembled items to the next production stage, resulting in a backup of other components being prepared for that stage, with further flow-on effects. In the wider community, we can imagine even more extensive ramifications of some people's failures to follow scripts, most obviously if they play roles in areas to do with communication and transport, but in many other areas also there will be multiple linked roles. Thomas noted that

> When persons facilitate the work of others there evolve expectations about how the others are to behave. More specifically, if a person facilitates another's role performance the other expects the first person to continue to be facilitative of his efforts, and not to hinder him. Because of these expectations, there arise forces upon persons to be responsible to others in order that the others experience minimal hindrance.
>
> (1960: 452)

These 'forces' are of course the same sorts of pressures as there are on us more generally to comply with social scripts: the likelihood of disapproval and sanctions. There will be strong prescriptions requiring conformity to the relevant scripts, often backed not only by social but also by legal sanctions.

INSTITUTIONALISED GROUPS, ETHICS AND INDIVIDUALS

Such intermingling of roles lies at the heart of institutionalised groups. The term 'institution' has a variety of uses, as shown in Marx's joke: 'Marriage is a great institution, but who wants to live in an institution?'[4] Whether or not it is a good joke, it shows how 'institution' can both apply to a set of social arrangements like marriage, but can also be interpreted to refer to a building like a sanatorium. Jepperson has noted how 'institution' can be used to refer to marriage, wage labour, the handshake, presidency, the motel and voting, as well as other things (Jepperson, 1991: 144). For our purposes, we can accept that an institution 'represents a social order or pattern' (Jepperson, 1991: 145), and that it most importantly 'reveals a particular reproduction process' (ibid.). Goodin has referred to institutions as 'organized patterns of socially constructed norms and roles, and socially prescribed behaviors expected of occupants of those roles, which are created and re-created over time' (Goodin, 1996: 19). Jepperson says that 'all institutions are frameworks of programs or rules establishing identities and activity scripts for such identities' (Jepperson, 1991: 146). To that extent they embody the sorts of script-based processes of prediction and prescription that we have discussed in the previous section, but the term 'institution' also has at least some connotation that the set of intermingled scripts and roles embodied in the institution is self-sustaining and self-reproducing. Thus, for example, commercial organisations include roles and scripts that not only prescribe that some members of the organisation recruit others, but also that some members – managers – articulate, develop and refine roles and scripts for themselves and others within the organisation. The implication is not that an institution is self-sufficient in all respects, but that subject to various constraints and greater or lesser influences from outside, it does reproduce the scripts and roles that give it its existence.

The institutionalisation of abstract groups like commercial organisations, government departments and nation-states means that they have continuity through time, and allocation of role responsibilities to specific members. It is this continuity and allocation of roles to individuals that means that we can attribute actions to the groups on the basis of actions being performed by group members with appropriately allocated responsibilities. When a president signs a declaration of war, a company purchasing officer a contract to buy a shipment of goods, or an official of a government department an order to provide welfare benefits to a specific family, the action can be taken as an action by the nation, the firm or the government. We can then evaluate those actions in terms of the same sorts of ethical principles we apply to individuals: the declaration of war may be justified as an act of self-defence, the purchase of goods an act that fulfils an earlier promise, or the provision of welfare benefits a fair way of compensating a family for disadvantage.

It is therefore very misleading to say that 'there is no such thing as society'. Society includes a variety of institutionalised bodies like government departments, welfare groups, commercial firms, trade unions and many

4 Groucho, not Karl.

others. The powerful effects of role prescriptions within them allow them to deal with large, complex issues. They can indeed have responsibilities for welfare, and multifarious other responsibilities also. Equally, if they can perform actions that create entitlements, then individuals or other groups can have obligations toward them. For example, if they offer services for payment, then *ceteris paribus*, those who receive the services have obligations to make such payment.

Our acceptance that some kinds of groups have both ethical rights and attendant responsibilities still leaves us with the question to answer: How does the application of ethical principles to institutionalised groups bear on the obligations of individuals within those groups? The fact that an action is performed by an institutionalised group certainly does not imply that it is performed by all individual members of the group, or that they have the same obligations that the group has. If a company buys a ton of wheat from a farmer, that certainly does not mean that the company's nightwatchman has bought a ton of wheat or has any obligation to pay for it. What is done by an institutionalised group may not be attributable as that specific action to any of the group's members. When a nation defaults on a loan, we cannot say that any individual has done so, not even the president.[5]

So far, it is as though we have created a parallel universe of activities by groups, to which we may apply ethical principles, as we may apply them in the universe of individuals, but it is not clear how applications of ethical principles in the universe of individuals relate to their application in the world of groups. We still need to consider how the ethical obligations to carry out role requirements are related to ethical assessment of the actions we attribute to institutionalised groups.

When Jones, the company officer, signs a cheque, he may do so because that is required of him as part of his role. Others expect him to carry out such an action in certain circumstances. In such circumstances, they may be disconcerted and disappointed if he does not do so, and *ceteris paribus* it would be wrong of him not to act as expected. But it is also true that Jones signing the cheque constitutes the company as paying a debt, and we can assess the action of the company in ethical terms. We may assume that it would be wrong for the company not to pay the debt, say because it has acquired goods to use in its operations, and now has to pay for them. So we can assess Jones' action as right, and the company action as right, and it appears that we are using the same general sorts of ethical principles.

Nevertheless, although the principles are similar, we are looking at two different sets of considerations in applying them. The expectations that his colleagues have of Jones are not the same as the reasons why the company ought to pay its debt. The company's debt accrues from things that it has done as a company. On the other hand, the fact that the company ought to

5 For more detailed analysis see in particular Jackson (1987).

pay its debt is one consideration Jones ought to take account of in signing the cheque, but it is not the only consideration. He also has to be aware that it has been properly drawn up, that it is within his delegated authority to sign, and so on. At the same time, others may have some responsibilities tied to the company action: seeing that funds are in place, that Jones' signature has been recorded at the bank, and so on. So, how does our evaluation of the company's obligation, and its meeting it, relate to our evaluation of behaviour by these various individuals?

We need to consider how institutionalised large groups function, to determine just how the application of such ethical principles to institutionalised groups bears on application of ethical principles to individual members of the groups. We cannot take the action of the whole and divide responsibility for it equally amongst the individuals in the institutionalised group, or attribute it wholly to each of them. Each individual involved in actions by institutionalised groups is subject to application of ethical principles in evaluation of their acts, but their individual acts are different from the acts performed by the group as a whole, and there is no immediate presumption that the same ethical principles apply in the same way to the individuals' actions as to the group they are associated with. Often, what will be at issue as far as individuals are concerned are the actions they have taken in authorising or certifying something that will then constitute the abstract group as having 'done something'. Thus, if a company pollutes a river with chemical waste, the actions by individuals that seem most clearly to be ethically important are the directions given to workers to tip the drums into the river, more than the workers' actions (the workers may not even know what is in the drums). But can we say more that that? Is there any clear basis for ethical evaluation of actions by other individuals who are members of the group?

A simple way forward is available here. In Chapter 1, I suggested that we may be praiseworthy or blameworthy through helping or hindering actions by others that are themselves praiseworthy or blameworthy. This may provide at least one sort of ethical link between the actions of individuals and the actions of groups, since individuals can help or hinder the actions of groups just as they can help or hinder those of other individuals. Just as with actions of other individuals, they may help or hinder them, encourage or discourage them, prevent them or allow them, and so on. If it is possible to apply ethical principles to institutionalised groups, one implication is that as individuals we have some moral responsibility to encourage and support morally good actions by such groups, and to discourage and restrain morally bad actions by such groups. That responsibility may apply to people generally, but be especially salient for group members.

So far as duties of beneficence are concerned, there is an obvious duty to encourage and support morally good actions by groups, and to discourage and restrain their morally bad actions. This seems straightforward. So far as institutionalised groups cause benefit or harm, we ought to facilitate or inhibit those outcomes, just because as individuals we have general obligations of goodwill towards others. However, there will be cases where not only beneficence but also other considerations like justice, honesty and fidelity may come into play. When a newspaper gives a false account about something, then (other things being equal) it is liable to blame for dishonesty, not just for the harm the story does. How are individuals' actions related to the actions of institutionalised groups in that kind of situation? If a newspaper publishes a false account of some event, then the maintenance technician on the printing press certainly does not have equal responsibility with journalists and sub-editors involved in preparation of the story. But it is not simple to apportion responsibility amongst the latter, either: Pamela, the sub-editor, may have assumed on the basis of his past work that Lee has checked his sources. Lee may not have seen the final version of the published story before it went to press. Chris, the new editor-in-chief, may have led staff to understand that circulation was more important than giving all sides of a story.

The situation seems to be rather similar to the question of what ethical responsibility people may have in regard to actions by other individuals they are associated with. There is a similar range of possibilities with regard to actions of groups. In some cases, even though I am an organisational member, I may know nothing of some actions the organisation takes. I may know, and approve, or disapprove, but have no hand in the action, and may or may not let my attitude be seen. I may encourage the action, facilitate it, or participate in it, and so on.

If the account given here is correct, then we see two dimensions of ethical evaluation that can be applied together in evaluating actions performed by individuals in organisations, in just the same way that they can be applied together in evaluating individuals' other actions in everyday life. One dimension is the obligation to avoid the inconvenience or harm to others that may be occasioned by failure to conform with role scripts, and the accompanying obligation to respect others' understanding of the social world that role scripts embody. The other dimension is the obligation we have not to assist in bad actions, and the possible obligation to assist in good actions. Just as these different sorts of ethical considerations might have to be weighed against one another in everyday life, so they may very often have to be weighed by individuals in organisations. It is true, as Hardin (1996) has pointed out, that there are difficulties to unravelling attributions of causal responsibility in complex social settings, but at least the complexities are ones we are familiar with in a variety of contexts, including attributions of responsibility in the law (Hart and Honoré, 1959). It is often hard to say how much responsibility an individual has for a group's action, but the difficulty starts to develop as soon as two or three people are gathered together. It is not a problem that is specific to institutionalised groups, or corporate actions. In Chapters 5 and 8, I shall say a little more about implications for moral decision making.

For practical purposes it is enough that as members of institutionalised groups individuals are subject at least to the same sorts of moral evaluation as they are in other contexts, and on the same sorts of grounds. These include the need to take account of others' expectations, having regard to principles of beneficence and respect, but they also include the need for people to consider the ethical character of organisational actions that are furthered or hindered by their own individual actions. This approach seems to be unexceptionable once we have accepted that it is possible to construe institutionalised groups as performing actions, and that such actions can be evaluated by reference to the same sorts of ethical principles as we use in assessing actions by individuals. If I assist you in charity work, or encourage you to publish false information about someone, then in considering what praise or blame I ought to receive, we may consider first the ethical merit or defect of your action, in terms of principles identified earlier, and then the nature of my assistance or encouragement. If we can first apply those ethical principles to actions of groups, we can then consider the nature of an individual's participation or contribution as a form of assistance or encouragement of the action performed by the group.

Just as with the actions of individuals, it is difficult to say how to regard people's approval for an action when they play no direct part in it (cf. Kutz, 2000: 187–89). This seems to be a very common occurrence when we attribute actions to institutionalised groups (Thompson, 1980: 907–8). Many individuals associated with the group may not play any direct role in the action, but may approve, or disapprove.[6] When my country invades Iraq, it may not only be the case that I did not do anything to support that action: I may actively have opposed it. When the firm you work for achieves a breakthrough in new medical technology, again you may not have supported the work, and indeed you may have opposed it. In terms of praise or blame, it is difficult to know what to say about the parts we have played. However, we have noted that this is also a difficulty for actions performed by individuals, and to that extent it is not a difficulty particular to the ethical relationship between the actions of individuals and of groups. Whatever we may want to say morally about people who approve another individual's action, without doing more to advance it, it is plausible to suggest that we may want to say something similar when they approve a group action, without doing more to advance it.[7]

SUMMARY

Overall, the account given here does not give simple, routine answers to questions about our social obligations in group contexts. Questions about

---

6 Aristotle distinguished the case of one who acts involuntarily, but with subsequent regret, from a similar case where the agent does not feel regret: Aristotle (1934: III, i, p. 123).
7 The general issues surrounding people's complicity in the actions of others have been analysed by Kutz (2000).

obligations in group contexts are no easier than questions about obligations in general. However, in this chapter I have aimed to provide a logical framework that makes sense of moral appraisal of actions by individuals who are members of institutionalised groups, relating those actions to actions of the groups themselves, but also taking into account the other pressures that create moral demands on individuals from their relationships with other individuals within the group. Others' expectations create moral demands on individuals, but so does the potential to further or hinder actions of the institutionalised group.

Thus, for example, we can modify and develop institutional structures in ways that make organisations themselves more or less likely to act in ethical ways. We can adjust the directions of commercial firms into courses that serve people or that harm them, we can modify their systems of internal governance to ensure that the actions we attribute to them are fairer or less fair, and so on. The situation is similar for all other institutionalised groups, whether they be nations, government departments or others. My focus in this book is primarily on individual decision making, but it is sometimes an ethical requirement on individuals in groups to press for different ethical directions by the groups of which they are members. As they do so, they may at the same time change the context in which other decisions are made by individuals, enhancing or reducing the chance of ethical decisions by those individuals also. Within institutionalised groups, pressures operate that can have important effects on people's actions, in ways that figure in moral evaluation. For example, in the next chapter I shall note conformity pressures that have important effects on individuals in groups. Through their actions, individuals within the groups can modify and develop organisational structures that change or moderate those effects. For example, Chapter 6 will note that we can devise corporate ethics programmes that support ethical action by individuals within organisations. The aim of this chapter has been to assist ourselves and others in what we do by first clarifying different sorts of ethical demands on us in institutionalised groups.

In the previous chapter I argued that we have obligations towards common-bond groups that we do not have towards common-identity groups. In this chapter I have modified that simple picture, as I have considered the nature of institutionalised groups. Institutionalised groups involve complex interlinked roles, and that is one key point that adds a new dimension to the obligations that individuals have in group contexts. Role requirements are generated by scripts that embody people's expectations about courses of action, and violating those expectations can generate inconvenience, harm and confusion, which may fly in the face of general moral requirements of beneficence and respect. Such requirements are not absolute. They are certainly important, but must be evaluated in circumstances that may involve other obligations also. In particular, it will be necessary for individual members of a group to consider how their actions bear on the actions of the group as a whole. If we accept that groups can perform actions that are subject to ethical evaluation, then individuals have obligations not to assist in bad actions by groups, and may have obligations to assist in good actions by groups, just as we have such obligations with regard to good or bad actions performed by other individuals. Obligations to assist or discourage group actions must be set alongside other obligations people have as group members, particularly those generated from role requirements; they should be neither subordinate to them in all cases nor over-ride them in all cases. They are no different in character from any other obligations of daily life that reflect the general moral principles discussed in Chapter 1.

The overall result is an account of obligations that individuals have in group contexts that shows how those obligations are not different in character from the other obligations of daily life, but at the same time shows how group contexts can give special prominence to some factors that generate obligations, such as the expectations that others have of us. In the next chapter I shall note some more details of such factors, and try to distinguish factors that have genuine obligatory force from others that tend to affect and motivate us even though it is questionable to what extent they generate real obligations. As I do so, we shall see that there are additional forces that combine with the tendency to align ourselves with common-identity groups that may confuse our understanding of obligations in group contexts.

4   Institutions, norms and ethics

Institutionalised groups are characterised by individuals' overlapping roles. Role requirements within institutions generate real obligations, but just as the allegiance we feel to common-identity groups may be out of proportion to any genuine obligations of loyalty that we have, so I shall argue that the obligations generated by role requirements of institutionalised groups may not be as great as the pressures we feel to conform to those requirements.

Our real obligations come from factors like others' expectations, and effects on group actions. This still leaves a significant task of ethical appraisal to be done in any concrete case, with various points to address. First, we must consider the extent to which an individual's action does in fact help or hinder some group action. Then, though, our overall ethical appraisal of the individual's action also has to take account of other factors in the situation, including obligations to other individuals, both group members and others. In practice, care and attention may be needed for us to discern what is right. It may assist us to identify some general factors that are often at work within groups, which may affect people's actions, and have a bearing on ethical appraisal of those actions, as well as suggesting ways to enhance and support ethical action both by individuals in groups and derivatively by the groups themselves.

We have already touched on some relevant factors. An especially notable one is our tendency to identify with groups of which we are members. Ingroup–outgroup dynamics then result, and sometimes shared personal relationships amongst members of such a group can strengthen our tendencies to favour ingroup members at the expense of outgroup members. When such a group is institutionalised, its dynamics may blend the three types of groups we have discussed. To the extent that a group is a common-identity group, research suggests that we tend to favour others who are members; if the group is a common-bond group, interpersonal relations amongst members move us by ties of personal loyalty; if the group is institutionalised, role prescriptions for members will generally require actions that sustain the continued existence of the group and favour its members over others.

The force and importance of such processes is clear, and well-known. They can be of great benefit, but have also had many appalling outcomes.

These processes are not confined to any time or place; they are common mechanisms of social life. But what we have said so far does not exhaust the processes that tend toward such problematic outcomes. This chapter looks at some others, and explores the way that such processes within groups can make it hard to distinguish ethical demands from other pressures. Some of the problems have arisen in stark form in documented cases of whistleblowers, where their exposure of unethical behaviour has been contested or opposed by organisational members. Later, in Chapter 8, I shall argue that stands of conscience that they and other individuals have taken in organisations illustrate some quite general points about ethical decision making and dialogue within organisations. In this chapter the emphasis is on distinguishing ethical demands from other pressures.

GROUPS AND CONFORMITY EFFECTS

Some of the pressures within groups are general pressures towards conformity. These do not especially revolve around the group's institutionalisation, but are important in institutionalised groups as in others. Consider Sherif's experiment on the autokinetic effect, for example:

> Sherif ... led individuals to a totally dark room and turned on a tiny bulb. This procedure creates the illusion that the stationary light is actually moving ... Sherif exposed people to a number of trials, each time asking subjects to indicate when the light began to move, when it stopped and how far it moved. Individuals were strongly influenced by the opinions of those around them. Indeed, Sherif was able to dramatically increase or decrease individuals' estimates of movement if he paid confederates to offer particularly large or small estimates. What was most impressive was that once people changed their estimates in response to group influence, they maintained similar estimates on subsequent judgments, even when they no longer were accompanied by group members. From this it would seem that people had truly changed their private perceptions about the amount of light movement they were seeing and were not simply going along with the group in order to avoid conflict.
> (Baron et al., 1992: 11–12; citing Sherif, 1936)

Other experiments have confirmed and extended the result. For example, experiments by Asch showed substantial conformity effects in the expressed judgments of people in group situations, at odds with their own perceptions (Baron et al., 1992: 64). Overall, 'conformity effects have been reported across such a wide range of judgements and subject groups that it represents one of the most substantiated and fundamental phenomena in social psychology' (Baron et al., 1992: 65). Possible explanations include individuals relying on others' judgment as a source of information, and their seeking others' approval and liking (Van Avermaet, 2001: 409). Various factors affect the degree of conformity people show (Levine, 1999).

This has implications for the design and governance of organisations and institutions. The idea of 'groupthink' has become well-known: 'a deterioration of mental efficiency, reality testing, and moral judgment that results from in-group pressures' (Janis, 1972: 9; see also Bovens, 1998: 128–30). There may be a combination of factors at work, including 'pressures on dissenters to conform to the consensus view', but also 'an illusion of unanimity and correctness' (Brown, 1988: 158). This can help explain the well-attested victimisation and intimidation of whistleblowers who have identified corrupt organisational practices (Glazer and Glazer, 1989; Provis et al., 1998). Rothschild and Miethe have commented that in many cases the responses appear to an observer to be 'out of proportion', and even to go to 'extraordinary lengths' (Rothschild and Miethe, 1994: 265, 261). If we are aware of these sorts of forces at work within institutionalised groups, we may counteract them by providing opportunities for dissent to be heard, and encouraging people to express alternative points of view. At the level of nation-states, which are large-scale institutionalised groups, liberal democracies aim to include such mechanisms in their institutional arrangements. One reason for doing so may be respect for individual liberty, but another is to guard against errors that are likely to occur as the result of conformity pressures on individuals (Benn and Peters, 1959: 218–20). Recommendations for governance of smaller-scale institutionalised groups like commercial organisations and government departments may also include encouraging diverse viewpoints, to guard against groupthink and the errors it leads to (Brown, 1988: 158–62; Lehrer, 2009: 216–18).

In institutionalised groups, however, pressures go beyond the general pressures for conformity, because of the presence of scripts and institutionalised roles. We noted in the previous chapter that scripts can have major effects on us. Others' failures to follow scripts can disconcert us and cause us both discomfort and inconvenience, so that we all are subject to disapproval and sanction if we fail to conform to established scripts without good reason. At the same time, acting consistently with our internalised scripts tends to confirm us in our own view of ourselves. The experiments by Sherif and by Asch alluded to above did not draw to any substantial extent on roles given to the experimental subjects, and largely avoided any script-based influences on the individuals. Some outstanding and well-known pieces of research in this area that do explicitly refer to roles are Stanley Milgram's experiments (see e.g. Milgram, 1974). Normal subjects showed an unforeseen and disconcerting willingness to inflict pain and harm on others when they believed that they were being instructed to do so by someone whom they perceived to have role-based authority. It may be that role-related conformity pressures go beyond other conformity pressures that are less clearly associated with role prescriptions. This is especially significant because of the omnipresence of roles in the lives most of us lead. It is possible that we often overestimate the extent to which individuals' behaviour results from their personal characteristics, and underestimate the extent to which it derives from roles they have, since, as Smith and Bond have pointed out, 'most mundane social behaviour occurs in the context of role enactments' (2003: 51).

For theoretical analysis, the normative force of roles is a major point. Ideally, the prescriptive force of role requirements should be placed, in some clearly defined way, within the context of ethical prescriptions, and distinguished from general ethical demands, which may have a far greater ethical weight. But as things presently stand, the same language is used in describing both role requirements and general ethical demands – terms like 'ought' and 'duty', for example – obscuring the distinction between the normative force of roles and general ethical requirements. This is not to say that role prescriptions correspond to no ethical obligations at all; as we saw in the previous chapter, role requirements do create genuine ethical demands, in so far as they shape others' expectations. But the demands of role prescriptions may go well beyond any genuine ethical force they have. For example, the role of a *mafioso* prescribes that he ought to do various things, but we would not agree that they are genuine moral demands, and indeed it is clear that actions prescribed by his role would be entirely contrary to generally agreed moral principles.

The fact that the language of roles is the language of duties and obligations, even though these may not be genuine ethical duties and obligations, makes it especially difficult to give a clear analysis of the ethical demands on members of organisations. Within an organisation, individuals have roles and duties associated with those roles. Because of the prescriptive force associated with social scripts, which we have discussed earlier, the pressures on individuals go along with the idea that in some way or other this is what they 'ought' to do. It is in this way that scripts and roles within an institutionalised group may be said to establish a 'local moral order' (Harré and van Langenhove, 1999: 1). Whether or not role prescriptions create genuine moral demands, their prescriptive force is often seen by participants as having the same weight as genuine moral obligations.

We need to separate the prescriptive force of local role requirements from genuine ethical demands, but that task requires careful analysis. The prescriptions at least present themselves in very similar ways to genuine moral demands, so that it may be misleading to suggest that 'when, and in so far as, individuals operate within institutional or hierarchical frameworks they are often less sensitive to ... internalised moral norms than they would be in their personal life' (Bovens, 1998: 126). The way that scripts and roles prescribe actions for people within such groups can give 'a picture of agency in which individuals create their own moral rules through the social interactions they experience with others' (Wolfe, 1989: 212). The difficulty may not be that people are less sensitive, but that they have difficulty in distinguishing genuine moral demands from other prescriptions. Shared scripts do have prescriptive force. Not only is there the likelihood of disapproval and sanction when we do not conform, there is in some way or other a degree of truth to the statement that this is what we 'ought' to do.

The fact that scripts and roles have prescriptive force leads to some intricate and difficult questions, which are key questions to address in considering the ethical implications of the social context of actions we perform as members of institutionalised social groups. If my role as an organisation member requires certain actions of me, then in one straightforward sense this is what I ought to do. However, it is possible for role prescriptions and other prescriptions of a 'local moral order' to run counter to genuine ethical demands. In considering this issue, we can start with the case where a role requirement would have me assist in ethically questionable conduct by an organisation.

INSTITUTIONS, LEGITIMACY AND NORMS

When another individual seeks support or assistance in a morally questionable act, there may be multiple considerations to take into account. If you ask me to help dump rubbish in a park, there are a number of factors that might be relevant, including the nature of my relationship with you (Are we friends, partners, mere acquaintances?), the significance of the act (What sort of rubbish is it? What will the effect be on the park, and on its other users?), and your reasons for wanting to dump the rubbish there (Why do you need to dispose of it? What other options do you have for doing so?). However, in the individual case it seems overwhelmingly likely that what I ought to do is at least try to discourage you, rather than assist you (cf. Cocking and Kennett, 2000).

How does this compare to the situation when I have a role within an organisation – an institutionalised group – that involves me assisting in activities of the organisation? There, to say I have that role is to say that there are scripts and role requirements that prescribe that I ought to do certain things, and in many cases those things will facilitate or support the organisation doing things. If those things are morally questionable, then my situation may differ in some quite significant ways from a case outside any organisation where another individual seeks assistance or support, because of the role prescriptions, and the extent to which these embody requirements of a 'local moral order'.

The accounts that Glazer and Glazer gave of many whistleblowers emphasise the extent to which they found themselves torn, for precisely this reason: they took seriously the prescriptive force of organisational role requirements, and found themselves having to weigh up those requirements against other normative requirements. They saw the organisational requirements as being in some sense legitimate, as having been in some way legitimised by their emergence from the role structures within the organisation (cf. Thompson, 1980: 913).

Several times, Glazer and Glazer noted that the conflict faced by the whistleblowers was between demands of their conscience and the requirements of the 'bureaucratic' organisation in which they were located. At one point, discussing the extent to which their whistleblowers were professionals, including scientists, lawyers, doctors, engineers and social workers, with commitments to the norms and values of their professions, the authors wrote:

> They had developed a strong commitment to upholding professional values that emphasize the significance of making decisions on the basis of their expertise and with primary responsibility to their constituents. When asked to subordinate these values to meet the requirements of the bureaucracy, many conjured up a 'red line,' a point they could not cross.
>
> (Glazer and Glazer, 1989: 69–70)

Later, they commented that 'the decision to challenge directly the authority of superiors is the most difficult one for an employee of a large bureaucratic organization to undertake' (1989: 79).

The emphasis on bureaucracy, and the conflict faced by members of bureaucratic organisations, echoes Weber's account of bureaucracy as an archetypal location of legitimate authority. Nowadays, the term 'bureaucracy' has predominantly negative connotations, linked to ideas of inflexibility and inefficiency (Albrow, 1970: 89–90; Hughes, 2003: 32), but Weber is known for his advocacy of bureaucracy as 'the purest type of exercise of legal authority' (Weber, 1947: 333). Such authority he saw as 'resting on a belief in the "legality" of patterns of normative rules and the right of those elevated to authority under such rules to issue commands' (Weber, 1947: 328). Weber's account of bureaucracy makes it a specific type of institutionalised group. The intermingled roles that go to make up an institutionalised group inevitably establish 'patterns of normative rules'. The rules are just whatever the roles require. Such patterns of rules may be found to some extent in any institutionalised group: that is entailed by the meaning of 'institutionalised'. Bureaucratisation adds extra emphasis to the hierarchy of authority, but does not create the normative element in organisational requirements. This emerges not from bureaucratisation but from institutionalisation. As soon as requirements on us are tied to some recognised role, there is some implication that we 'ought' to comply with them: that is the sense in which they have prescriptive force.

There are two problems: a practical, empirical problem, and a more abstract theoretical problem. The empirical problem is the increased psychological pressure on us to comply with the requirements. Glazer and Glazer referred to Milgram's accounts of the difficulties of rejecting authoritative instructions (Glazer and Glazer, 1989: 79–80; referring to Milgram, 1974: 10). The difficulty does not rely on full bureaucratisation. The involvement of the experimental subjects in Milgram's experiments did not constitute them as members of a bureaucracy, but did place them in substantial role relationships:

> By engaging in the experiment, the naive participants had unwittingly entered into a powerful role relationship between themselves (as the follower) and the experimenter (as the leader). The experimenter is perceived as the expert who has done this study many times and knows what he is doing while the participant is unfamiliar with the situation. Consistent with this view was the finding that obedience rates fell considerably when another participant was asked to play the role of experimenter or when the experimenter left the room and communicated with the naive participant over the telephone.
>
> (Martin and Hewstone, 2003: 350)

The effect was significant even though the experimenter's role authority was not supported within a bureaucratic context. The psychological pressures that whistleblowers have to contend with are magnified still further if it is. The problem is not confined to bureaucracies, or even to institutionalised groups. There may not even be a clear line between other pressures for social conformity and the pressure from scripts and roles (Martin and Hewstone, 2003; Nowak et al., 2003). Nevertheless, there are some especially important considerations about pressures from scripts and roles, and they loom especially large in contexts of bureaucratised authority.

To address that practical problem effectively, we also have to deal with the theoretical problem. If we want to develop ways of mitigating or opposing pressures that do not have moral weight, we have to say which pressures do and which do not have moral weight. This is the theoretical problem, the difficulty of distinguishing the prescriptive force of a 'local moral order' built out of institutional role requirements from genuine ethical demands (Wueste, 1994).

The idea of a local moral order can be developed as a set of local norms, which may or may not emerge from intermingled roles. That norms may be associated with intermingled roles seems clear:

> Rules develop in the course of a relationship, and many relationships emerge out of mutual role enactments which are bounded by roles and normative prescriptions generally accepted by all the actors. If one wishes to predict and understand the social behaviors occurring in that situation, one needs to know about its norms.
>
> (Smith and Bond, 2003: 55)

However, social psychologists may refer to group norms even in the absence of differentiated role descriptions (Brown, 1988: 52; Forsyth, 1990: 160–63; Baron et al., 1992: 11–12). According to this usage, Sherif's experiments on the autokinetic effect establish group norms, even though the individuals in the experiment do not constitute a recognisably institutionalised group. In this sense, the situation is the same with group norms as with pressures to conform with perceived role requirements: they are not confined to institutionalised groups, but may be especially salient there.

In groups generally, a major reason for the development of norms is that this 'reflects the development of group standards that serve as frames of reference for behaviors and perceptions': 'A group facing an ambiguous problem or situation lacks internal consensus, but members soon structure their experiences until they conform to a standard accepted by the group' (Forsyth, 1990: 161; citing Sherif, 1936, 1966; Sherif, 1976). We can see various explanations of how group norms may develop, and this explanation perhaps refers to one of the most basic, 'to reduce uncertainty and confusion when the environment seems unpredictable, unusual or threatening' (Baron et al., 1992: 12).

That explanation shades into a slightly different one, the explanation of norm emergence that refers to the function of norms in solving coordination problems (Nowak et al., 2003). A simple and familiar example is which side of the road to drive on. It does not matter very much whether we all drive on the left or on the right, but it is quite important that all of us within a single community drive on the same side of the road. Once we have a rule of driving on the left, it contains a positive feedback loop that helps the rule sustain itself: I drive on the left not just because it is the traditional thing to do, but because I know that other drivers will do so, and I must do likewise to avoid a collision. People's expecting one another to drive on the left causes them to do so, and their doing so sustains the expectation that they will do so. Although there are legal rules that prescribe driving on the left, those rules are neither necessary nor sufficient for me to do so. The need to avoid a collision is the key factor in my behaviour. Driving on the left is the use of a convention to solve a 'coordination problem', the sort of problem that arises whenever different people have to coordinate their actions to achieve some mutually desired result.[1]

Many such regularities are taken for granted and only dimly noticed. They may have to do with language and other forms of symbolic communication. A hand movement could have some intrinsic significance, like a blow, but gestures are often of no intrinsic significance. They have their significance because people use them to convey certain intentions or feelings. Because people do use them to convey such intentions or feelings, they are interpreted as intending to convey such intentions or feelings, and because they are interpreted in that way, people continue to use the gestures to convey those intentions and feelings (see e.g. Schiffer, 1972). Other examples

---

1 For a seminal study, see Lewis (1969). Bicchieri (2006) has contrasted conventions with norms, but also notes that the distinction is blurred (p. 38), and for our purposes we do not need to emphasise it.

come to mind quite easily. For example, in some cultures a certain impression is conveyed by wearing a suit and tie, but in other cultures such an impression may be conveyed in different ways. In either case, it is a matter of convention how the impression is conveyed.

These norms embody regular ways of perceiving and behaving, for people in the group, but the implication of referring to them as norms is that they are not just regularities: they have prescriptive as well as predictive force. Like role requirements they can be stated by saying that in some sense or other this is what people ought to do.[2] Within a particular group, they may include matters like dress and hairstyle (see e.g. Brown, 1988: 42). However, it is hard to see how norms to do with bodily adornment or hairstyle and the like have any genuine moral force. In cases like Milgram's experiments, or some dilemmas faced by whistleblowers, it seems as though what a role prescribes that I ought to do runs counter to genuine ethical requirements. In cases like hairstyle or earrings or top hats, it is not so much that the prescription of a group norm about what I ought to do runs counter to ethics: rather, it simply does not matter in ethical terms.

These points are not new. We have used the term 'local moral order' to refer to sets of prescriptive norms, but it could be replaced by John Austin's phrase 'positive morality':

> The name *morality*, when standing unqualified or alone, may signify the human laws, which I style positive morality, as considered without regard to their goodness or badness. For example, such laws of the class as are peculiar to a given age, or such laws of the class as are peculiar to a given nation, we style the *morality* of that given age or nation whether we think them good or deem them bad.
>
> (Austin, 1998: 96, italics in original)

We may speak of a 'local moral order', or of 'positive morality', without subscribing to it ourselves, but we still owe an account of what ethical force such norms may have, bearing in mind a range of possibilities from conventions about which side of the road to drive on to local norms about dress standards.

WHEN DO PRESCRIPTIONS HAVE ETHICAL FORCE?

Even if detached academic examination discerns no force to norms about bodily adornment, hairstyle and the like, there is no doubt that they can be influential. In that respect they resemble role requirements, as illustrated in

---

2 Norms that arise out of habitual behaviour may embody what Weber (1947: 341) characterised as 'traditional' authority.

Milgram's experiments. Both the empirical question and the conceptual issue loom large. Empirically, the influence of norms on people's behaviour can be just as substantial as the bureaucratic role requirements faced by conscientious whistleblowers, even if they are only to do with hairstyle and bodily adornment. Conceptually, both with role requirements and group norms, we have to ask when prescriptive force reflects a genuine ethical demand.

Ethical force vs institutional legitimacy

It might be suggested that this question can be posed as the question of what creates legitimacy, whether for authority in an institutionalised group, or for a norm in any group. Such questions arise in groups of all types. Within commercial organisations, Jackall noted, 'business cannot be conducted without formal authorization by appropriate authorities' (1988: 39). The question then arises: What is an appropriate authority? The idea of an 'appropriate authority' has been even more salient in the case of nations, where discussion and debate have proceeded for hundreds of years over the idea of 'legitimacy'. We can go back to seventeenth- and eighteenth-century conflicts, and even earlier, regarding what authority in a community was legitimate (for vivid illustration, see Thomson, 1974), and the issues have not abated, as shown by debates over civil disobedience and by differences of opinion about the rights of states to invade others in the name of a 'war on terror'. It is one face of Kennedy's issue, the question of what obligations of loyalty we have to institutionalised groups, which we noted to be a general form of the problem of political obligation. As modern technologies allow large organisations to gain greater hegemony over communication and information flows amongst their members, there is potential for greater and greater concentrations of power in the hands of dominant members of those organisations, but their maintenance of control still relies on perceptions amongst organisational members and others that they have a legitimate right to exercise authority and power within the organisation, and so the question of what actually makes such authority and power legitimate continues to be salient and important.

This general idea of legitimacy is at the root of questions about the extent to which actions by certain individuals within a group may be taken to be actions by the group itself, and so allow us to consider applying ethical principles to it. When a country's government is legitimate, the things done by its duly authorised officials count as things done by the country: incurring debts, entering into treaties and so on. 'Duly authorised officials' are those whose roles have been allocated to them by others with legitimate right to do so. The debate over sources of legitimacy reflects the fact that there can be different views about whether certain individuals do have such rights. For example, at various times there was debate over whether the monarch could authorise certain other individuals to collect taxes, or whether the consent of Parliament was necessary (Stone, 1972; Waley, 1975: 15). On other occasions, there were questions about whether the monarch could make appointments to bishoprics, or whether these could be made only by church authorities (Brooke, 1975: ch. 13). It is a general sort of question that has great importance in institutionalised groups.

However, it is possible to distinguish the question of what makes for legitimate authority within an institutionalised group from the question of when prescriptions have genuine ethical force. Certainly, the contested question within institutionalised groups, what authority is legitimate, often has had ethical overtones and implications. Once some authority or prescription is accepted as legitimate within a group, it becomes a source of great influence and power, and to say that some authority within the group is 'legitimate' authority is to say that within the group it is accepted as a basis for deciding what ought to be done: it is the basis for a 'local moral order'. Nevertheless, it is an error to equate prescriptions of legitimate authority within a group with prescriptions that necessarily have genuine ethical force. A concentration camp commandant may have had authority that was legitimate within the institutions of which he was a member, but it is still possible that that authority was morally repugnant and without any genuine ethical force (Wueste, 1994: 106, 109).

Ethical vs group prescription

We have noted two sorts of problems about role requirements and group norms: empirical ones associated with conformity pressures, and conceptual ones because of the need to separate prescriptions that do have ethical force from others that do not.

As noted above, the conceptual problem is difficult because we use the same language to refer to genuine ethical obligations and to institutional role prescriptions: terms like 'duty', 'ought' and so on. 'Legitimate' is another example of a term with dual usage. The term 'legitimate' could be construed as meaning 'legitimate in ultimate ethical terms', or could mean 'legitimate within such-and-such an institutionalised group'.[3] The word 'ought' can be used to refer to whatever is prescribed by local group norms, or to what accords with genuine moral demand. The distinction is blurred by the fact that the two forces of 'legitimate' or of 'ought' sometimes coincide: in those cases where what is prescribed by legitimate institutional authority is indeed what one morally ought to do. To try to avoid confusion that might derive just from terminology, we may speak of institutional authority as authority that is 'perceived as legitimate'. I do not mean to imply by this phrase 'perceived as legitimate' that it either is or is not legitimate in ultimate

---

3 And so, as Ladd said, 'actions are subject to two entirely different and, at times, incompatible standards' (1970: 501).

ethical terms. It simply denotes institutional legitimacy as a form of power that sometimes carries ethical legitimacy and sometimes does not.

One question then is how it may be that sometimes perceived legitimacy fails to have any genuine moral force when perceptions of legitimacy emerge from role scripts and from people's expectations, and if, as I have argued, others' expectations can create genuine obligations for us.

However, the answer to that question is fairly plain. While others' expectations can create obligations for us, they do not always do so. In particular, they do not do so when the expectations are that we shall do something that is clearly unethical. Obligations created by others' expectations may in part be created by inconvenience or harm or disappointment that others will suffer if we do not act as they expect, and may in part be created by the need to respect others' understanding and picture of the world. Neither of those sorts of factors seems to have any weight if others' expectations are that I shall do something that is clearly unethical, and it is not clear what other factors might then have any weight, either. The concentration camp commandant's claim to have legitimate authority over inmates is without any genuine moral force, because the perceptions of legitimacy on which the claim is based are tied to expectations that others will do things that are clearly immoral. The scripts that prescribe camp guards' compliance with the commandant's instructions about treatment of inmates may embody expectations about how people will act, but these expectations do not have moral weight.

Often, the distinction between institutional legitimacy and genuine ethical requirements is blurred by the fact that in establishing and maintaining institutions it is usually our deliberate intention to have prescriptions of organisational authority coincide with what ought to be done in genuine moral terms. It is blurred further by the fact that sometimes the prescriptions of legitimate authority will have genuine moral weight, but still be countered to some extent by other ethical considerations. An order given by a properly constituted institutional authority may tend to improve production of beneficial goods or services, but still confront opposed considerations of fairness or due process, for example.

It might be suggested that this is always true, that whenever we find ourselves confronted by normative requirements that are based on group standards or role requirements that contradict general ethical principles we have an instance of the 'dirty hands' problem discussed in Chapter 1. That problem, as we discussed it, occurs where people confront conflicting ethical demands: opposing requirements that each have genuine ethical force. However, in some of the cases we have been considering the normative requirements associated with group standards or role requirements do not have any significant ethical force. When we consider a role requirement that one should inflict unnecessary pain on others, as in Milgram's experiments, it is hard to see how the requirement could be a moral or ethical one at all.

In other cases, for example a group norm that prescribes that men should wear their hair cut short, as we have seen in various cultures at various times, a norm seems to have little ethical significance, but may have weight in some circumstances: it may be good for me to wear my hair cut short to avoid grieving my parents, for instance. It can often be the case that group standards gain some moral significance in such a way, just as gestures of no intrinsic significance may become important when people use them to convey intentions or feelings. But such standards do not have any inherent moral force, just as there is no inherent superiority to driving on the left or the right side of the road. The circumstances can give genuine moral force to such requirements: it is not just imprudent but morally wrong for me to drive on the left if to do so risks harming others. In this case, what gives moral force to the requirements is the principle that we ought to avoid doing harm to others. In another case, it might be proper for me to conform with the expectations others have of me, because they would be unfairly disadvantaged otherwise, and it would be a principle of fairness that gave moral force to the requirement.

Thus, the conceptual problem of separating prescriptions that do have ethical force from others that do not cannot be solved by any simple rule. In one way, the problem simply dissolves: there are no unique ethical demands on us within organisations. But dealing with the issue in practice requires moral sensitivity: an understanding of when others' expectations do or do not create obligations for us, and an awareness of circumstances that may give social norms some moral weight. In Chapter 8, I shall say a little more about the general need for developing such moral sensitivity. In the next section of this chapter, I turn to the more specific sort of situation that confronts us as members of institutionalised groups like corporations and other organisations.

Obeying orders

To begin with, nothing that has been said implies that there can be no moral force to 'formal authorisation by appropriate authorities'. If someone with duly constituted authority in an institutionalised group issues an instruction or gives an authorisation, that immediately creates widespread expectations amongst group members. Those expectations then form a basis for group members to arrange their own activities and then, quickly, the extensive, interlinked expectations amongst group members (shared, often, by others outside the group) create genuine obligations on group members. In a later chapter I shall look further at how such expectations create obligations for us, but the essential point is the one made already: failure to conform to others' expectations can lead to their harm and discomfiture.

Often, through that process, instructions or authorisations prompt actions that lead to worthwhile outcomes, whether they be improved efficiency, creation of new products or services by a corporation, rectification of injustice by a government department, or something else. To the extent that the final outcome of action by the institutionalised group will be a good one, individuals have obligations to help; in general, they will do so by carrying out the requirements of their roles.

Here, there is no need to explore the differences amongst different types of institutionalised groups. For instance, there is no need to enter into distinctions like those of Parsons between 'bureaucracies' and 'associations' (Knoke, 1990: 8). Enormous amounts have been written both about different types of social groups, and the importance of groups in achieving worthwhile outcomes (e.g. Sandler, 1992: 19). The differences amongst different forms of institutionalised groups are very important in understanding social arrangements, in developing social policy and in planning by government agencies and private sector corporations, but we have no need to explore the differences in detail. In various ways, the different sorts of groups have unquestioned importance for human welfare, but in general terms our obligations are similar. As group members, we have opportunities to assist with many good things. To that extent we often need to shape our actions to organisational policy, according to the instructions of other members whose role it is to guide that policy.

On the other hand, though, there are not many occasions where ethics might suggest blind obedience to orders. Perhaps there are some, where we can have reasonable faith that authority knows what it is doing, and there is no time or opportunity to look more closely. Most often, though, we need to attend to the whole situation we are in, open to possibilities that we can see other demands as well as official authority. We need, then, to evaluate all the demands that come on us, and the argument has been that, within institutionalised groups of all sorts, obligations are likely to fall upon us from three directions.

First, we always need to take into account such general moral principles as beneficence and respect for persons. As an organisational member I still have obligations to avoid harm to others and to care for them. Whether I am a casual passer-by, a building caretaker, a professional engineer engaged in consultancy work, or the company CEO, I still have some obligations of care to a child I see fall and hurt herself.

Second, we have obligations from others' expectations of us, especially expectations associated with roles we have as members of institutionalised groups, and including expectations generated by authoritative instructions. Underlying these obligations are the same general moral principles of beneficence, respect for persons and the like, but focussed by the salience that role requirements have for institutionalised groups, and the importance that social scripts have for us within these groups, both by allowing us to understand events and our own place within the group, and as a basis for our decisions and actions. As a professional engineer engaged in consultancy work, I have some other obligations that the casual passer-by does not have, when we see the child fall. Most often, that will pose no problem. In this situation, it probably has no implications: my other, professional obligations may have no effect on what I ought to do to help the child. However, in Chapter 6 we shall look more closely at cases where conflicts of obligations do arise as a result of role prescriptions.

Third, our membership of institutionalised groups means that we have obligations to assist the group to do good things and avoid doing bad things. The actions we perform as group members commonly assist performance of actions by the group as a whole. Not always: sometimes what I do may oppose the acts of the group, or it may be neither help nor hindrance. When I chase the cricket ball and prevent it reaching the boundary, the other team may still have scored four by their active running, and my action has neither helped nor hindered my team's quest for victory. But if I am batting and I score a vital run, or, on the other hand, I throw my wicket away, then on the one hand I have helped and on the other have hindered the team's pursuit of its aim. As a worker in a manufacturing enterprise, when I realise that a product has some potential to harm consumers, I may call attention to the problem, or conceal it. In the first case, I may have helped the firm to avoid the harm it might cause; in the second, I have hindered the firm from meeting its obligations to consumers. In the first case I have met and in the second I have failed to meet some of the obligations I have as an individual.

Once again, these obligations are founded on the same general moral principles, but as those apply to actions by the group as a whole, coupled with general principles about obligations we have to help good actions and oppose bad actions. Within organisations, my obligations as a group member often are especially salient, because the group is especially organised to coordinate individuals' actions towards group aims. The arrangement includes authority structures that shape people's expectations and actions for purposes of coordination in pursuit of those aims. By and large, I have obligations to comply with authoritative instructions because they shape others' expectations of me and create a situation where my compliance will contribute to worthwhile actions by the group as a whole.

However, on that account, my obligations are still based on the same general moral principles as all our other obligations. In particular, our organisational roles do not draw their ethical force from any different source than the other everyday obligations we have, and neither do authoritative instructions given to us as organisational members. The practical difficulty is that we are prone to be influenced by social conformity pressures and tendencies to accept authority perceived as legitimate, to an extent that outstrips the genuine obligations we have as organisational members. We often do have very extensive and substantial obligations, but sometimes we are carried away by these other pressures, partly because of our human psychological makeup and partly because of the difficulties there are in distinguishing real from counterfeit obligations. Milgram's experiments, for example, explained vividly how it was possible for ordinary German men and women to be drawn into the moral quagmire of Nazism.

We have some predisposition to obey duly constituted authority, and there is little need to emphasise that often we have obligations to do so. If we regularly do otherwise, people are confused, their plans in disarray and coordinated action almost impossible. There are also some situations where that is precisely what happens, both in whole communities like contemporary Somalia, and in some dysfunctional organisations, which quickly fade from sight. In these cases, the air of legitimacy has faded from duly constituted authority and people's lack of inclination to comply with it breaks down possibilities of coordinated action. But in the sorts of institutionalised group we are concerned with the greater likelihood is that we overemphasise authority and those who hold it. Jackall wrote that 'In all the companies that I studied, the most common topic of conversation among managers up and down the line is speculation about their respective CEO's plans, intentions, strategies, actions, style, public image, and ideological leanings of the moment' (1988: 22).

Our tendencies towards excessive respect for authority can extend to resentment of others when they withhold their own respect. Glazer and Glazer found that several of the whistleblowers they studied had been in situations where they had perceived things differently than others, and 'their superiors had a tendency to define dissent as insubordination and disobedience as rebellion' (Glazer and Glazer, 1989: 71). The conformity pressures that operate very strongly in groups, and the tendency we have to identify ourselves with groups, and favour members of our own groups above others, are associated with disapproval of group members who fail to show loyalty to the group, and to respect marks of group identification, including adherence to group norms and official authority.

For principled leaders, the issue is how to encourage group members to maintain commitment to one another and to the aims of the group, and to accept the prescriptions of organisational authority that are consistent with moral requirements, but not expect blind obedience from others on account of their own organisational position even though they believe that their own view of events and policies is sound. The task is not an easy one, but there are leaders who carry it out successfully. The next section will consider what it involves.

INSTITUTIONS, NORMS AND CORPORATE SOCIAL RESPONSIBILITY

The role of leaders is important in developing organisational culture as well as organisational policy (Schein, 1992). Much has been written on leadership and it is not necessary to add more here. However, good leadership can certainly be assisted by a clear view of what ethics requires. There are some areas where our present discussion may assist with that. One aim of the present account is to contribute to discussions of corporate social responsibility, and the associated responsibilities of individuals. It is still possible to find some defenders of the view promoted by Milton Friedman that corporations only have responsibilities to their shareholders (Friedman, 1970), but there is nowadays widespread consensus that commercial enterprises have wider responsibilities than that (see e.g. Shaw, 2005: ch. 5; Crane and Matten, 2007: 48; Boatright, 2009: 369). There are many efforts to foster social responsibility by business enterprises, including some major initiatives in regard to corporate reporting, including not only the well-known 'triple bottom line' (e.g. Elkington, 1999), but many others.[4] By and large, the reports envisaged give accounts of corporate activities in a range of areas of ethical significance, and can be seen as aiding ethical evaluation of the activities. The question that still remains in many situations is what the relationship is between ethical evaluation of the activities of the corporation and the actions by individuals within it.

In some cases, there is no major difficulty, because there are actions by individuals that are clearly unethical (see e.g. Sims and Brinkmann, 2009). In other cases, however, it is less clear what individuals have done wrong, even where corporate action is problematic. Solomon has referred to this as 'the System Problem' (1994: 124–25). In many cases there are ethical problems about corporate action even though it seems as though all the individuals in the company have done their own jobs quite correctly:

> The system problem presents us with the dilemma that, even if people are just doing their jobs, the overall result may nonetheless be bad. In the most dramatic imaginable cases, of course, there are the moral dilemmas such as the lieutenant in the military who is ordered to do what he knows to be wrong. But the system problem is present in every large enterprise – university teaching, working in a large hospital, running even a medium-sized city – as well as in every business that is more than 'small' … Watching out for the system problem is the ultimate job – and ultimate dilemma – of every manager, who, on the one hand, has particular responsibilities to carry out on a day-to-day basis, but, on the other hand, has or ought to have the well-being of the company as a whole in mind.
>
> (Solomon, 1994: 125; for some vivid recent examples of system problems see Cassidy, 2009)

We might just add the caveat that it is not just the well-being of the company that is at issue, but general requirements of ethics. That aside, though, Solomon's point reminds us of the 'many hands' problem identified by Thompson. The interlinking of actions in institutionalised groups makes it hard to attribute responsibility to individuals for group actions.

Elsewhere, Solomon (1992: 160–67) has also discussed the issues that arise in organisations from people identifying with their roles, and identifying their duties with the requirements of their roles. He comments on 'the need

4 See e.g. the Global Reporting Initiative website at www.globalreporting.org/Reporting Framework/

for maintaining the larger picture of the place of one's job and the corporation in society as a whole' (1992: 165). The aim here is to give an account that may help us do that, by seeing how the requirements of our organisational roles are founded in the same sorts of basic moral considerations as other moral requirements on us, and, at the same time, to see how this can help with 'the system problem'. The expectations others have of us, and the inclination we have to accede to formal organisational requirements, work together to set role requirements firmly in our minds and obscure the fact that all the moral requirements on us have the same general foundations in considerations like beneficence, fairness and respect for persons.

In that respect the account is a little like utilitarian accounts that sought to provide a single common currency for all moral decisions, such as the pleasure or happiness of people in general. Classic utilitarianism has been undermined by some intractable problems, but it is still possible for us to aim for an account that unifies and simplifies our understanding of complex moral problems as much as possible. Our decision making will still be a form of pattern recognition rather than calculation of utilities or mechanical rule following, and there will still be hard decisions, but we may at least be able to see all the relevant considerations as part of the one overall picture, rather than focussing first on one picture that is only part of the problem, then on another, and so on. We may therefore be aided in avoiding the sorts of fixation or ethical myopia that some writers suggest is often a crucial factor leading to moral failure in the corporate world (see e.g. Goodpaster, 2007: ch. 1, 3).

Of course, the 'system problem' cannot be remedied simply by people reading the account of it given here, but it at least can be seen for what it is: primarily, a need to discern causal relationships, more than a need to rectify and improve role requirements. If we accept that there is a moral requirement on us to help good corporate actions and oppose bad ones, then the issue comes down to the question of what effects our actions might actually have in any specific case: and this question will not be resolved by examining formal role requirements or scrutinising official norms and policies. We shall have to take account of a lot of very complex causal relationships, including the effects of our actions on others, noting their expectations and perceptions, which are shaped in part by official roles and norms, but also by their own perceptions of likely effects. The issue will sometimes be a very difficult one, but it is not unique to evaluating moral requirements. It comes up in all sorts of contexts in organisations, when we are working out the best ways to do things. We can try to improve systems, by clarifying people's expectations of one another, and by creating new expectations through new roles or changes in old ones, but the process is not unique to ethical matters.

In addressing the system problem in general, it can often be stultifying to focus too much on official authority and formal authorisation or instruction. That has been commented on well enough in matters of product development, quality control, service delivery and so on. The point here is just that it is equally true in matters of corporate social responsibility. Modern production systems have increasingly moved to rely on individual employees accepting responsibility for quality and efficiency. It would be a mistake to imagine that ethics ought to be treated differently, if the present account is correct. Ethical considerations within organisations are not more arcane or difficult than other issues. Other kinds of issues can also be complex and difficult, and it is no surprise that ethical issues can be, but at least we can see that solutions do not lie especially in obedience to official authority. Good leadership will recognise that, and provide support for individuals.

SUMMARY

The thrust of this and the two preceding chapters has been to notice major psychological influences that affect us in group contexts, but to distinguish them from genuine ethical demands. The fact that there are such influences is well attested in psychological research, and evident also in everyday life. Our tendencies to identify with groups we are members of, our susceptibility to influence by institutional authority, the pressures on us to conform to group norms, all affect us every day. Often, the outcomes are innocuous, but history books and news programmes vividly convey the terrifying results that occur quite regularly.

In particular, for example, religious wars and racial oppression show how actions we are inclined towards by identification with a large abstract group can be further prompted and rationalised by role prescriptions and by authority that is perceived as legitimate within the institutionalised group. A terrorist *jihad* or a disproportionate response to allegations of terrorism both may be contemporary examples where these factors prevail, and so may the irrational responses to whistleblowers who set out to remedy organisational shortcomings, only to be ostracised and attacked.

A good deal of the explanation for these cheerless events seems to be the combination of psychological pressures we experience from group identification, perceived legitimacy and role prescriptions. These pressures are made harder to combat by the conceptual problems of distinguishing them from genuine ethical demands. These three chapters have aimed to show how the distinction can be made, while still recognising the difficulty of making it.

Thus it has been argued that common-bond groups may create obligations of loyalty that common-identity groups do not, even if we feel some ties of loyalty towards common-identity groups. Obligations towards institutionalised groups may be grounded by instrumental factors, such as their effectiveness in creating goods and services, but there is no apparent reason why such a group should merit loyalty for its own sake. In determining our obligations as members of institutionalised groups, the important consideration is not any tie of loyalty, but the extent to which we help or hinder the group in doing good or bad things.

Within an institutionalised group, roles and role requirements also create genuine ethical demands, as people shape their actions around expectations of what others will do. Failures to meet those expectations can both confuse others and harm them. To that extent, the ethical force of role prescriptions can be set alongside the ethical implications of helping the institutionalised group carry out some action or other, and we can come to an overall conclusion about moral requirements. In an era when corporate social responsibility is increasingly salient in practice and in academic discussion, that is no small thing, since it allows corporate employees to see a way forward in terms of their own individual responsibilities.

For that approach to be effective, however, we have to acknowledge that roles and role prescriptions can also have a force that goes beyond genuine ethical requirements. There are enormous pressures on organisational members to conform to group expectations, beyond any genuine ethical requirements. Added to the psychological pressures of group identification, there are tendencies to conform with group norms, and with authority that is perceived as legitimate. To distinguish genuine ethical requirements from these pressures is no easy matter, since role requirements and institutional structures are cloaked with the same language of duty and legitimacy as genuine moral imperatives.

Nevertheless, once we have a satisfactory account of the basis for our genuine ethical obligations, of loyalty to groups, of assistance to organisations or of meeting others' expectations, we have a basis to distinguish genuine moral obligations from other pressures. We shall still be called on to exercise pattern-based moral judgment, *phronēsis*, rather than calling on any routine or calculative decision process, but at least we shall be able to see what considerations are morally relevant, and how they bear on one another. They are largely encapsulated in the principles discussed in Chapter 1.

The points so far considered address points to do with our obligations in situations where we are members of social groups of one kind and another. Inevitably, much of the discussion has been quite abstract. It has been noted that in real situations some factors occur together which can be separated for the sake of discussion (for example, the fact that a group of one kind, like an identity group, can also be a group of another kind, like an institutionalised group). A variety of the different factors occur together in work organisations. The next chapter considers an example of a fictional work organisation that displays a number of the factors we have considered. In doing so, it allows us to consolidate some parts of our discussion and opens the way to further develop some other parts.

5 A hypothetical case

Endeavour organisation

The purpose of this chapter is to do three things: first, to consider the abstract ideas of the last three chapters in a more concrete situation; second, to show some links between those ideas and some further issues in the literature; and, third, to suggest the importance of an account of ethical decision making like that given in Chapter 1, when we are considering the ethical issues that arise in groups and organisations. For a concrete example that raises a number of the points considered so far, imagine that Jean is an employee of the fictional 'Endeavour' organisation.

Jean tends to identify herself as a member of Endeavour. She is pleased when she sees news reports of its achievements, she is happy to tell people that she works for Endeavour, and on occasion she even wears her t-shirt with the motto 'Endeavour Forever'. If she learns that someone she meets is also associated with Endeavour, she naturally tends to favour them over others, even if she has no other association with them.

On the other hand, there are some individuals she works with at Endeavour, whom she has known for many years, and with whom she shares quite close personal relationships. They have coffee together and sometimes meet socially with their families. They share their true feelings about matters within Endeavour, sometimes lamenting its shortcomings, talking about problems they have, ranging not only over things to do with Endeavour but sometimes over personal difficulties. They are aware of one another's shortcomings (or at least, of some of them), but sympathise and support one another in hard times, as well as sharing moments of humour and congratulation.

Of course, their work at Endeavour is defined by their positions and roles in the organisation. As a middle-ranking project officer and team leader, Jean has reporting relationships to her line manager but also a responsibility to provide reports to senior organisational officials. She has responsibilities also to members of the team she leads, ranging from task allocation and team organisation to leave approvals and budget oversight, and other role-related relationships throughout the organisation, with members of central units like information technology and human resources and with ancillary staff like cleaners and security personnel.

Thus, like most real organisations, Endeavour shares characteristics of common-identity groups, common-bond groups and institutionalised groups. The fact that these characteristics overlap in real situations is compounded by the other multiple factors that impact on decision making by members like Jean. For example, Jean sometimes has to attend meetings where she and other members of Endeavour have to determine organisational policy on a particular issue. She may go into those meetings with a point of view, but then find it difficult to maintain her initial stance when she hears others with different ideas. On such occasions, she finds herself influenced by the course of the discussion and is convinced by the ideas others are putting forward, without being quite sure why. On other occasions, she voices assent with the general opinion, even though she has private reservations. But this does not always happen. Sometimes, one or two others at such a meeting will join with her, and together they will maintain a minority viewpoint, and sometimes even convince the majority to change their own view, but it is often a struggle to avoid going with the flow, and Jean is not always sure whether she is just being stubborn when she maintains a different position, or if she does actually have a better understanding of the issues than others.

It is not only at meetings when Jean sometimes wonders if she is being idiosyncratic. She is happy enough to wear her Endeavour t-shirt at a barbeque, but some of the organisation's standards strike her as unnecessary, like having to use official templates for all letters and presentations, and enforcing dress standards when they seem irrelevant (such as during times when she has no contact with members of the public, or when meeting with groups who probably would not care anyway). Some of her colleagues do not worry about such things, but others take them quite seriously, and last week her colleague George made a comment that was only half-humorous when she wore a casual polo top ('Looks comfortable; everything else at the dry cleaner?').

Those are common sorts of experiences for members of modern organisations, and are in keeping with points we have discussed already. But how do they bear on the ethical decision making Jean has to engage in from time to time? In what follows we shall consider some specific examples.

1. Last week, Mikhail, a member of Jean's team, came to her to seek advice. Another organisation, General Services, has offered him a position. He has an important role in one of the team's current projects, and is worried about the effects on Endeavour and on other team members if he leaves. He told her that he is grateful to Endeavour for the opportunity it gave him when he first arrived in the country, and he is also aware that Joseph, one of the other team members, will have some difficulty carrying on alone. She could not discuss it with Mikhail then, but has promised to meet with him this afternoon.
2. Meanwhile, this morning, she had to attend a meeting about production strategies. There is a proposal being considered for a new product, which

most people at the meeting are supporting, but she is concerned about a potential weakness that may pose a danger to users. She points to some general data about the strength of the material being used to make the product, which support her misgivings. However, most people at the meeting seemed to think that she is being alarmist, and point to the extensive history of the use of similar materials without any problems. The meeting was adjourned, and will continue tomorrow. Jean has to consider how firmly to press her opposition.[1]

3. Ursula, a longstanding colleague and friend, and a project officer in a different team, has a quarrel with George, who is leading a project that involves members of several teams (although those individuals still report to their local team leaders, like Jean). He has given Ursula a draft of a report that he wants her to finish. It takes some key performance indicators, and compares Endeavour's rating with several other organisations. Ursula read the draft and told George that she thinks that it is being too selective in the factors it considers. Endeavour does well on these factors, compared to the other organisations. However, there are some different factors where the reverse is true, which are not mentioned in the report. Ursula wants to include them, and thinks it is dishonest not to. George said that the report is for public release, not for internal use, and because of that it is not appropriate to include the other factors. He said that the other organisations could prepare reports of their own if they wanted to, and that Ursula's role was to prepare a report that would paint Endeavour in as good a light as possible. Jean and Ursula are discussing the issue over lunch.

4. Not of especially pressing urgency today, but a background preoccupation that continues to worry her from time to time, is the tension Jean experiences between her responsibilities as team leader and her own individual work analysing data, preparing reports and considering projects. She sometimes feels that she ought to be giving more time to the members of her team. Lin (one of her team members) has hinted quite clearly that he does not believe that Andrea (another team member) is pulling her weight. Jean knows that Andrea has some problems at home, but she has not found time to sit down with Andrea and speak to her about them, and the effect they are having at work. Counteracting this, Bronwen, Jean's own line manager, relies on her for quite a lot of detailed analysis. It calls on Jean's technical expertise, she enjoys it, and Bronwen tells her that at the moment it is important to Endeavour's work. However, this analytical work draws her away from issues of team management.

In each of these four vignettes, a number of different factors are entwined. In that respect, they resemble real situations, where various considerations

---

1 This case of Jean and the new product is also discussed in Provis (2010b).

often have to be distinguished and perhaps weighed against one another. Imagination may be required in solving such ethical problems, just as in solving others (see e.g. Johnson, 1993; Werhane, 1999). In addressing such issues, I suggest that we cannot hope to identify rules to follow, but we can see kinds of things that are relevant, what general ethical principles bear on them, and how the problems may be approached.

1. MIKHAIL AND THE JOB OFFER

What factors should Jean consider in advising Mikhail? Mikhail and Jean have a good relationship. She will be sorry to see him go. Joseph can take over the main part of Mikhail's work, but Jean will have to arrange some extra support for him. She feels a moment of irritation. Two or three weeks ago, she and Mikhail had both applauded a staff presentation by Endeavour's CEO, where he concluded by announcing awards to long-serving staff, and extolled their loyalty. Now it seems that Mikhail is casting aside pretensions of loyalty to Endeavour, and to her.

The irritation passes quickly. It is true that she has helped Mikhail a lot since he came, but it is equally true that he has worked hard in the team and has amply repaid the support she has given him. She has no good personal grounds to discourage him from going.

Are there any good reasons she can point to from Endeavour's point of view, rather than her own personal point of view? Losing Mikhail's services will mean some delay to the current project, and some extra costs in arranging his replacement. Nevertheless, it is a situation familiar to many people with experience as managers, where we have been able to put aside thoughts of loyalty to the organisation and respond to another individual, taking their interests into account as the primary consideration. Have we been wrong in doing so? Should we pay greater heed to requirements of organisational loyalty? Should Mikhail be loyal to Endeavour, for the sake of their past relationship? It is not clear how much weight that sort of factor ought to be given. Although in some respects it is like a human person, institutionalised groups such as Endeavour do not merit loyalty for their own sake. One cannot develop the same sorts of relationships with an institutionalised group as a whole as one can with individual human persons: relationships of friendship and the like (Duska, 2004: 308; Provis, 2004: ch. 6), and that reflects the differences between an institutionalised group and a human person. On the account given in Chapter 2, there may be loyalty requirements to couples and small groups where people's individual identities are intermingled, but not to abstract identity groups or institutionalised groups.

This analysis runs counter to some accounts. Kennedy's exhortation, 'ask not what your country can do for you – ask what you can do for your country', reminds us that sometimes institutionalised groups like nation-states are seen as proper objects of commitment, giving rise to obligations of loyalty.

The same sort of commitment is sometimes expected toward other institutionalised groups like commercial organisations. Sometimes, individuals are expected to show great loyalty to organisations, and leaving is viewed as treason (Donaldson, 1982: 110). Baron gave an account of the loyalty expected in the Phillips Corporation, where 'of course, a loyal employee would never leave Phillips unless it was absolutely unavoidable' (1984: 1). Fielder has commented that while the Phillips example is extreme, it is not uncommon (1992: 71). The same idea is conjured up by the description that Deal and Kennedy gave of the National Cash Register Corporation:

> [I]t was a living organization. The company's real existence lay in the hearts and minds of its employees. NCR was, and still is, a corporate culture, a cohesion of values, myths, heroes, and symbols that has come to mean a great deal to the people who work there.
>
> (Deal and Kennedy, 1988: 4)

NCR is depicted as having a personality that deserves loyalty, a personality created by its corporate culture. The culture encourages employees to identify with it, to see their own identity bound up with it as though in a close personal relationship. The collection of values, myths and heroes heightens the sense of identity that employees feel with the organisation, and the reality they give to it in their hearts and minds. Nevertheless, it is hard to see how it makes the situation qualitatively different from the identification that experimental subjects felt for groups that were essentially fictional.

Have corporate cultures changed since Deal and Kennedy were writing? Since then, globalisation has increased, and strategies of human resource management have developed apace. Firms have adopted flexible employment practices which sometimes include greater use of temporary or contract labour, or techniques of outsourcing (Stone, 2008: 71–72). We might expect that there would be less emphasis on employee loyalty, simply because it would be harder to demand it in such an environment. Bélanger and colleagues have referred to 'the problems of engendering loyalty in a "market-driven workforce", which is now accustomed to the lack of employment security and is probably more circumspect about any enduring attachment to the objectives of particular firms' (Bélanger et al., 2002: 45; citing Cappelli, 1999; see also Sennett, 1998: 25; Edwards and Wajcman, 2005: 85).

It is still true that firms continue to need dependable long-term workers (Boxall and Purcell, 2007: 76–77). That may create some pressures for managers to get workers to identify with the company, using techniques of culture management (Brown, 1995; Appelbaum, 2002: 134). But that can only create a sense of obligation in employees, not genuine obligations. If managers succumb to the pressures they have on them, trading on others' tendencies to identify with the firm as an abstract group, that may create ethical problems, as employees are persuaded falsely that they have moral commitments they do not really have. We shall consider such problems below, in Chapter 7.

Certainly, so far as genuine obligations go, there are no reasons of loyalty to Endeavour as an abstract identity group that oblige Mikhail to stay. On the other hand, what about other individuals in the team? That could be less clear-cut, if Jean and Mikhail can see that there will be extra demands on those individuals, which Jean cannot alleviate. We do have obligations to other individuals, obligations based clearly in a number of principles, such as avoiding harm to them, being fair to them, and respecting them. If Mikhail's departure could properly be said to 'leave them in the lurch', if perhaps he had led them to rely on him, and there was no way to replace his contribution, then perhaps he ought to think again.

Does that suggest too 'nice' a degree of moral concern? Is it not the case that in the contemporary world of flexible labour markets and job mobility, we ought to expect Mikhail to be able to change employment without any concerns for things like that?

Others' expectations are often an important ethical consideration in social life, and if we live in times where there are widespread expectations that people may change jobs at short notice, then that can affect what is ethically reasonable. The fact that such expectations are common can ease Mikhail's way forward. People who work in organisations may need to take account of such possibilities, and plan accordingly. That applies especially to managers who have responsibility for such matters: a team leader like Jean, for example. Knowing that such moves are common, she needs to ensure back-up is available if someone leaves. This is important for organisational effectiveness, but the responsibility is also a moral responsibility, if her failure to carry it out will disadvantage other team members. At the same time, she lessens the obligations that Mikhail has to others in his team.

The fact that managers are able to construct organisational arrangements so as to affect other individuals' obligations to one another is important for several reasons. Fostering a team spirit seems like a generally positive thing to do. However, there can be a danger when team arrangements are developed and fostered and promote interpersonal relationships amongst team members. Often unproblematic, such arrangements raise moral questions if they are contrived to benefit the organisation. Rather than ensuring that team arrangements are structured to leave employees as much personal flexibility as possible, they can be structured so that team members are closely interdependent, reliant upon one another, with associated obligations to one another. The temptation for managers is to use such arrangements to get enhanced effort from workers. Teamwork played a significant role in development of new 'high performance workplaces' in the 1990s, with organisations devolving decision making to teams who share knowledge of issues and problems in specific areas of production (Bélanger et al., 2002: 39–40). Often team arrangements are welcomed by workers (Edwards et al., 2002: 74–75), but sometimes they may be initiated 'as a way to get workers to pressure each other to work harder' (Appelbaum, 2002: 133). Such arrangements are morally problematic, and we shall consider them in

Chapter 7, together with other efforts that exploit individuals' real or fancied obligations.

In thinking about the ethics of team loyalties, we should also note that terms like 'teamwork' or 'team loyalty' can be used in various ways. The idea of a team conjures up images of collaborative relationships and perhaps some worthwhile interpersonal bonds. But just because of its positive connotations, 'team' language is used to refer to a range of different arrangements. Jackall depicted quite vividly the extent to which managers in some large firms are expected to be 'team players' (Jackall, 1988: 49–61), but his discussion emphasised the requirements on team members to accept organisational demands and requirements of social display, rather than interpersonal loyalty to other team members. Abandonment of individuality, long office hours, acceptance of role requirements: these and some other characteristics Jackall identifies stand out just because they are not linked with any requirements of loyalty towards other team members as individuals. Quite the contrary: it is the absence of any genuine loyalty that stands out.

Arrangements like that seem problematic just because they are devoid of worthwhile friendships and loyalties. On the one hand, it can be wrong to foster unnecessary commitments between individuals, to constrain and motivate them for ulterior purposes. On the other hand, as Jackall showed, there is an opposite extreme of competition and individualism which is also to be avoided.

In Mikhail's case, however, so far as the case has been described, we can assume that it falls between these extremes. There may be worthwhile collaborative relationships, but we do not know of any commitments or obligations that Mikhail has towards other individual team members that he might violate by accepting the job offer. Of course, in this case as in most others, we can imagine all kinds of factors that might make a difference. Mikhail might have given some undertakings that override the general expectation that people may leave when attracted elsewhere. On the other hand, whatever others' expectations, he might have major family commitments that he can only meet if he takes the job with General Services, and so on.

But let us assume that there are no such other circumstances that make a moral difference. There is still another sort of consideration we have discussed that might be something for Mikhail to take account of. Institutionalised groups do not merit respect for their own sake, but they often have great instrumental worth. As a result, there may be indirect reasons for concern about Endeavour, to do with the importance of the project Mikhail is involved in, and how hard it may be to complete the project without him. This circumstance occurs quite often in organisations, as people move on. Does Mikhail have any obligations in the matter from this point of view?

As an institutionalised group, Endeavour organisation may be held responsible for doing good or bad things, and Mikhail may assist or hinder it in doing those things. If the organisation were doing something very good, and Mikhail's assistance was crucial to its success, he might need to consider that as a source of obligation. Similarly, if it were doing something bad, and Mikhail's actions were able to play a key part in preventing it.

On occasion, those are real considerations for some individuals. How to weigh them in practice may not be easy, but we can see some of the things that are relevant: how significant is the organisation's activity, how important is my contribution, what other options are there, and so on. In the next section we look further at such issues. However, I have already suggested that there are reasons for Jean, as a manager, to have arranged things so that Mikhail's work could be done by others when he has other commitments or obligations. The implication is that if Jean has lived up to her responsibilities as a manager then she can reassure him, discuss the best ways for him to hand his work over to others, and give him her good wishes for his future work at General Services.

2. THE NEW PRODUCT

What should Jean do tomorrow, when the discussion continues about the proposal for the new product? This morning, she had a distinct feeling that she was on the outer, and that if she persists in opposition to the project she will harm her reputation, while the project will go ahead anyway.

This sort of case would be no news to many of the whistleblowers whose stories were told by Glazer and Glazer and by others. Admittedly, the case differs from ones where corruption is at issue. There is no hint that other individuals in Endeavour are seeking personal profit outside legal or ethical standards, or that Endeavour itself is so hypnotised by success or profit that its managers will simply push aside considerations of public welfare and consumer safety. In that respect the case is different from ones like Frank Camps' concerns about the Ford Pinto, as Glazer and Glazer report it. Camps was trying to have a potentially life-threatening flaw in the Pinto rectified, but his superior was too concerned about reduction of his bonus to pay any heed (Glazer and Glazer, 1989: 18).[2] That case raises questions about authority and dissent within institutionalised groups, and the issues of legitimacy alluded to earlier. It also raises questions we shall touch on below about the way that institutionalised groups can shape incentives for their members, and the ethical implications. But those things are not at issue here. Jean simply feels that others at the meeting are being affected by the mood of the group, and the wish to move forward. They may be influenced by a desire for organisational success, and their own role in it, but if they could see a clear safety issue then they would accept the implications.

---

2 The Pinto case has been extensively discussed and analysed. For a summary of the literature and the actual events, see Danley (2005), who has argued that some of the criticisms of Ford are unjustified.

This case is less like the situation reported in Frank Camps' case than the case of the *Challenger* disaster. Like the Pinto case, the *Challenger* case has been discussed and analysed at great length (see e.g. Elliot et al., 1993; Vaughan, 1996; Allinson, 1998). There is little suggestion that those involved in decision making about the ill-fated *Challenger* launch were motivated by mere self-interest. They may have had some concerns about their careers, and the extent to which their careers might be hindered, one way or another, but by and large the ethical issues are rather different. They are to do with estimates of risk, organisational communication, care for danger and the like.

In many social situations, we are confronted with a similar interplay, where we have to make some estimate about the facts of the situation, at the same time as we have to work out how to communicate our estimate and its implications, bearing in mind not only the probabilistic assessment we have made of the facts, but also the ethical concerns that are tied to it, and the attitudes and positions of others in the situation. The factors include those we have discussed: personal loyalties that individuals have to one another, general social pressures towards conformity, people's tendency to identify with groups,[3] and obligations generated by roles within the organisation. Sometimes, these pressures reinforce one another, as they may have done in the *Challenger* case when Robert Lund was told to 'take off his engineering hat and put on his management hat' (see e.g. Werhane, 1999: 49), thereby calling on both social identification and role expectations. What makes such a situation especially difficult is the problem of discerning which pressures are associated with genuine obligations, and which are not.

One way to put the point is to say that Jean has to decide how far to press her view. Her situation is very much like Roger Boisjoly, the engineer at Morton Thiokol who voiced concerns about the *Challenger* launch, with specific fears about the effect of low temperature on the O-ring seals, which in the event did fail, causing the disaster. We have to make a judgment about the outcomes, the costs and benefits of maintaining a position.

For us, important points have to do with the nature of moral reasoning in complex social situations. In Chapter 1, I suggested that good ethical decision making often proceeds by recognising patterns rather than through step-by-step reasoning. The difficulties with step-by-step reasoning in complex social situations emerge forcefully in this case. If Jean were to reason about things in a step-by-step way, she might try to separate out the different sorts of considerations, and deal with them one by one. First, what are the probabilities that x, y and z are the case? Second, what are the ethical issues tied to x, y, and z? To what extent does x involve harm to others? To what extent does y involve keeping a promise? To what extent is z unfair to others? Third, when she has come to a view about what it will be best to do, how does she approach others?

---

3 Including one part of the organisation rather than another: see below, p. 133.

Such step-by-step reasoning might be fostered by a consequentialist approach. Prominent consequentialist Philip Pettit distances consequentialism from the 'actuarial' approach mentioned in Chapter 1, but he has also identified an alternative non-consequentialist approach that is worth noticing here (Pettit, 1997). He notes that, whatever moral values we may have, there are two approaches towards them: an approach that considers just what will promote those values, and an alternative approach that 'honours' such values, even if that may contribute nothing towards promoting them. Without being able to look at details of Pettit's arguments here, we may take it that Jean might honour her values by standing out against the proposal for the new product, even if she had no assurance that doing so would be of any use. Should Jean do that?

Such cases are not unreal. Pettit notes as an example the tension between pacifists who adopt a course in the belief that it will promote peace, and others who eschew war whatever the outcome (Pettit, 1997: 126). In the news not so long ago was the case of a climber encountered by others on Mount Everest. The climber was in difficulties. The others did not try to assist, because, as one of them said, 'there was nothing they could do for him' ('Climbers Everest Decision Agony', 2006). Subsequently, Sir Edmund Hillary said 'On our expedition 50 years ago, [we] would have never considered leaving a man like that' ('Death on the Mountain', 2006).

Here, the implication is that Jean might not only have to weigh up consequences. She might have to 'honour' her values, rather than basing her decision on an estimate of likely outcomes. Within social groups, we shall sometimes have to make decisions about whether to stand up for something we believe in, even in the face of a majority view. We can expect that group dynamics will create situations where if we are conscientious in trying to come to a point of view we shall find ourselves opposed by a majority, often by a large majority. It will often be hard to assess the consequences. On the one hand, the fact that the majority support a proposal may be a sign that we ought to reconsider: we may simply be mistaken. On the other hand, if the majority opinion is swayed by the pressures of group conformity, standing out against it may hearten others to do the same.[4] But calculating the effects of doing so may be impossible, in practice (Elster, 1989: ch. 4).

Taking further the point that often we do not use step-by-step, calculative reasoning in arriving at decisions, in recent years attention has been given to the need for managers like Jean to make intuitive decisions in situations where they are under time pressure or face situations of high complexity like this one (Dane and Pratt, 2007; Sadler-Smith and Sparrow, 2008). Sadler-Smith and Sparrow have said

---

4 'Conformity effects are undermined when the deviate finds that she or he is not alone in disagreeing with the majority' (Baron et al., 1992: 65).

While models and computers may be good at aggregating and analyzing data, intuition (since it derives from integrative pattern recognition and holistic judgments) may be the only avenue open to managers to weigh, aggregate, and make sense of intangibles involved in judgments where there are 'deeper core values that underlie a decision'.

(Sadler-Smith and Sparrow, 2008: 317; quoting
Schoemaker and Russo, 1993: 28)

So it is for Jean, in her meeting. She will have to make a judgment that combines assessment of the whole variety of factors that arise in this complex social situation. Rather than coming to a decision through clearly articulated, step-by-step reasoning, she may be led by her commitments and experience to a single, intuitive judgment.

This is not to say that such intuitive judgment is ineffable, unquestionable or unable to be theorised. As noted in Chapter 1, cognitive psychologists and others have examined ways in which such judgment may develop as pattern recognition based on the use of templates or prototypes. In Chapter 8 we shall say more about Clark's point that development of moral expertise is made possible partly by collaboration and language use: even though moral reasoning and decision making may be forms of pattern recognition, they are also 'quintessentially a communal and collaborative affair' (Clark, 2000: 274). In coming to a decision, Jean can think about these issues in the sorts of terms we have been using in this account, and discuss them with others.

At present, the point is that our ability to make intuitive choices allows us to deal with complex social situations. The complexities include difficulties of prediction, and outcome assessment, but also the need to recognise multiple role demands and to evaluate the moral status of pressures like group identification and personal relationships. The role of the analysis in earlier and later chapters of this book is to separate and examine some of the different considerations that apply in real situations, so that detached reflection can improve the intuitive judgments often required for action.

In complex social situations in particular, the new understanding may lead to progress because it can help to develop avenues of social support for good decisions. Thus, for example, if we consider the *Challenger* case, we can see that an engineer like Roger Boisjoly, who repeatedly voiced concerns about the prospective launch, might have been sustained in his opposition to the launch by a professional code of conduct, which articulated expectations that went beyond local organisational norms. Such a code gains from providing social support from a known professional community, as well as from providing linguistic resources that can aid in articulating concerns. In experiments, conformity with a majority declines markedly when an individual has an ally (Brown, 1988: 95), and professional codes or standards can provide a source of perceived allies: many whistleblowers have found support in standards they learned during professional socialisation (Glazer and Glazer, 1989: 97). The fact that decisions in complex social situations are often based on intuitive pattern recognition does not show us precisely which decisions are correct, but it does enable us to see that such resources can improve decision making. Chapter 8 adds a little more to this point.

Overall, then, Jean's decision about the new product will depend on full details of the circumstances, and her judgment will emerge not from following rules or calculating outcomes, but from an understanding that is based both on her own direct experience and on present and past social exchange. Her experience and social exchange may also have involved professional development, and that may have both exposed her to codes or standards that have further refined her understanding and commitments, and also have given her a sense of wider social support when she has to deal with conformity pressures in her own specific organisation. Ultimately, the decision will be her own, but analysis and discussion can inform and affect it.

While this part of the case study consolidates our account of decisions about obligations in group settings, it also extends it. It shows entwined pressures towards social conformity and role responsibility when faced with opposed concerns about general moral issues, combined with difficulties about prediction and evaluation of risk. It notes that decision making in such a context may be a matter of intuitive pattern recognition, but also that such decision making can be guided by language and socially developed conceptual resources. As we proceed further with our discussion, it will be important to bear in mind that language and conceptual resources are significant in another way when we have to make decisions in group contexts. Previous chapters have emphasised that others' expectations are a major source of social obligations. Language and discussion are important ways in which people's expectations are shaped. That point will prove to have further importance as we go on to notice further ramifications of the significance that others' expectations have for our moral obligations.

3. URSULA AND THE DRAFT REPORT

Jean knows how Ursula feels about making a balanced report. Last year, she was involved in putting together a report on the performance of an earlier range of products. There was nothing to be ashamed of in the figures. The products had been robust, and effective, and their price had been reasonable. But competitors' products had been more versatile, and less costly to run. There was general acceptance of those points and they were key factors in planning the new models, so in that sense openness about competitors' strengths was beneficial to Endeavour in improving its own performance. But there had been a question of what should be included in a public report. How much should be acknowledged regarding their products' weaknesses, and the strengths of competitors'?

Ursula and others are of the school of thought that says to include all the facts, as objectively as possible. But that view encountered the objection from George and others that the report was to become public, and that competitors would use the report for their own advantage, to Endeavour's detriment. When someone of the former camp voiced an opinion that honesty was never wrong, it was derided. Examples were offered of reports produced by competitors that completely avoided any mention of Endeavour's products at all, let alone their strengths. Someone else quoted the view that the Golden Rule 'is simply not feasible as a guide for business' (Carr, 1968: 146), and the comment by other writers that 'to take risky or imprudent action on the basis of moral ideals, when others cannot be trusted to do the same, may be admirable, but it goes beyond the obligations of morality in practice' (Dees and Cramton, 1991: 136).

George's approach might be prompted in part by identifying with Endeavour and its interests. The tendencies that we have to identify with large, abstract groups may be increased in competitive situations (Forsyth, 1990: ch. 13; Brown, 1988: ch. 7). We are all too familiar with the extremes of patriotic fervour that we tend to show in times of war, or when our country is attacked in any way. The same sorts of behaviour can be conjured up by competitive markets, where firms are identity groups for their members and opposed interests and actions of other firms strengthen members' identification with their own groups. Many psychological studies have shown such effects of intergroup competition. Conformity pressures may increase, and group members tend to evaluate actions of their own group more favourably in moral terms (e.g. Forsyth, 1990: 412).

However, these points do not directly cast light on Ursula's problem. She needs to detach herself from pressures of group identification and social conformity, and consider other aspects of the situation. The decision to be made by Ursula is about actions of hers that contribute to an action by Endeavour, a large institutionalised group. The report in question will be published by Endeavour, not by the individuals like George and Ursula who are members of the group. On the account given above, their actions can be evaluated by reference to two factors. First, there is the question to what extent each contributes to or assists in performance of the action by Endeavour. Second, there is the question whether Endeavour's action itself is right or wrong.

So far as Ursula's actions are concerned, we can see various points. She has expressed concerns, but George has over-ridden them. We can take it that the requirements of her role imply that ultimately she needs to comply with George's wishes. Failure to do so would violate local norms and perhaps explicit contractual arrangements she agreed to when she accepted employment. Apart from exposing herself to possible sanctions, she would potentially violate undertakings that she has given, and show lack of regard for others within the organisation who rely on orderly processes to arrange their own work. On the other hand, if Endeavour's action in publishing the report would be ethically problematic, she may be culpable for assisting in that corporate action, even though any blame attaching to her would be mitigated by the efforts she made to oppose the corporate action. From her point of view, she would need to take into account her view of whether the corporate action would be wrong and if so how serious it would be. To some extent, her situation would be similar to Jean's, in the previous case, where Jean had to work out how forcefully to oppose the new product.

The difference in this case is that we may be able to say a little more about the corporate action Ursula is potentially assisting. The case of Jean and the new product involved technical risk assessment, but the facts of this case are more visible. The issue Jean and Ursula are discussing is how to evaluate the corporate action, by trying to determine criteria for what to include in the report.

Here, we are assuming that we wish to act in an ethical way. It is easy to find cases of public communication where writers or speakers do not seem concerned about that. A prodigious literature has grown up about the history, techniques and effectiveness of political propaganda (Jowett and O'Donnell, 1986), while business ethics still grapples with questions about honesty in advertising (see Maciejewski, 2005). There is little question that there are many cases of unethical public communication: the issue is how to distinguish them from what is reasonable and acceptable. Can we add more to our understanding of factors that distinguish ethical from unethical communication in group contexts?

In Chapter 1, I suggested that honesty in communication may be tied to respect for persons, because respecting others involves consideration for them as autonomous agents with scope to make responsible decisions, but what that means in practice can depend on circumstances. It means in particular that we have to consider how others will actually interpret what we say, and what use they may make of it. What I say to you can be evaluated by what I know you will understand by it, not merely by what others are likely to understand in different circumstances. Audience expectations seem to be the crucial factor, and what can reasonably be known about those expectations. Courts recognise this in what is required of parties to contractual exchange: we may not assume that an ordinary customer has the same understanding and expectations about goods as another experienced dealer, for example (Duggan et al., 1994).

That creates difficulty with something like Ursula's report. With a public statement, or a publication, different individuals may interpret it differently. Communication to an audience whose characteristics are known only in general terms creates difficulties that go beyond issues in small-scale interpersonal communication. In the latter, we can take account of our knowledge about the others who form our audience, and we can use feedback from them to check whether we are understood correctly. In a public communication, often we shall have no specific knowledge of the individuals who comprise our audience, and no immediate opportunity to check how we are understood.

One option is to consider what is known about people's general expectations. Within an organisation, people share many expectations: we have noted how such shared expectations create norms of behaviour. It is an important fact that people can share expectations more widely, in a whole community and beyond. In Europe, many such expectations have long traditional roots, perhaps traceable back to the Greeks, especially in matters of law and government. Solon initiated reforms in Athens that took root over time. Osborne has commented that 'What Solon did ... was establish a baseline of expectations, and a set of procedures which all citizens could reasonably expect to see followed' (2004: 68), and subsequently 'the pattern of expectations established in the Greek mainland was spread both to the territories conquered by Alexander to the east, and to the territories of the Roman conqueror to the west' (2004: 135). The printing press and modern internet technologies are only the most prominent ways in which shared expectations can be spread widely, and if we know of such widely shared expectations then they may create a basis for decision about what to anticipate from an audience for public communication.

These public expectations of what is reasonable and acceptable have great bearing on the ethics of public communication. For example, in advertising, 'puffery' is accepted where we can predict confidently that people will not rely on the strict or literal truth of what is claimed: puffery is 'mere exaggeration that any reasonable adult would understand as a "mere exaggeration"' (Bettinghaus and Cody, 1994: 28). Similarly, in the case of Ursula's report, it might be that any reasonable adult would anticipate that a report from Endeavour would skip over the weaknesses of the company's past products, and so therefore to exclude that data would not be a matter of deception.

On the other hand, however, we know that in some cases people can be misled by such public documents. Nowadays, company reports are hedged about with cautions and disclaimers, born from hard experience of the mistakes that people make. In addition, a report can always contain an invitation to readers to enquire further, if they wish to, and an option for Ursula would be to suggest something along those lines: an address, a phone number or the like. Then, if people contacted her, she would have opportunity to identify them more precisely, and the need they have for full information. To do that would recognise the nature of communication as a process that is not usually over and done with in the promulgation of a single message, but a to-and-fro process, where we can deal with others' needs and abilities as they become gradually more apparent.

For us, the general point is that we need to be realistic about the expectations others have. In what follows we shall consider some further issues that revolve around people's expectations, but the requirement to be realistic about others' expectations is one significant general point. In the present case, Jean and Ursula need to consider how likely it is that others might be misled, and what harm might come to any who were. As the case has been described, it does not seem very likely that people will be misled, or suffer harm as a result, if Ursula complies with George's wishes. In that case, her path is clear, and Jean may advise her accordingly. But it will not always be so. This case, like the case of Jean and the new product, shows how individuals in organisations need to consider a variety of factors if they wish to act in an ethical way. In the following case, Jean has greater difficulty.

4. JEAN'S CONFLICTING RESPONSIBILITIES

As they finish their lunch, Jean starts to think about the work she has to do in the afternoon. The major issue now is the position she will take on the new product. She needs to go back through some of the figures about the temperature effects on the materials. It is not especially easy data to analyse. She enjoys the technical problems, and has always been able to absorb herself in them, a challenge she has enjoyed. But it has become harder and harder to cope with, as she has other kinds of responsibilities as well. She has to find time soon to speak with Andrea, and Bronwen wants to be briefed on some other technical issues. The regular, fortnightly team meeting is scheduled for first thing tomorrow morning, and she has not given any thought to the issues raised last time, promising herself she would deal with them nearer the time of this coming meeting. She cannot put that off any longer. In particular, she has to collate the preferences people have sent to her for their annual leave. It is not a purely mechanical chore: she has to consider the prospective demands on the team, with attention to who will be needed during which periods, and to what extent different individuals can cover one another's absences, as well as the personal needs they have, based on school holiday periods and so on. She has to fight against an inclination to regard it as trivial: she knows that it is important for the individuals, and some of them have already started to make plans based on what was said at the last meeting.

In many respects, juggling these different demands is just what Jean and lots of other managers like her are paid for. Ordering priorities, planning and coordinating jobs, arranging resources, briefing others in a clear way that allows them to do their own planning: the demands are similar in many contexts, from building construction to domestic tasks and family life. In social contexts these sorts of problems have two characteristics that go beyond simpler forms of juggling demands and priorities. First, the different demands may include elements of moral obligation: satisfying one demand and the obligations tied to it may require sacrificing some other obligation. Second, the extent to which individuals encounter conflicting demands may be a matter of people's decisions about how institutionalised groups are formed and structured.

It is important that the juggling of these social demands goes beyond some of the other juggling and prioritising that we constantly have to do. When Jean arrives home in the evening, she has to deal with competing priorities. She would like a cup of tea, but if she takes time for that, then she will not have time to mow the lawn before dusk. When she goes to mow the lawn, she discovers that she needs mower fuel, and if she goes to get some then she will not have time to prepare the meal she had been looking forward to. But if she does not mow the lawn now, she will need to do it on Saturday, when she had intended to go to the market. To some extent, such conflicts are frustrating, but dealing with them is the stuff of life, and Jean can simply decide to forsake the cup of tea, or Saturday's marketing, or whatever she values least. When she does so, she may feel some passing tinge of regret, but can face that easily enough, even in some more weighty issues. It is up to her to decide on her priorities, and if she decides that mowing the lawn so that she can go to the market is what she wants most, then she need have no qualms about her choice. How much care she takes over the decision is up to her, and if she decides to toss a coin then no one can reasonably suggest that she ought to have done otherwise.

In the social context of her work life, however, many of the problems are more difficult, because they involve moral obligations. She cannot merely decide that one thing is more important than another, without having some regard for moral principles like fairness and honesty and avoidance of harm to others. When she said at the team meeting two weeks ago that she would do certain things, that was to some extent a promise. The need for her to speak with Andrea is something she needs to do partly out of fairness to Lin, and partly because she is concerned about Andrea's problems, and believes that Andrea may want help. The research work she has to do on the new product may avoid dangerous consequences. And so on. Here, the juggling we have to do does not only involve us working out our own priorities, but moral priorities.

Potentially, Jean is involved in a 'dirty hands' problem, the sort of problem we confront when we have to violate some important moral commitment in order to achieve a good and desirable result. Speaking with Andrea will probably take some time, and may mean that she cannot deal effectively with the problems of the new product. Checking the figures on the strength of the product's materials could mean forsaking commitments she has to Andrea both in her role as team leader and as a close personal acquaintance. Sometimes, such issues can be dealt with by ordering them in terms of urgency: the product meeting is tomorrow; probably Andrea's situation will be made no worse by a twenty-four hour delay. But sometimes that kind of solution is not possible. It may be that when Jean returns from lunch she finds Andrea in tears in her office, and the issue is now as urgent as the product research.

In real situations, we may often be able to find solutions. But sometimes, we cannot. Sometimes, the situation is structured in a way that means that whatever course we take will forsake some person, value or principle. In such cases, we face a moral challenge, and in making a decision we go beyond what we do in ordering our own priorities. This kind of issue is endemic to life in institutionalised groups, because of the extent to which such groups revolve around role relationships, which give rise to expectations that people have of one another. When Jean is faced with the conflicting expectations that others have of her, it may well be that some of those expectations have no ethical weight. George's expectations about how she will dress may simply have no significant ethical weight at all. Even if he is offended, her comfort may be just as weighty as his discomfort, and she has no obligation to consider his comfort more than her own. Even if his expectations reflect some local Endeavour norm, that does not necessarily create any significant moral obligation for Jean to conform. On the other hand, the expectations team members have of her on the basis of what she said at the last team meeting may well have some weight, because they may have shaped their own plans and actions around her words.

It is a familiar fact that others' expectations of us can be demanding and stressful. What may be less familiar is to consider how far they create genuine obligations for us, and the issues that arise when these obligations conflict with others. We move to look further at that issue in the next chapter.

SUMMARY

The aim of this chapter has been to show how some of the points put forward in previous chapters can be relevant to analysing ethical issues in a complex work organisation. The situations outlined are intended to be ordinary situations that will be familiar to those of us who work in organisations.

What were the points? Regarding Mikhail and the job offer, they were primarily to do with loyalty, and I argued that the account given in preceding chapters could help us to distinguish real from counterfeit obligations of loyalty, putting aside demands for loyalty to abstract groups, but retaining our commitments to other individuals.

In the case of the new product, Jean has to combine issues about her involvement in groups with issues about persuasion and conscientious action. The conformity pressure that we constantly face in groups gives some special point to the case, combined as it often is with the need to think about consequences and weigh ideals. The complexity of the situation emphasises the need to use *phronēsis*-like intuitive judgment in making some ethical decisions, and that will be a requirement also in some of the other problematic situations we touch on. Nevertheless, articulating relevant sorts of principles and considerations can assist judgment, as part of a communal, language-based theorising process that is important for developing sound intuition.

In the case of Ursula and the draft report, we note the fact that competitive environments can exacerbate tendencies toward social conformity and identification with a group, but determining genuine obligations is assisted by the account of Chapter 3, which separates two considerations: What is the ethical status of the corporate action in question, and how far does the individual's action assist the corporate action? What the individual ought to do will be affected partly by answers to those questions, but also by the other obligations that confront her, including those imposed by role requirements, which emerge from others' expectations. In this case, there may not be an ethical problem, but to reach that conclusion here, where the corporate action has to do with public communication, we need to gauge people's general expectations, and perhaps include some safeguards for individuals who might be misled.

The fact that others' expectations create obligations for us is also at the heart of the issue of Jean's conflicting responsibilities. Within organisations, people can have multiple expectations of us. Not all of these create obligations for us, necessarily, but some of them do, and sometimes those obligations are in conflict with one another or with other obligations we have. In the next chapter we examine in more detail some issues to do with the emergence of multiple obligations from others' expectations.

6 Conflicts of obligations

At the end of the previous chapter we noticed that Jean cannot avoid some situations where she has conflicting obligations. In groups, especially in institutionalised groups, it is not uncommon to face this problem. Jean may have to deal with cases where her role-based obligations conflict with personal obligations she has to other individuals like Andrea, or with other general moral obligations, or where different role-based obligations conflict with one another. In this chapter I examine such problems in more detail. First, I focus on some sources of conflicting obligations, their importance, and the requirement that we should avoid such conflicts when we can. But given that we cannot avoid all such conflicts, I turn second to consider how they may be dealt with. Often, we must rely on the obvious fact that some obligations are more important than others, but just saying that is not enough. In practice, to choose the best course of action we need moral understanding and judgment. This sort of judgment is not reducible to calculation or step-by-step routine. Nevertheless, it is consistent with this that organisations can take steps to assist people with decision making in difficult situations. It is a shortcoming when they fail to do so, but even more of a shortcoming when they ignore such problems or establish systems of incentives that make conflicts more likely.

In considering the difficulties we face in dealing with conflicts of obligations, we begin to see more clearly the shortcomings of views that reduce decision making to calculation or routine. A theme of this book is that understanding the moral commitments we have in group contexts may run contrary to neoliberal and managerialist schools of thought. I will develop that theme more fully in Chapter 8, but I start to touch on it here. Those sorts of views emphasise structured decision processes that can be articulated in quantitative economic terms. Neoliberalism seeks extension of market arrangements to govern decisions more widely, while managerialism suggests that similar management techniques can be applied in widely different organisations, from manufacturing enterprises through banks to hospitals and schools. These and related views tend to downplay the sort of judgment and experience that are highlighted in this chapter.

CONFLICTING OBLIGATIONS: SOURCES AND IMPLICATIONS

It is not uncommon for managers and other members of organisations to face conflicting obligations (Grover and Moorman, 2009: 58–59). Cases involving nurses provide some clear examples. For us, theirs are useful examples. In many other sorts of organisations, there can be a temptation to say that some of the pressures we feel are not genuine obligations at all. For example, I have argued that the orders of a concentration camp commandant create no obligations at all, even if they do embody official organisational policy; and in the case of Jean's Endeavour, arguably she has no moral obligation to comply with organisational dress standards, even if demands of prudence and convenience lead her to do so. But there is less scope for argument about many of the requirements faced by nurses in hospitals. There, considerations of respect for others and concern for their welfare cannot be lightly pushed aside. As a result, several brief examples involving nurses figure in this and following chapters.

In the following example, we can notice that a hospital nurse is not only an employee but a member of a profession, and both can generate obligations. In this case, we see nurses involved in conflicting obligations because of their conflicting roles, and, as Grover has said, 'of the many different ways to resolve role conflict, one is to lie' (Grover, 1997: 74). In one study,

> Practising nurses read scenarios of nursing situations and then were asked how likely they were to report a specific behavior from the scenario in a chart, to supervisors, and to peers. An example of a scenario with a high degree of professional role conflict is one in which a nurse is instructed to administer a certain drug level that will make the patient uncomfortable. The nursing demands to make patients comfortable conflict with institution demands to follow orders. The lying resolution to the conflict is to give a dose the nurse deems appropriate and to report giving the amount ordered.
>
> (Grover, 1997: 75)

The result showed an increased likelihood for nurses to lie in such a conflict situation: they simply deal with one role demand by misreporting the extent to which they have complied with it. Lying may seem obviously to be an unethical solution to such a problem, but such is the nature of dirty hands situations, and many other situations of conflicting obligation: whatever one does is wrong.

Conflicting obligations often emerge from different roles people have. In that example, they emerge where a professional role collides with an organisational role. The various possibilities for conflict are multiplied by the large number of roles we can have. I may have obligations as a father, as a professional engineer, as a supervisor of others at work, as a member of a work team, as a citizen of a particular country, as a player for a particular soccer team, and from many other roles. Within institutionalised groups, the conflicts of obligations that I may then experience are tied to the phenomenon of 'role conflict' mentioned by Grover. Forsyth has said:

> In some instances group members may find themselves occupying several roles at the same time, with the requirements of each role making demands on their time and abilities. If the multiple activities required by one mesh with those required by the other, the individuals who adopt these roles experience few problems. If, however, the expectations that define the appropriate activities associated with these roles are incompatible, *role conflict* may occur.
>
> (Forsyth, 1990: 115, italics in original)

Terminology is not always used consistently, but there is general agreement that such conflict may occur either from conflicting expectations on someone within a single role, or from conflicting expectations generated by different roles occupied by a single individual (Katz and Kahn, 1966: 184–85; Forsyth, 1990: 115–16). It may include 'role overload', where

> The focal person ... finds that he cannot complete all of the tasks urged on him by various people within the stipulated time limits and requirements of quality. He is likely to experience overload as a conflict of priorities or as a conflict between quality and quantity. He must decide which pressures to comply with and which to hold off. If it is impossible to deny any of the pressures, he may be taxed beyond the limit of his abilities.
>
> (Katz and Kahn, 1966: 185)

Although role conflict itself has been widely noted, the fact that it can involve conflicts of obligations has been less often emphasised. Various sorts of difficulties with it have certainly been recognised. Katz and Kahn referred to studies that showed that work-based role conflict was associated with 'low job satisfaction, low confidence in the organization, and a high degree of job-related tension' (Katz and Kahn, 1966: 190; cf. Forsyth, 1990: 116–17). Tensions and stress involved in role conflict can be bad, just as any excessive tension and stress can be harmful, and Clutterbuck is quite right to have said that 'HR has at least a moral responsibility to ensure that employees are not trapped in jobs which generate unreasonable, continuing levels of stress' (2003: 116). However, the source of stress and tension is not just the fact that one is subject to conflicting pressures; at least to a significant extent, it is that the injunctions have prescriptive force, which one believes one ought to comply with. R. D. Laing captured the point in the description of a 'double-bind' situation: 'The "victim" is caught in a tangle of paradoxical injunctions, or of attributions having the force of injunctions, in which he cannot do the right thing' (Laing, 1969: 144). For Laing, of course, the point is that such a situation can generate mental illness. For us, however, the point is that in ethical terms it is something like a 'dirty hands' situation.

Certainly, problems of conflicting obligations are not generated only by roles people have. We may have some obligations that are generated by one or more roles, but others that emerge from different considerations. Take the following case, given by Kopala, of a hospital nurse:

> Due to short staffing and heavy patient acuity, the nurse knows that she will not be able to complete all that needs to be done for her patients during the shift. The nurse knows that the supervisor will not grant overtime to 'finish up,' telling nurses who ask to 'Prioritize. Do what is essential.' The nurse must decide whether to work overtime without pay in order to provide the care she feels her patients deserve.
>
> (Kopala, 2004: 163)

It may just be a 'feeling' that the nurse has, as we could feel a need to finish any job of work at the end of the day, but the case implies more than that. It implies a feeling of obligation grounded in the need the patients have, or the expectation they have been given that their problems will be dealt with. The obligation that the nurse feels may not be tied to her role but quite directly to the needs of the patient, in a context where the nurse is the only person situated to be able to meet those needs adequately.

However, even this conflict does also involve some other role requirements. One option she considers is to work unpaid overtime. That is unfair on her, and to some extent harmful to her, but may also involve her in further role conflict, because of the roles she has outside of her employment, roles as a parent, a partner, a carer for an aged parent, or others. The opposed demands of work, family and other parts of life have become more and more salient in many Western communities as hours of work have become extended over wider periods (see e.g. Pocock, 2003), but the possibility of such role conflict was used as an example by Katz and Kahn in 1966, noting that inter-role conflict may occur where

> demands ... on the job for overtime or take-home work may conflict with pressures from one's wife to give undivided attention to family affairs during evening hours. The conflict arises between the role of the focal person as worker and his role as husband and father.
>
> (Katz and Kahn, 1966: 185)[1]

---

1 We are struck nowadays by the gendered form of the example, and that can remind us that the expectations associated with roles are not fixed but mutable, and that they evolve over time, partly through people's increasing renunciation of expectations that others have of them.

Although conflicting obligations do not necessarily emerge from requirements of different roles, this is a very common source for them. As a result, the difficulty is very great in institutionalised groups, because of the extent to which established scripts and roles are part of such groups, and the costs we may incur through forsaking membership, which sometimes render it impracticable to escape. Work organisations are the clearest case. In the final case of the previous chapter, Jean can escape the obligations that crowd in on her only by leaving her job. Other cases may occur whenever there are worthwhile benefits to membership of the group, whether it be a social club, trade union or professional association. It is always likely that the scripts and roles that make up the institutionalised context may create expectations and obligations for members, some of which may be distasteful. Often, obligations are not welcome: 'obligation is thraldome', Hobbes said (1968: 162). There are many situations where it is quite reasonable to avoid unnecessary obligations, just because they are burdensome. However, the fact that our obligations can be distasteful, because of the demands they make, is not as problematic as the fact that there can be conflicts amongst them. When there are, people encounter moral dilemmas, sometimes serious, requiring potentially anguished efforts to resolve them, and engendering remorse at failure to do so, alienating them from the demands of ethical action, breeding cynicism and apathy.

Here it is possible to confuse conflicts of obligations with conflicts between obligation and self-interest. Robbins and colleagues referred to a study that found that many business executives had faced 'the dilemma of having to choose between what was profitable for their organisations and what was ethical' (Robbins et al., 1994: 384; referring to Brenner and Molander, 1977). Whether or not that accurately describes the findings of the study, it implies a misconception: that profitability is typically not an ethical consideration. In fact, corporate executives have a role obligation as well as a personal interest in doing what is profitable for their organisations (Boatright, 2009: 19–20). The result can sometimes be difficult decisions, as they have to weigh some obligations against others, decisions that can be all the more difficult as they also face pressures from tendencies to identify with their organisations or other social conformity pressures. It is all too easy for observers to count errors as simple instances of self-interest, where they may rather be illustrations of inadequate moral intuition where the demands on that intuition are substantial and complex.

The situation is similar to 'conflicts of interest' that stem from conflicting roles: a company director with a role in another company, perhaps, or a judge of a court who is the member of the board of an association that is party to some proceedings in the court (Orts, 2001: 144). Although this sort of issue has ever-changing features, it is not new. Moore and colleagues have commented that 'conflicts of interest have been a fixture in the economic and political landscape almost from the outset of capitalism' (Moore et al., 2005: 1), but in fact such problems occurred quite clearly even before capitalism became dominant. Feudal society was based on ties of personal commitment, in which one man swore allegiance to another, his lord. Bloch devoted a chapter of his *Feudal Society* to 'The Man of Several Masters' (Bloch, 1965: ch. XV). He began the chapter by noting that similar Japanese feudal arrangements embodied the maxim that 'A samurai does not have two masters', as 'the ineluctable law of any system of personal allegiance, strictly conceived' (Bloch, 1965: 211). In Europe,

> The commended man could change his lord, if the person to whom he had first sworn fealty agreed to release him from his oath. To pledge himself to a second master while remaining the man of the first was strictly forbidden. Regularly, in the partitions of the Empire, the necessary measures were taken to prevent any overlapping of vassal engagements, and the memory of this original strictness was preserved for a long time.
>
> (Bloch, 1965: 211)

It is clear that the ties of allegiance were conceived as matters of moral obligation, both general obligations common to all such relationships, and specific types related to the content of particular vows (Bloch, 1965: ch. XI). The prohibitions against commitments to two masters were therefore aimed at dealing with conflicts of obligations, as can be seen in the later Middle Ages as the prohibition came more and more often to be violated, with the foreseeable result that individuals found themselves confronted by inconsistent obligations: in many cases, because their two lords were at war with one another. It became necessary to put in place strategies to deal with such conflicts, just as it may be necessary to put strategies in place to deal with modern conflicts of interest:

> When two of his lords were at war with each other, where did the duty of the good vassal lie? To stand aside would simply have meant committing a double 'felony'. It was therefore necessary to choose. But how? A whole body of casuistry developed ...
>
> (Bloch, 1965: 213)

In modern times, extensive consideration has been given to conflicts of interest, and principles developed for avoiding or dealing with them (see e.g. Davis and Stark, 2001; Moore et al., 2005). The medieval analogy with such modern conflicts of interest standards and principles is very striking. It reflects quite clearly the sorts of difficulty that arise when people are confronted by conflicting obligations, and the fact that strategies can be developed to deal with such conflicts when they are foreseeable. To a large extent they are similar courses of action as we might use to escape role conflicts more generally: for example, to redefine role requirements, say, by removing the requirement to make decisions in certain sorts of cases. Nowadays, perhaps the most important part of developing such strategies is to recognise the nature of the conflict:

part of the reason that conflicts of interest have been allowed to become so pervasive is that most people think of succumbing to a conflict of interest as a matter of corruption, when in fact it is much more likely to result from processes that are unconscious and unintentional.

(Moore et al., 2005: 3, referring to Chugh et al., 2005)

Strategies to deal with foreseeable conflicts are not always simple or trouble-free, but they may at least allow the development of moral intuition that is guided by a realistic understanding of the difference between pressures that reflect genuine obligations and other pressures that do not. In what follows, I shall suggest that where pressures do reflect genuine obligations, some cases are easier to deal with than others. We need to consider cases within organisations, but cases also where work-based organisational obligations conflict with obligations within our families and with others outside our work life.

In doing so, we need to bear in mind the sorts of reasons why it is important to deal with conflicts of obligations. One sort of difficulty is the fact that they can make people's fulfilment of role requirements less reliable, and so reduce trust in associated institutions, such as law courts or corporate boards. Another, wider, reason is the stress they produce for the individuals involved. It seems likely that such situations can be tolerated better by some individuals than by others (Katz and Kahn, 1966: 194–96; Stroebe and Jonas, 2001). However, that might be partly because some individuals are more fully sensitive to conflicting demands than others are (Katz and Kahn, 1966: 194). From an ethical point of view, there may be queries about the methods that we use to free ourselves from such stress. Davies and Harré are speaking about self-conceptions rather than roles, but their comment is equally applicable: 'to act rationally, those contradictions we are immediately aware of must be remedied, transcended, resolved or ignored' (Davies and Harré, 1999: 49). Whether rational or not, some of those solutions may be morally better than others. If I am in a situation where, one way or another, I am necessarily involved in 'a violation and a betrayal of a person, value, or principle' (Stocker, 1990: 18, cf. above, Chapter 1), then I must at least try to work out which is the greater call on me. Coady's comment sums it up very well: 'you are damned if you do and damned if you don't, but one route can still make more moral sense than the other' (Coady, 1990: 272). To remedy or resolve a problem may be a good thing to do, but to ignore it may not be. We at least need to consider what route does make most moral sense.

In some cases, one obligation must be set aside, at least for the time being. In others, perhaps we can find a remedy: perhaps we can ask a colleague to perform a task for us, to allow us to do something else. But we cannot, ethically, just ignore one or other of the conflicting demands, as if it is of no weight or significance. To say that it is an obligation is to say that it is of at least some weight and significance. If we ignore them in our present action, we may have some residual need to apologise or otherwise rectify the fault. That is a general point about dirty hands cases. The reason for the terminology is partly that after acting we are to some extent or other left with dirty hands, a need to rectify things so far as we can, and a reason to feel some concern if we cannot. Ross referred to that concern as 'compunction':

> When we think ourselves justified in breaking, and indeed morally obliged to break, a promise in order to relieve some one's distress, we do not for a moment cease to recognize a *prima facie* duty to keep our promise, and this leads us to feel, not indeed shame or repentance, but certainly compunction, for behaving as we do; we recognize, further, that it is our duty to make up somehow to the promisee for the breaking of the promise.
> (Ross, 1930: 28; cf. Stocker, 1990: 17)

The fact that in such situations we sometimes have to make very difficult choices, ones that properly cause us to feel some concern, is a reason why role conflict and associated conflicts of obligations may be demanding and stressful. Just how stressful these situations are will undoubtedly be tied to how much is at stake, and how significant the obligations are.

Nevertheless, it is not only because they are stressful and demanding that we have reason to avoid such situations. To the extent that in such situations we must fail to comply with some obligation or other, we do not simply have reason to avoid them; we have an obligation to avoid them if we can. This seems to be a clear implication of the fact that in them we are violating some obligation we have. The obligation I have to keep a promise is equally an obligation not to make a promise that I know I cannot keep. The obligation I have not to harm others is equally an obligation not to harm them directly, and an obligation not to put myself in a situation where I cannot then avoid harming them, one way or another. When I am driving, I have an obligation to avoid collision with other vehicles. I also have an obligation not to put myself in a situation where I cannot avoid collision with them. Again, the obligation I have to be fair to others is equally an obligation not knowingly and avoidably to put myself in situations where I cannot avoid being unfair to someone: I ought not encourage someone to do a job of work for me if I know that I cannot reward them adequately, for example.

There is an important distinction to be made between situations where I have conflicting obligations, and cannot fulfil all of them, but could not reasonably have foreseen that this would happen, and other cases where I might reasonably have foreseen such conflict and could have taken steps to avoid it. If I have promised my son to watch a televised football match with him, but am suddenly and unexpectedly called to assist a neighbour in distress, there is a difference from a case where I made that promise to my son, but carelessly forgot that I had already promised my daughter to help her with her homework. As Cullity has noted,

> The difference is that in the second situation but not the first, I cannot give an adequate justification of the actions through which I ended up

facing that choice. And this makes it misleading to say, without quali-
fication, that I can justify breaking my promise in the second case. I can
give what we might call a 'proximate justification' of the action, given
the circumstances of the choice, but I am also answerable for those
circumstances, and I cannot justify the actions that got me into those
circumstances.

(Cullity, 2007: 67–68)

Homely domestic examples of promises I have made to my son and daughter
may be unproblematic enough. I can assuage my son's disappointment in
one way or another, expect his forgiveness, and carry no great burden of
guilt. But other cases matter more. The idea of dirty hands is especially
associated with life in politics because such significant cases arise there. In
politics especially there can be clashes of different loyalties and commitments, and it is often very easy to contract political debts and obligations
that cannot all be met. A leader may promise to keep interest rates down,
and later find that to do so will lead to higher inflation. If the promise is
kept, the inflationary pressures will cause economic damage; if it is not,
constituents who have relied on it in taking out mortgages will be both
harmed and betrayed. Better not to make the promise in the first place, but
the temptation may have been great. In the caucus, a member may promise a
vote to a colleague, and then find that another better candidate is unexpectedly running for the position. Again, better not to have made the promise, but parliamentary life revolves around such commitments. Politics is
an area where such problems have been especially discussed, but of course it
is not only in politics that they can be of substantial concern. They arise in
work organisations like Jean's situation at Endeavour, and in any other
institutional context where intermingled roles and significant outcomes may
blend to create tensions that are important but hard to deal with.

If I can reasonably be aware that I may become involved in a conflict of
obligations, and do nothing to avoid that conflict, then when subsequently
I find that I am unable to meet the moral demands on me it may be that
I shall indeed be warranted in feeling more than merely the 'compunction'
that Ross refers to. If I have allowed myself to fall into such a situation
where I could have avoided it, then it may be that shame, repentance or even
remorse are the appropriate feelings to have. I have failed to take moral
demands seriously enough, perhaps through laziness, perhaps through lack
of moral concern. Does this emphasis on obligations give moral concerns too
much weight? On the contrary, the weight they ought to have is in many ways
the point. We ought to avoid putting ourselves in situations where we have too
many obligations. Otherwise, we run the risk that we shall be unable to deal
with them as seriously as we ought to. It is no more onerous to consider
possible effects of incurring obligations than it is to make plans for other
aspects of our lives, and to take obligations seriously is only to consider them
amongst other matters as we make those plans. There are certain respects in

which obligations have over-riding force: they take precedence over inclination and mere preference, but so, too, do demands of our physical lives, the needs for food, shelter, rest and so on. Again, the general point that we need to seek harmony amongst our obligations and ends is an old one: for Aristotle, 'one's character is integrated and stable to the extent to which one can form systematically related intentions that realize one's general ends' (Sherman, 1989: 76).

COMPARING OBLIGATIONS

True, we may rightly ignore some demands that present themselves as obligations. In some circumstances, for example, we might conclude that a supervisor's instruction has no moral weight: as in the case of the concentration camp commandant, the organisational legitimacy of an instruction does not necessarily create a genuine obligation. We can imagine cases where a supervisor may be acting from caprice, or even malice. But in general it will require some attention and thought to distinguish counterfeit from real obligations. In the case of Kopala's nurse, there is no reason to think that the supervisor is acting from caprice: the instruction may be the only way the supervisor has to deal with the limited resources available. The organisation's limitations on overtime payments may just be a fact about funding levels. The supervisor's instruction is forced by the fact that if the nurse works overtime then the hospital will not have funds to meet the consequent legal requirement for payment. The supervisor's instruction satisfies all the requirements we can hope for, and the nurse has some genuine obligation to comply with it.

So what more can we say about dealing with such conflicts of obligations? The most prominent factor is the different force that even genuine obligations may have. Because nursing practice impacts so directly on other individuals, nurses are often faced with conflicting obligations, but even here the obligations may not be major ones. At one extreme, there are examples like Corinne Warthen's, to be discussed later. She found herself in a moral dilemma over instructions to dialyse a terminally ill patient. But at the other extreme, there are regular homely situations like one case found in a hospital, where a nurse did what she believed she ought to for patients while simultaneously blaming herself for what she described as an 'extravagant' use of bath towels.

> You're always told how much it costs for linen and that sort of thing ... I like to put an extra towel over their shoulders to keep them warm while I dry them with the other towel, so that may not be cost conscious.
> (quoted in Provis and Stack, 2004: 6)

The case is simple, but we see in it an individual who is at least to some extent confronted by a moral dilemma. She accepts that she is bound by the policies and directives of the organisation that employs her, but she also senses an obligation to the individuals for whom she is caring, an obligation grounded in a care for the other person that reflects beneficence or respect, which runs counter to the requirements of the organisation. On the other hand, the obligations she has to deal with are not of very great weight. Her difficulty is real, because whatever her choice she potentially feels some regret, some sense of failure to meet all moral requirements, but the issue is not a major one. If this obligation to the patient confronted the need of another patient whose life was in danger, she would not hesitate.

That some genuine moral obligations are less weighty than others is obvious, but important. It is only through accepting that point that we can make sense of the possibility that reasonable decisions can be made when obligations conflict. Such decisions are sometimes straightforward, but sometimes not. Often, we can see that although there are conflicting calls on us, each of which has some genuine moral weight, nevertheless there is one that has clear priority. But often the situation is not simple.

As an example, consider the autobiography of Wang Ling, who has recounted some aspects of her work as a judge in China. She gives an account of an incident where her fiancé was disappointed at her refusal to use her position as a judge in the Nanchang Railway Transport Court to help one of his family: 'He scolded me, saying that I didn't understand his love, that I owed him so much yet would not repay him' (Wang, 2002: 154). Chinese *guanxi*-based culture emphasises the significance of obligations based on personal acquaintance (see e.g. Kipnis, 2002). For Wang Ling it was clear what her overriding duty was, but the situation was not necessarily an easy one.

Perhaps in a case like that we are inclined to say that Wang Ling had no genuine obligation at all to her fiancé. But that inclination may be the product of Western familiarity with the strong rules that have grown up around the roles played by judges in the legal system (Luban, 2001; Orts, 2001: 144). Such rules are important in sustaining judicial institutions, and have to overcome the pull of conflicting demands like those of friendship. Blum more than most has recognised that demands of friendship often create obligations: indeed, he has argued the case succinctly. He nonetheless accepts that often the obligations associated with friendship run counter to impartiality, suggesting that 'institutional-role contexts are ones in which impartiality is demanded of us' (Blum, 1980: 49). He gives the role of judge as one prominent example. If a judge has a special connection with a party to proceedings, then there is an obligation on the judge to step aside. Similarly, Blum suggests, impartiality is demanded in a number of other roles, such as a captain of a ship, a doctor or a nurse. In taking this approach, Blum is reflecting long-established views. Aristotle, for example, recognised the special claims of friendship or close attachment, but accepted that these may be outweighed by other obligations (Sherman, 1989: 122).

Nevertheless, individuals with those roles have some obligations to friends and family as a result of their personal relationships. The threat of partiality is to some extent a recognition that personal relationships and roles like those of 'friend' or 'family member' tend to create obligations, and the need to step aside is the need to avoid the call of such obligations in making decisions where they might bias judgment.

The continued presence of obligations based on personal relationships is evidenced by the fact that on some occasions they may outweigh role obligations. In various situations, it is tempting to suggest that one type of obligation always turns up trumps. Some managers might say that organisational demands and duties to external stakeholders always take precedence. Some others might say that family obligations always have priority. That sort of approach is tempting, but too easy. My obligation to keep my promise to my son to get home early to watch a televised football match may be outweighed by an urgent and important problem at work, but may itself outweigh a lighter and less pressing issue, such as my need to mow the lawn.

In the Endeavour example, perhaps Jean has an obligation to Lin and to other members of the team to remedy Andrea's poor performance, but an obligation to Andrea to take account of the troubles that Andrea has at home. Can we say automatically that one of the obligations always and necessarily has priority? The implication of saying that would be that no elaboration of the circumstances could have any tendency to alter the judgment. To begin with, it would render irrelevant factors of interdependence such as the importance of the team's work to organisational outcomes, the community well-being that is contingent on them, or the inconvenience and stress on other team members that is occasioned by the problems with Andrea's work. In addition, it would be like saying that it did not matter whether Andrea's difficulties were the fact that her partner had cancer and her child some major problems at school. If one set of obligations always takes priority, none of those factors are relevant to an ethical decision.

It is impossible to say that such considerations are not relevant, but if they are then we cannot say that one sort of obligation always takes priority over another. Similarly, where Kopala's nurse may have obligations to patients but conflicting obligations to members of her own family, we may need to consider what is at stake both for the patients and her family, what promises she has made to her family, what other options are available for patients, and so on. In many situations, there may be a point where we have to rely on a rule of thumb about what sort of thing is best to do, but a rule of thumb provides guidance about what is probably best, all things considered, not a licence to assume that other things are never important.

This account is consistent with our discussion of ethical decision making in Chapter 1. It is consistent with envisaging ethical principles as statements about the sorts of factors that are often relevant to decision making, and not as rules that provide a basis for routine, algorithmic decision making. It is consistent with the idea that we make decisions by recognising patterns amongst the factors identified by such principles, and not by mechanical, step-by-step reasoning. It runs contrary to some tendencies in many

organisations, towards routinisation, quantification of performance measures, and focus on outputs. It highlights one shortcoming of managerialism,
construed as the idea that management of one organisation is much like
management of another, calling on techniques like those just mentioned (see
e.g. Considine and Painter, 1997), because it points out the need for individuals in organisations to understand the details of concrete situations when
working out what to do. It also runs contrary to focussing just on obligations that are generated within the organisation. Such focus can stem not
just from managers' efforts to get compliance with organisational requirements, but also from our tendencies to identify with organisations as
abstract groups, and from the fact that organisational obligations may be
better defined and more obvious than other, equally real obligations we have
towards others outside the organisation.

Dealing with conflicts of obligations

Conflicts of obligations require understanding and moral judgment but
even then are inherently problematic for the individuals who have to deal
with them, and are more likely where people have multiple roles, as they do
in modern organisations. The extent to which such situations occur depends
on the ways in which institutionalised groups are designed and structured.
Often enough, the sets of scripts and roles that make up the institutions
emerge over time, with little explicit thought. Conventions of language, of dress,
of technological design, and many others, provide cases where arrangements
just grow up. But often they are matters for deliberation and choice. Thus,
for example, Forsyth noted measures such as that 'the workplace can ... be
designed so that potentially incompatible roles are performed in different
locations and at different times' (1990: 117), and that some organisations
'develop explicit guidelines regarding when one role should be sacrificed so
that another can be enacted, or they may prevent employees from occupying
positions that can create role conflicts' (1990: 117–18).

Certainly, we cannot expect to remove all conflicts of obligations, and
there will always be a need for judgment and moral understanding to deal with
them. However, there are still many cases where foreseeable, avoidable role
conflicts face employees with moral dilemmas. One of the best-documented
sorts of case is where individuals are confronted by conflicting obligations in
their roles as employees, on the one hand requirements to comply with
instructions regarding the quantity or rate of the work they do, and on the
other hand obligations they feel to colleagues or organisational clients. Kopala's
case is a hypothetical one, but not so far from others that are documented
where individuals find themselves subject to conflicting obligations in their
employee roles. Van den Broek studied a call centre staffed by professional
social workers whose work was to receive and evaluate reports of child
abuse. Like Kopala's hypothetical nurse, these employees found themselves
caught between the obligations placed on them as employees to complete a

certain quantity of work within a set time, and the obligations they felt as part of their professional role responsibilities. One of van den Broek's interviewees went so far as to say that their supervisor had 'no understanding or respect for the fact that there are humans and human lives involved, children's lives' (van den Broek, 2003: 245).

Various other examples can be found in the literature (see e.g. Thompson, 1980: 914). Apart from cases generated by required work rates, there are such cases as those where people's natural relationships with clients generate conflicts. Solomon gives an example where a manager who has responsibility for acquiring items the company needs has a relationship with a supplier who has done business with the company for many years. The relationship is a perfectly respectable personal relationship, built up over years of them dealing with one another. Now, the supplier's bid is not quite the lowest, but is as low as the supplier can go. Solomon has suggested that the personal relationship is at least something to consider:

> Such examples abound in any aspect of business – which is to say, most of business – where personal relations are not only inevitable but essential, between a bank loan officer and her long-standing clients, between any retailer and his customers, between every manager and his or her reportees.
>
> (Solomon, 1992: 165)

But such relationships can generate obligations, and we can say the same things about that manager's situation as we said about Wang Ling's, above: the personal relationship cannot just be set aside as of no account.

In situations of this type, there is often no substitute for developed individual judgment. One reason for development of bureaucratic structures and processes in organisations has been the aim to avoid individuals' having to exercise judgment in deciding what to do. By proliferating rules, individuals can be guided in more and more difficult situations, and resolve conflicts by reference to the rule book or procedure manual. But the rule book never covers all eventualities, constant efforts to extend it consume more and more resources, and individuals spend more and more time finding the rule that applies to the case at hand. This is one of the problems that neoliberal programmes of 'reinventing government' sought to address (Osborne and Gaebler, 1992). But these programmes have fallen into another trap: instead of proliferating rules, they try to quantify results (Power, 2004), pushing aside some important moral considerations. The resolution of the dilemma requires appreciation of the fact that in many problematic situations decisions need to be made neither by following rules nor by calculating outcomes, but by exercising pattern-based moral judgment.

In these situations, corporate ethics programmes may help. Such programmes often centre on codes of conduct, but to work effectively they also need to include support mechanisms like training and help lines (e.g. Treviño and Nelson, 2007). What is appropriate varies from organisation to organisation, but one general point is implicit in what we have seen about the complexity of decision making in group situations, and possible conflicts between authoritative instructions and ethical demands. There are no routine, rule-based ways to escape from such conflicts. Good ethics programmes will help employees develop their capacity for ethical judgment in situations that cannot be dealt with in routine, mechanical ways (Michael, 2006: 496; Stansbury and Barry, 2007: 253–54). For example, perhaps mentors or experienced managers may through their experience have come to develop judgment that can deal with both the demands of ethics and the complexity of organisational life. If we accept that good ethical judgment and decision making are based on pattern matching that is improved and deepened with experience, then organisations can turn to experienced people who are recognised as having good, relevant ethical judgment, because others in the organisation will benefit from their advice and example in dealing with the ethical dilemmas that confront them. Choice of people for such a role is not simple, but may be possible (Adobor, 2006). Opportunities for organisational members to benefit from that advice and example can be provided in a systematic way by ethics programmes which accept that conscientious employees can be faced with dilemmas in doing their jobs, dilemmas that cannot be resolved just by closer adherence to policies or more detailed codes. (In Chapter 8, I will say more about development of moral judgment that is relevant in such situations.)

One way or another, when such conflicts are predictable, there is some requirement to put arrangements in place to deal with them. The need to avoid the stress of conflicting demands is one reason, but another, perhaps less noticed, is the need to avoid people being put in situations where they have conflicting moral demands on them, just as we, as individuals, ought to avoid such situations for ourselves where we can. It is not sufficient to expect individuals involved in such conflict to deal with it by learning to manage the demands and pressures that it involves. It is important to consider the environment and situation that create such stress (Newton, 1995; Doherty and Tyson, 2000: 109–12) but textbooks on organisational behaviour sometimes give the impression that the major issue to be considered about role conflict is that it is a source of stress. They may identify role conflict as one amongst several other causes of stress (e.g. Robbins et al., 1994: 338; McShane and Travaglione, 2003: 226), and then turn to ways of dealing with stress, which include both organisational and individual strategies, but pay no special attention to the fact that this particular source of stress puts individuals in situations of moral conflict that are bad in themselves, regardless of the fact that they are sources of stress.

Such an approach gets things the wrong way round. We may expect moral conflicts to be sources of stress, and should be concerned if they are not. If we fail to experience some degree of stress when we are in situations where we have conflicting obligations because of the different expectations that others have of us, then we are to some extent failing to be sensitive to those expectations and to the moral pull on us that they create. To the extent that organisational behaviour texts suggest a strategy of selecting staff that are best able to deal with stress, they run the risk of encouraging selection of individuals who are less sensitive to genuine ethical demands (cf. Robbins et al., 1994: 350; Thompson and McHugh, 1995: 341).

The requirement to address such matters will involve some cost. It will involve time and delay, and probably the commitment of other people to consider issues thoughtfully or to arrange alternative courses of action that will free individuals from conflicting demands. In cases that emerge from conflict between demands of different roles, it may be necessary to draw on other people to perform some of the role requirements. In commercial organisations, it will typically involve some cost to put in place clear arrangements to deal with role conflict, costs occasioned either by extra time or extra staff. There is then some incentive to avoid such costs. The sorts of case envisioned for Kopala's hypothetical nurse, and the situation of van den Broek's real social workers, are good examples. They are involved in conflicts amongst the obligations they have to different patients or callers, which is a foreseeable conflict, and avoidable through the employment of additional staff. That involves extra cost. However, to avoid the cost is not just stressful for the employees involved (which is certainly important), but incurs the moral burden of forcing people not to meet obligations they have.

Of course, resources are limited. Sometimes, it will not be possible to provide them. A nurse may have obligations to manage the care of several patients, and the arrangements in place may have been worked out to allow the nurse to call for backup if necessary. If some unusual circumstance means that it is not available, then that may confront the nurse with a conflict of obligations to different patients that could not reasonably have been avoided, any more than it would have been possible to avoid the conflict of obligations I was faced with when my promise to my son had to take second place to my neighbour's distress. The problem arises only when such a conflict is reasonably foreseeable and avoidable. Then it is important to bear in mind that it is not fully and satisfactorily dealt with by encouraging and schooling individuals to cope with the resulting stress. That can amount to encouraging and schooling them to neglect or downplay ethical obligations of genuine significance.

Even more problematic than neglecting role-based conflicts of obligations is the situation in which people are actively encouraged by contractual means to develop opposed obligations. The possibility is certainly not a new one. As we saw, it was frequent during the Middle Ages. Bloch expressed surprise that the problem of conflicting obligations based on multiple allegiances became widespread so quickly, and that

> Historians are inclined to lay the blame for it on the practice, which grew up at an early date, of paying vassals for their services by the grant

of fiefs. There can indeed be no doubt that the prospect of obtaining a fine and well-stocked manor induced many a warrior to do homage to more than one lord.

(Bloch, 1965: 212)

This may well have been one factor that led to the eventual decline of the system of personal allegiances within which people became obligated to others, in favour of the system of more flexible obligations that is to be found in capitalism. But the same problem can arise within modern organisations if people are encouraged to incur obligations that may conflict. There were incentives for medieval lords to seek homage from vassals, to obtain service and resources from them, and there can be incentives for modern organisations to give their members roles that may result in conflicting obligations. The clearest sort of incentive is cost restraint: saving resources by multiplying individuals' roles.

However, there are some cases that are even more deeply problematic, where organisations may trade on actual or potential conflicts amongst individuals' obligations in order to maintain control or enhance work performance. There is potential for this within job and organisation design, for example, when team structures are contrived so as to make employees dependent on one another. For example, Leidner has recounted her observation of how hard-working most of the people were in part of her study of the fast food industry, and goes on:

> Considering workers' low wages and limited stake in the success of the enterprise, why did they work so hard? Their intensity of effort was produced by several kinds of pressures. First, it seemed to me that most workers did conceive of the work as a team effort and were loath to be seen by their peers as making extra work for other people by not doing their share.
>
> (Leidner, 1993: 77)

The same point was touched on earlier, in Appelbaum's comment that team arrangements may be initiated to get workers to pressure each other to work harder (Appelbaum, 2002: 133; see above, Chapter 5). The interdependence of team members does not necessarily lead to role conflict, but it does create the potential for it, by extending the extent to which individuals have expectations of one another and resulting obligations to one another. The additional obligations workers have to one another then also may clash with other obligations they have outside the organisation: most obviously, to friends and family members. The worker who has to pick up her children from child care now has the additional problem that in doing so she lets down her co-workers.

The general implication of discussion in this chapter is that we need to be alert to the fact that such role conflicts can involve genuine conflicts of moral demands, and should not be dealt with as just one amongst many forms of stress on individuals in organisations. Sometimes, such arrangements will emerge without anyone being aware of the mechanisms involved. If we do notice the potential for them to occur, and encourage them nonetheless, then we seem to be doing something especially culpable. It is culpable to do something wrong, but especially culpable to encourage another to do something wrong, or to be placed in a position where in all likelihood it will be impossible to avoid doing something wrong.

In situations like the one described by Leidner there is another concern as well. It may be ethically problematic not just that individuals can have conflicting obligations as a result of their interdependent roles, but also that they are cajoled into obligations to one another as a way of increasing the benefit to a third party. I take up this issue in the next chapter.

SUMMARY

In Chapter 1, we noticed the 'dirty hands' problem, conceived as the general problem that arises where we have conflicting obligations and we cannot meet all the moral demands on us. The complexity of life in groups creates wide possibilities for us to be involved in conflicts of obligations. Such situations are especially likely in organisations, because it is in these institutionalised groups that we often play multiple roles. This fact gives rise to well-recognised possibilities of role conflict, but because we generally have obligations associated with our roles, role conflict may not only be stressful and demanding; it may mean that we fall short of what is morally required of us.

The obligations we have that may conflict with others are not all engendered by organisational roles, but include personal commitments and other sources of obligations. Nevertheless, the likelihood of them occurring within organisations makes it especially important to pay attention to the possibility there. Within organisations, we ought to arrange things so far as possible that neither we nor others do face such moral conflict. Procedures to allow people to avoid conflicts of interest are an example, but so are other efforts to avoid people being involved in role conflict. If we can see the prospect of ourselves or others being involved in a conflict of obligations, we ought to take steps to avoid it actually occurring, so far as we can. When we are involved in a conflict of obligations, then we necessarily fail to meet one or other of them, and if we could have foreseen and avoided the conflict then we are culpable for not doing so.

Nevertheless, there are some occasions when either we cannot foresee or cannot avoid conflicting obligations. In that case, we have to work out what to do. Such situations are not susceptible to routinised decision making, but require us to exercise moral judgment. It is obvious enough to say that some obligations are more important than others, but to judge which are which in concrete situations is not always easy. We may be able to develop such judgment for ourselves, but organisations can also foster the development of moral judgment, and to do so is the aim of a good organisational ethics programme.

An organisation can then support and develop good judgment by individuals in situations where they are faced with conflicting obligations, as well as trying to avoid placing them in such situations. But there are cases where organisations do exactly the reverse, exacerbating the moral difficulties that individuals confront. Sometimes, they do so inadvertently, for reasons of cost or efficiency, but sometimes they may even do so in order to exploit the efforts individuals then make to fulfil all the obligations they have on them. This is especially problematic.

For ourselves, as individuals, we may then see several requirements. One is to develop moral judgment that allows us to deal with conflicts of obligations that we cannot foresee and avoid. Another is to be alert to prospective moral conflicts and avoid them if we can: even if we choose the best course of action in that situation, we are culpable for allowing the situation to arise in the first place. A third is to consider the effects we have within our organisations, and the extent to which we assist in avoiding moral conflicts for ourselves and others.

7   Obligations, exploitation and identity

In the previous chapter I focussed on the extent to which organisational roles can create multiple obligations for us, and the consequent likelihood that we may face conflicts of obligations. Nowadays, some such conflicts are salient in the context of 'work–life balance'. I considered the need for organisational arrangements to minimise such conflicts, and to assist people in dealing with them when they do arise. Towards the end of the chapter, I also noted in the case from Leidner (1993) that sometimes organisations may not just allow but profit from such conflicts amongst their members.

The case described by Leidner shows some benefit accruing to an organisation from the obligations that its members felt to one another. In itself, that is not problematic. Families may well benefit from the obligations that people in them feel towards one another, and so do countless other groups and organisations. It is often the essential feature in successful performance by a sporting team that its members feel mutual commitment to one another, and as a result contribute great effort to their shared aim. There may be a problem because the generation of extra obligations for employees makes it more likely that they will be involved in conflicts of obligations. However, the arrangement also hints at another issue. We may ask whether the deliberate arrangement of others' obligations to one another for instrumental purposes is of ethical concern in itself.

In this chapter I discuss this question of the institutional manipulation of obligation, suggesting that the answer is tied to people's understanding and consent. That is unsurprising, but the issue turns our attention to some other cases where people influence others by contriving real or apparent obligations for them. Cases where team members' obligations to one another are turned to organisational purposes are one example, where their obligations are based in the mutual expectations they have of one another, but other cases revolve around people's perceptions of social identity. This raises further questions, since I argued above that typically our loyalties to identity groups are not genuine but counterfeit obligations. Similarly, people's perceptions of legitimacy can be used as means of influence, even when they reflect no genuine moral requirements.

CONSENT AND EXPLOITATION

It is no surprise that people's relationships with one another may be drawn on to achieve organisational purposes. The importance of such relationships has been noted by many writers on management: for example, Deal and Kennedy wrote that 'one of the strongest influences on people is the influence of their personal ties with others' (1988: 164). The situation described by Leidner is far from unique. Some moves towards team-working in commercial organisations trade quite explicitly on the mutual obligations and commitments that are deliberately developed amongst individuals. For example, some versions of 'just-in-time' (JIT) work systems are reported to do this. In their account of 'human resource maximisation' in such systems, Delbridge and Turnbull have commented that the systems 'harness the peer pressure of fellow team members to ensure compliance with company objectives' (Delbridge and Turnbull, 1992: 63).

> Any failure to supply the 'customer' just-in-time with perfect quality goods is noticed immediately in the absence of buffer stocks and brings an immediate response. Thus the objective is not simply to illustrate to the worker that he/she has 'let down' a fellow team member, but to bring peer pressure to bear *within* the team, as a team leader at a UK engineering firm explains:

>> he makes his endshield and passes it on to the next bloke who's got to put the screws in and he says 'You stupid bastard it's got no bloody thread in there' ... the final assembly of the whole product is within 50 yards of him. So he's immediately going to go over there and give him a bollocking.
>> (quoted in Oliver and Davies, 1990: 562–63)

> The pressure of one's peers extends to other aspects of work such as attendance, as there is often no cover for absentees under a JIT system and other team members (or the team leader) must cover for the absent worker. A list of absentees, and their reasons for absence, is frequently posted in a prominent position on the shopfloor to bring further pressure to bear in what has been described as 'an intensive ideological campaign' by management to illustrate to all employees how fellow team members are 'hurt by absenteeism' (Parker and Slaughter, 1988: 106) ... In sum, team work facilitates management's ownership of the workforce, both mind and body, and this invasion of the worker's psychological space tends to blur the distinction between voluntary and mandatory behaviour.
> (Delbridge and Turnbull, 1992: 63–64; quoting Oliver and Davies, 1990 and Parker and Slaughter, 1988; see also Beaumont, 1993: 193 and Delbridge, 1998: 115–19)

The suggestion that the distinction is blurred 'between voluntary and mandatory behaviour' reflects the fact that expectations that employees have of one another are to some extent used to replace direct instructions and sanctions from official organisational authority. What ethical concerns are there about this arrangement?

Benefits to third parties

To begin with, consider the situation in general terms. One possible reason why there might be some concern about the institutional use of peer obligations is the fact that benefits accrue to a third party as a result of one person incurring obligations through the expectations of another. Often, people exchange commitments just because they see mutual benefit in doing so: that is the essence of contract arrangements, and a reason why an enforceable contract requires giving some 'consideration'. But the case here is where people are encouraged or inveigled into entering into mutual commitments by a third party, who is not directly involved in those commitments, but who benefits from them being made. The team workers have obligations to one another, but it is other third parties who benefit. Patterns of mutual obligation are fostered, and benefit accrued from them, by those who are not directly involved or implicated by them.

Consider a simple analogy (adapted from Provis, 2004: ch. 10). Bob gets Tricia to agree to water the garden if Pat weeds it, and Pat to agree to weed it if Tricia waters it. All three will share the produce. If either Tricia or Pat fails to do what the other expects, then the garden fails. Tricia would be letting down Pat if she did not do her part, and vice versa. If they both play their part, there will be enough for all of them; if either of them fails, there will be nothing. Bob gets his share of the produce without doing anything more.

Is there an ethical problem? Tricia has made a promise to Bob and to Pat. Pat has made a promise to Bob and to Tricia. The obligations that Pat and Tricia have emerge from those promises. The promises the two have made have created mutual expectations that they have of one another, and if either of them fails to play her part, then their shared endeavour will fail. On the other hand, if each keeps her promise, then each achieves the benefit she was led to expect. So far, the arrangement seems like a good one, and similar to many where people make promises to one another for their mutual benefit.

But is there a problem about Bob's role in the arrangement? If he is the owner of the garden, and has to exert some effort in making the arrangement with Pat and Tricia, and explains it in full to them at the outset, then it is hard to see how there might be any ethical problem. Or if he is disabled, and cannot weed or water the garden, then it can be seen why Pat and Tricia would knowingly wish to enter into this arrangement. But if those assumptions are significantly weakened, we might see things differently.

Imagine that Bob is able-bodied, the garden is on common land, and it was in fact quite easy for Bob to make the arrangements with Pat and Tricia. Then, there is no particular reason why Bob should not do some of the work himself. In such a case, it may be that he did not reveal everything to them: perhaps just explained to each the basic terms of what she would receive in exchange for what she was to do. Pat and Tricia still do the same work, and receive the same benefit. Is there a problem?

The case is reminiscent of the Marxist idea of exploitation, seen as Bob's appropriation of 'surplus value' created by the labour of Pat and Tricia (Eaton, 1966). In the simple case of Bob, Pat and Tricia, the latter two might come to a new agreement between themselves, removing benefit to Bob. To the extent that the situation is analogous to a Marxist picture of capitalist production, that option would amount to worker expropriation of the means of production. In practice, we know that there are major difficulties with the feasibility of that option. Here, though, the question is not directly about remedies but about ethicality.

It might be suggested that it is unfair for Bob to appropriate a share of the result from Pat and Tricia's work, just because Bob does not contribute proportionately even though he appropriates a share. A key issue is the extent to which 'just deserts' can be based on factors like ownership and on different sorts of effort and work: in particular, on 'entrepreneurial' work as opposed to direct production. However, these considerations are not especially affected by the fact that the productive effort by Pat and Tricia emerges from obligations they have to one another. They apply equally, if at all, to any cases where Bob appropriates part of their output. Are there any considerations that especially turn on the fact that it is the others' obligations to one another that yield benefit to Bob?

Consent, obligations and respect

An important part of the issue lies in the extent to which the obligations people incur have their informed consent. This notion is a familiar one (for application in different areas see e.g. Feinberg, 1986: 305–15; Duggan et al., 1994: ch. 2). It is perfectly possible for people to enter into arrangements in which they have obligations to one another that benefit both themselves and some third party. If you and I enter a sporting team, we may be well aware that our on-field performance will involve mutual obligations to one another, and that our efforts not to let one another down will enhance our performance. It may, at the same time, enhance the reputation, status and career of our team manager. There seems nothing problematic in itself about any of that. The issue of concern is contrivance that allows exploitation of others' commitments and moral obligations without their informed consent.

The general point here is that, so far as we can, we ought to allow others to gain full understanding of what may be involved before they commit themselves to a course of action. There are multiple reasons to accept that we ought to allow others to gain full understanding of the situation before they commit themselves in ways that will involve them in obligations. The requirement is implied by ideas of beneficence, fairness and respect for others. Of these multiple reasons, respect looms largest (see e.g. Bowie, 1999: ch. 3). Such matters are tied to considering others' status as moral agents with responsibility for their decisions and actions.

However, the situation here is a little like the situation discussed in the previous chapter, where we ought not allow ourselves to be caught in conflicts of obligations, but that does not free us of a need to determine a course of action if we are caught. Here, it may be that Bob ought not contrive mutual obligations for Pat and Tricia without their informed consent, but they still have to determine a course of action when they find themselves in that situation. In the previous chapter, I addressed cases where individuals had to deal with conflicts of obligations, arguing that such conflicts must be avoided where possible, but when they do occur we have to use developed moral judgment to work out what course of action is appropriate. The situation here may involve something similar: not a conflict of obligations, so much as a conflict between obligations and rights.

The difficult case is where Pat and Tricia do not agree what to do. If Bob's contrivance of the arrangement did not have their informed consent, then we may assume that they have no obligations toward him. If they then agree to abandon the arrangement, there is no moral problem. But what if one wants to continue and the other does not? Is there a right to withdraw that outweighs the obligation to continue?

The possibility is perfectly real. Suppose that in fact Pat and Tricia are team-workers in the sort of arrangement described by Delbridge and Turnbull. In such a team-working arrangement, Pat might want to leave work early, but Tricia might not. Perhaps Pat just decides to forsake the overtime payment that is available, but Tricia needs the money. In the sort of case we are envisaging, the work can only be performed if both are present. We can assume that Pat has no moral obligation to the employer, but she may still have an obligation to Tricia. In practice, in cases like that described by Delbridge and Turnbull, the question is whether any special moral problem is created if the participants cannot easily change the situation where they make moral demands on one another.

Situations of this type are likely to be created not only in workplaces that have an explicit commitment to JIT work systems or to 'human resource maximisation'. In any workplace where people's tasks are interlinked, it is possible that we have obligations to complete our tasks because of the inconvenience or harm that others may suffer if we do not complete them. In many cases, the consent we have given to the arrangements may be limited: not because anyone has contrived the arrangement or deceived us, but just because the complexity of social environments may hinder us from seeing implications of what we agree to. We may have genuine obligations, but ones we have not fully and freely consented to.

Does our imperfect consent lessen the weight of the obligations we have? I noted in the previous chapter that obligations are not all of equal weight or force: otherwise, it would be hard to make sense of decisions when we have to deal with conflicting obligations. If an obligation has been contracted without full and free consent, does that lessen its weight? Perhaps lessen it so much that it can be set aside entirely?

There is some analogy with a right of self-defence. This was one of the secondary moral principles mentioned in Chapter 1. If another's behaviour threatens to harm us, we have a right to protect ourselves. This principle does not apply only to physical threats, but to other threats. We noted that it may apply to a threat to use private information against us, and it would apply also to threats of humiliation or belittlement, and many others, so long as our defence is proportional to the threat. In the present situation, we might ask if it justifies some form of defence against exploitation. In general, we may certainly have a right of self-defence against another's action, even if the other's action has been instigated by a third party. In the case of Pat and Tricia, perhaps the right of self-defence may justify Pat forsaking her obligation to Tricia. Circumstances affect what rights we have, and here circumstances by which the obligation was established are relevant in determining whether to comply with it. If Pat does not comply with her obligation, then Tricia is wronged. But Pat has been wronged by being placed in this situation, in the first place. That is a relevant consideration that she may take account of when making a decision what to do.

Once again, there is no routine, automatic way for Pat to make a decision. The obligation she has to Tricia is a real one, and cannot just be ignored. She must feel some compunction about a failure to comply with it. But the way in which the obligation came about is a relevant consideration, which she may take into account in her decision. Once again, decision making requires developed moral judgment.

There are thus two respects in which the situation resembles cases of conflicts of obligations dealt with in the previous chapter. One is the fact that for the individuals involved there is likely to be a call for developed moral judgment, without a solution from routine, calculative or rule-based decision processes. Aggregation of preferences or technocratic processes will not deal with the problem. The other is the fact that we have obligations to avoid situations of this type arising in the first place.

In the previous chapter, we dealt with conflicts of obligations that may sometimes take us unawares, when some unanticipated confluence of factors finds us committed in contrary directions. Here, the problem is quite different; the conflict arises because of others' contrivance. That fact directly affects decision making in the situation. It does not remove the obligation that Pat has to Tricia, but it is one factor that Pat may take account of. More important, however, that fact is itself especially problematic in moral terms. It is not only a failure to give moral demands the attention they deserve; it is subordination of moral demands to other ends, the use of ethical concerns for other purposes.

To the extent that people's ethical commitments and obligations are importantly tied to their existence as persons, exploitation of people's moral obligations and ethical commitments for the gain of a third party is problematic because it uses these obligations and commitments as means, rather than ends, and is to that extent of concern for the same general sort of reason as Kant suggested that it is of concern to treat persons as mere means rather than as ends. In treating people's commitments and obligations as means, we disregard the importance persons have as beings whose moral dimension is fundamental to who they are. If, in making a request of you, I fail to have regard for the fact that you have made a promise to someone else, I show lack of regard for your status as a moral being whose ethical commitments and obligations are important.

For managers, it is not merely wrong to exploit others' obligations for gain; there is a positive requirement so far as possible to avoid people having unnecessary obligations to others. This is the sort of requirement Jean satisfied in Chapter 5 when she was able to face Mikhail's departure with equanimity because she had fulfilled her obligation to ensure that others were not relying on his contribution.

Disregard for the importance of people's moral commitments and obligations shows not only a lack of regard for them as individuals; it shows lack of regard for the moral status of persons in general. To encourage individuals to enter into relationships that involve them in mutual expectations and commitments, like the closely interdependent role relationships described by Delbridge and Turnbull, fails to heed the importance of people's obligations to one another. To that extent, it shows a lack of regard for individuals as persons, and also fails to respect ethics as a matter of concern in human life. In doing so, it may reflect a tendency to assimilate matters of obligation and commitment to matters of inclination and preference, a tendency embodied in rational choice theory, which I discuss further in the next chapter.

EXPLOITATION AND SOCIAL IDENTITY

We may have concerns about contrivance of obligations because of the lack of respect it shows for the moral status of persons in general. On the same grounds, we may also have concerns about influencing persons by using counterfeit obligations: demands that they feel as moral commitments but which are not genuine obligations. I have contended above that commitments to large abstract groups are not directly sources of moral obligation, in the way that commitments to specific other individuals and small groups may be. Nevertheless, it is possible for a third party to gain through using or contriving people's commitments to abstract groups, just as it is possible to do so through using or contriving genuine obligations that people have to one another.

Here, we need to go a little further into some points already touched on about the ways that groups and social identity are important in explaining people's motivation and behaviour. To begin with, we may note that the importance of groups is well-recognised by writers on motivation. In the context of work organisations, Lahiry has noted that

> Groups are the building blocks of organizations. This being the case, organizations are most likely to change for the better if they target improvement efforts at groups of employees. Widespread efforts at team building are one example of this trend.
>
> (Lahiry, 1994: 50)

Similarly, as Staw discussed the old topic of 'how to manage an organization so that employees can be both happy and productive' (1991: 264), he commented that 'much of organizational life could be designed around groups, if we wanted to capitalize fully on the power of groups to influence work attitudes and behavior' (1991: 272), going on to say that:

> We know from military research that soldiers can fight long and hard, not out of special patriotism, but from devotion and loyalty to their units. We know that participation in various high-tech project groups can be immensely involving, both in terms of one's attitudes and performance. We also know that people will serve long and hard hours to help build or preserve organizational divisions or departments, perhaps more out of loyalty and altruism than self-interest. Thus, because individuals will work to achieve group praise and adoration, a group-oriented system, effectively managed, can potentially contribute to high job performance and satisfaction.
>
> (Staw, 1991: 273)

A focus on groups within organisations can be partly a matter of attention to interdependent team roles, as in the cases described by Delbridge and Turnbull, but they can also build on the fact that individuals may be highly motivated by group identification. Brown quotes a factory shop steward:

> I went into the army. I had no visions of any regiment to go in or different kind of preference for tank or artillery. But once I was in the artillery, to me that was the finest regiment. Even now it is and I've left the army twenty years ... I think it's the same as when you come into a factory. You get an allegiance to a department and you breed that. And you say, 'fair enough I'm a Development worker', and you hate to think of going into Production ... Once someone gets in a department you've got that allegiance to it.
>
> (Brown, 1988: 21)

One problematic result can be intra-organisational competition that is at odds with organisational effectiveness (Riley, 1983: 428). However, such competition can also be used to foster greater effort and commitment, with positive effects on overall organisational aims.

The power of group identification as a motivating factor for individual behaviour has been more clearly articulated in the context of wider social movements. Brysk has pointed out that, in a political context, theoretical models of people's behaviour often fail to capture reality if they offer explanations that refer solely to rational decision making grounded in material interest:

> When the political will of peasant communities overcomes the wealth and weapons of a superpower, as in Vietnam or Afghanistan, we may be told that nationalism transformed 'hearts and minds' – but not why or how. When the most marginalized sectors of poor societies mobilize around Islamic fundamentalism in Iran or liberation theology in Haiti, their stories and symbols are seen as a code for more material interests, even though the participants repeatedly sacrifice earthly rewards in pursuit of their vision.
>
> (Brysk, 1995: 560)

There are problems with 'rational choice theory': the idea that people's actions can generally be explained as utility-maximising rational choice, even though that theory is common as a basis for economic theorising and public policy (see e.g. Elster, 1989: ch. 3; Udehn, 1996: ch. 2; Frank, 2004: ch. 1). One problem is that people's social identity can play a significant role in their action and decision, and this is at odds with rational choice theory.

We shall discuss rational choice theory further in the next chapter. There we shall focus primarily on its aspect as a prescriptive theory, its recommendation of some ways rather than others for people to make choices. However, it also has an aspect as a descriptive theory, regarding the ways in which people actually make decisions. In particular, it downplays the significance of such factors as people's social identity. James Montgomery has given a useful discussion about the difference between rational choice theory and other ways of understanding people's choices (the following summary draws on Provis, 2007).

To begin with, Montgomery notes that rational choice theorists tend to model mutual cooperation and trust in terms of repeated Prisoners' Dilemmas, where self-interested actors sustain cooperation through 'calculative trust': 'I trust you because I calculate that your short-run benefit from an opportunistic defection is outweighed by your long-run benefit from continued cooperation.' However, he notes, 'experimental evidence raises doubts whether cooperation in PDs is based upon calculative trust' (Montgomery, 1998: 93; citing Dawes and Thaler, 1988; Sally, 1995; Rabin, 1998).

Montgomery notes that the outcomes of Prisoners' Dilemma trials are significantly affected by the instructions given to participants, even when the rules governing their potential losses and benefits are not affected. If behaviour is primarily to be explained in terms of participants calculating how their interests are best served, it is difficult to see how factors other than their potential losses and benefits can have such a substantial effect.

What is especially notable in these experiments is that the sorts of effects in question are produced by changes to instructions that seem relatively minor. For example, there are significant effects from labelling one course of action 'cooperation', rather than just identifying it by a number or a letter. In one notable experiment, some pairs of subjects were told that they were playing the 'Wall Street Game', and others that they were playing the 'Community Game', with no other differences between the situations they were presented with:

> Given the usual game-theoretic presumption that labels are irrelevant, the experimental results are striking. While only one-third of the subjects in the Wall Street condition cooperated in the first period, more than two-thirds of the subjects in the Community condition did so.
> (Montgomery, 1998: 95; citing Samuels and Ross, 1993; Ross and Ward, 1995a, 1995b)

In some respects, this reminds us of work about the psychological phenomenon of 'priming', where 'recently and frequently activated ideas come to mind more easily than ideas that have not been activated' (Fiske and Taylor, 1991: 257). Some research has found that self-interest can be 'primed': when people were exposed to certain stimuli (like conversations that highlighted considerations of self-interest for those present), they were more likely later to cite self-interest as a reason for a particular political position (Young et al., 1991). However, Montgomery's discussion may also remind us of the points about group identity that have been discussed above. Both in minimal group experiments, and in the Prisoners' Dilemma simulations referred to by Montgomery, we see significant effects on people's behaviour produced by apparently small variations in the way the situation is described.[1] Montgomery suggests that the difficulties that rational choice theory has in explaining such phenomena might lead us to consider sociological 'role theory' as a better alternative for conceptualising them.

Our earlier discussion of social roles emphasised how they embody scripts, which include cognitive elements predicting how people will act, and normative elements prescribing how they ought to act. We noticed also that institutionalised groups are made up of people playing interrelated roles, as well as noticing that people tend to identify with abstract large groups. Within institutionalised groups, identification with a role and identification with a group can often go together: the shop steward quoted above by Brown shows

---

1 A point that may be recognised in Confucian ethics by the importance that has been given to the doctrine of *zhēngmíng,* usually translated as 'Rectification of Names'.

both, in his thought, 'fair enough I'm a Development worker'. What now needs to be emphasised is the strength of that social identification as a motivating factor for people's behaviour. On this view, individuals view themselves as embodying socially constructed roles, partly because of the recurring need we have to understand our place in the world.

Because it is such a significant factor in people's motivation, it is therefore no surprise that group identification may be seized on as a matter to take account of in organisational design, as well as in other contexts. To influence people through calling on their social identities is a common and widespread device. From governments that call on people's awareness of themselves as citizens of this rather than another state, through religious groups that remind people of their differences from others, political parties that emphasise the points that distinguish their followers from other groups, sporting teams that draw heightened commitment from members and supporters by the rites and rituals of group identification, to the management of commercial organisations through attention to groups within them, such influence is ever-present. Some writers have considered the extent to which members of organisations can be encouraged to act in ethical ways by promoting the salience of one social identity rather than others (Treviño et al., 2006: 963), but more attention has probably been given to the encouragement of productivity and loyalty: 'One of the most significant and robust empirical findings derived from social identity research is the discovery that heightened organizational identification generally leads to improved task performance and organizational citizenship behaviors' (Ellemers et al., 2003: 16–17). However, there are significant ethical questions that emerge from efforts to influence people by getting them to identify with social groups like work organisations, just as there are ethical questions like those discussed above about influencing people through their personal ties in common-bond groups and the mutual obligations they have to one another. The questions are about effects of group identification, but are made more complex because these effects are not all of a piece.

Identity, self and ethics

Late twentieth-century political theory drew attention to the positive function of identity in political processes (e.g. Phillips, 1993: 17), but modern 'cosmopolitanism' has equally emphasised the negative role of social identity in group conflict and war (e.g. Pollock et al., 2002). Roger Brown referred to the 'paradoxical fact that people who oppose group discrimination of any kind sometimes favour group assertion' (Brown, 1986: 551). We need to consider this tension before we go further, and its implications.

Brown noted that there is a reasonable explanation for the paradoxical fact he refers to, as positive social identity for under-privileged groups has the potential to foster awareness of injustice and action to remedy it. Similarly, Phillips has noted that 'radical pluralism', contrasted with the conventional pluralism that revolves around ideas of interest groups, instead 'focuses on groups that are defined by a common experience of exclusion or oppression, thus on identities that are often secured in direct opposition to some "other"' (Phillips, 1993: 17).

In this context, to speak of a person's identity is to speak of his or her self-understanding as a creature with some continuity through time and a place in the world. One of the clearest and best statements of the idea is by Stanley Benn, who has tied together the idea of a person's identity with the ideas of their interests and projects, at the same time making a similar point to Montgomery's about the way that rational choice theory does not provide a full basis for understanding human action. While rational choice theory tends to explain people's behaviour in terms of the pursuit of interests, and is often conceived simply in terms of preference satisfaction, a more complete account of interests must tie the idea to these other ideas:

> A person's interests in this sense are not merely objects or objectives to which he as subject addresses himself; they provide the strands of his identity over time, through which he is able to see continuity of meaning and pattern in what he is and does. In what he is today he perceives the residues, the successes and the failures, of yesterday's projects, but equally the interests which inform his present projects reach forward into a future he is still fashioning and which he can understand as also as his own just because he can see how its features would express his present interests. For this reason it is quite inadequate to understand his projects merely in terms of the gratification he will enjoy, or how much better it will be for him, if they are successful. His projects are an exteriorization of himself, projections, indeed, of himself into the world; his identity as a person, qualifying for respect not only from others but also from himself, depends on his sense that they are indeed his own, informed by interests which together constitute him an intentional agent with an enduring nature, not simply a stream of experiences, even of remembered and envisaged experiences.
>
> (Benn, 1988: 106–7)

The same idea is at the root of Sennett's discussion of 'the corrosion of character': the suggestion that modern socio-economic developments tend to undermine this sense of self. To contrast the present with the past he tells the story of Enrico, whom he interviewed years ago. Enrico was a migrant who had worked for years at the same job, gradually saving to buy a house, improve conditions for his family and provide for his sons' education. Predictable, and to some minds boring, his life nevertheless had meaning in his own terms: 'He carved out a clear story for himself in which his experience accumulated materially and psychically; his life thus made sense to him as a linear narrative' (Sennett, 1998: 16).

If this account is correct, then respect for persons is closely linked to respect for the identity they construct for themselves, and beneficence, promoting the good for persons, is creating and sustaining the conditions under which they can best construct and maintain that identity. It is therefore of fundamental ethical importance on both counts, and we misconceive ideals of public policy if we allow them to revolve around preference satisfaction that does not foster individuals' construction and maintenance of that identity.

However, what remains a significant question is how individuals' social identity is related to their identity in this sense of self-understanding as distinct persons with continuity over time. We can accept that such self-understanding must often involve understanding of oneself in relation to others. In Chapter 2, I noted that our relationships with others can be of great importance, and of great ethical significance, but I also noted that it is hard to say that our relationships to large abstract groups can be of equal importance, since the sense of self which that sustains can be equally engendered by groups that are essentially fictitious. To that extent, self-understanding that emerges from identification with such abstract groups seems of much less value than a sense of self that emerges from relationships within common-bond, face-to-face groups.

Here, we find a clash between the fact that a sense of social identity can be an important source of social mobilisation, on the one hand, against the fact that it can develop into an affinity towards an abstract social group, and thereby develop into a sense of self that does not ultimately have moral value. It is clear that a sense of social identity can be a basis for collective action by members of oppressed and disadvantaged groups (as well as Brysk, 1995, see e.g. Kelly and Kelly, 1994). But if it is, its moral value seems to be basically instrumental, allowing achievement of other values, rather than valuable for its own sake. It may allow members of such groups to become aware of disadvantage, and assist them to take action to remedy it, but does not seem to be of value in itself. If it were, it would be necessary to admit also that patriotic social identity was of moral worth for individuals who are members of well-off and advantaged groups, and more widely that a sense of social identity would be of worth for any individual, whatever factual basis it might have.

This is not to say that it is unimportant for people to understand the extent to which they are members of particular abstract groups (see e.g. Solomon, 1992: 161–62). That certainly may be important, but it is not clear that it is more fundamentally important than it is for people to understand facts about their physical nature, or geographical situation. It may be very important for members of an oppressed or disadvantaged group to understand their situation. That situation may have emerged from them having been classified as members of a particular group, perhaps with stereotypical characteristics attributed to them, which rationalised their oppression. If so, understanding of that history may be important. But it does not thereby become of greater moral importance than for any people to understand the historical and natural circumstances that have led to their conditions of disadvantage, or, for that matter, their conditions of privilege.

Influence and social identity

A variety of empirical studies have demonstrated the significance of social identity as a source of motivation. Its force may be explained by the extent to which it sustains a sense of self for an individual, but the sense of self that it sustains is divorced from that sense of identity which Benn so aptly describes by reference to the projects and activities in which an individual is engaged, and which is built also out of personal relationships with others. We are all too familiar with tactics of persuasion and influence that build on individuals' social identities, often to their detriment. The best-known are the calls to patriotic military service, built around

> The old Lie: Dulce et decorum est
> Pro patria mori.[2]

But the same sentiment equally underlies Kennedy's call, referred to in Chapter 2: 'ask not what your country can do for you – ask what you can do for your country'.

We can accept that there may be a variety of circumstances in which it is perfectly reasonable for people to embrace some identity with an abstract social group, and for it to underpin collective action they take towards some shared goal. Support for sporting teams can be enjoyable, and can foster good and worthwhile activities. Support for an underprivileged group can be of more fundamental importance in emancipating them from disadvantage, injustice and hardship. People's identification with work organisations can enhance effort and achievement, and boost valuable organisational outcomes, whether they be manufacturing, scientific research or charitable endeavours. However, as is shown by cases where appeals to patriotic social identity are used to persuade young people to military service in unjust wars, the motivational force of people's identification with abstract social groups can also be misused.

On that basis, we can return to the point where we began to consider ethical implications of influencing people through their identification with abstract social groups. We came to this issue after considering cases where people may be exploited through contrivance that builds on genuine moral obligations they have. It is also possible for people to be exploited by calling on their social identities, as we have just noted, through calls to their

---

2 Wilfred Owen's conclusion to his heart-wrenching depiction of gas warfare in the First World War trenches of France, 'Dulce et Decorum Est' (in Owen, 1963). The original Latin ('sweet and fitting it is to die for one's country') is from Horace, *Odes*.

patriotism, for example. It is possible that on occasion calls to collective action in national self-defence are wise and justified, and do well to refer to people's social identity, but it also seems clear that not all are justified, and that on some occasions governments or elite groups can draw on patriotic fervour for their own ulterior motives rather than in the interests of their audience. Similarly, it is possible that on some occasions there can be reasonable and justified calls made to members of work organisations, political parties, religious groups and others, calling on the individuals' identification with the group, but on other occasions such calls may be questionable.

In the previous sort of case we considered, with the example from Delbridge and Turnbull, people were exploited by others contriving obligations for them: genuine obligations that made real moral demands on them. The concern was partly about the lack of respect this showed for them as individuals, and partly about lack of respect for the moral status of persons in general. The general lack of respect was shown in the use of moral commitments for ulterior ends. In the present case, there is still a concern about the lack of respect for persons in general, but here that is because people are encouraged to think and act as though there are moral commitments where in fact there are none; again, in some cases, for ulterior ends.

In this sort of case there is no genuine obligation associated with illicit appeals to social identity. When a political leader calls a 'khaki election', or a military recruiting poster cries out 'Your country needs you!', then in all likelihood there is no obligation to heed the patriotic call. There may be reasons of prudence, especially in the atmosphere of hysteria that such calls can generate (see e.g. Boulton, 1967). In some cases, there may also be reasons of moral obligation. But if there are, they will be instrumental reasons, because heeding the call will play a part in some action that is good or obligatory for some other reasons. For example, it may be that I shall play a part in collective action to achieve some common goal, and that reasons of fairness require me to play my part with others. But my duty is not created by any identification I may have with the abstract group, any more than I would have an obligation created out of my identification with a fictional group. It may be that I have an obligation grounded in the personal relationships I have with others in the group, but then the obligation is grounded in reasons of personal loyalty and commitment to those other individuals, not out of my identification with the abstract group of which we happen to be members. If my country is engaged in a just war, I may well have an obligation to fight, but the genuine moral obligation I have is grounded in fairness to others and in obligations to friends and family, not in abstract patriotism. If my company is struggling to survive in a competitive marketplace, I may have an obligation to work hard as part of its efforts, but if so then that is because I have obligations of fairness and loyalty to others involved in the company, not any duty grounded in identification with the company itself.

Here, the grounds of our genuine moral obligations are different than the forces that will often give us the strongest motivation. It may well be that the obligations I have to fight in a war will stir me less than the sight of my country's flag, or its rousing anthem, or a fervent speech by a Churchill or a Hitler. But that is no more surprising than the fact that I may well be more strongly motivated to pursue my pleasure or relaxation than to carry out some duties I have. It also means that it is not surprising that people may use others' social identities as a basis for persuasion and influence. On the surface, then, there is no greater problem in efforts at influence that trade on people's social identities than there is in appealing to our tendencies to seek pleasure or relaxation.

The special problem arises to the extent that there is a tendency for us to believe that we have obligations tied to our social identities. There is no particular likelihood that we may perceive our inclination towards pleasure and relaxation as duties, but there is some likelihood that we may perceive ourselves to have obligations to abstract groups: phrases like 'patriotic duty' do not ring strangely on our ears, and management literature routinely aims to produce commitment from employees that can amount to a sense of duty. Brewer has commented that 'once identification with a job and an organisation occurs, employees accept values, attitudes and actions that are significant to them but are principally those of the organisation' (Brewer, 1993: 36; referring to Turner, 1982). The problem then is not one where a third party obtains benefit by contriving mutual obligations for others, but the problem that one party influences another by getting the other to perceive obligations where there are none. The similarity between this and the earlier sort of case, and a factor that makes them both problematic, is that in each case people are treated in ways that undermine respect for moral commitments and for the moral status of persons in general. The difference is that in dealing with the earlier sorts of case we have to judge the weight of genuine obligations, affected by the fact that we have not freely consented to them. In the latter, we have to set aside some alleged obligations entirely.

ETHICS, INFLUENCE AND PERCEPTIONS OF LEGITIMACY

It is not only through playing on others' sense of social identity that it is possible to motivate them and get them to perceive duties where there are none. The fact that people are motivated to favour abstract groups of which they are members, and to work for their benefit, is tied in practice to our perceptions of legitimate authority. In theory, the two may be separated. Milgram's experimental subjects seem to have complied with the instructions they were given because they perceived the experimenter as an expert, and not because of any specific group affiliation, or group-related authority. In many cases, however, perceptions of authority will be tied to social contexts where the authority emerges from group membership and group identification. Most obviously, such perceptions of authority will be tied to membership of a community with a recognised government. Cialdini has commented:

> To Milgram's mind, evidence of a chilling phenomenon emerges repeatedly from his accumulated data. 'It is the extreme willingness of adults to go to almost any lengths on the command of an authority that constitutes the chief finding of the study' (Milgram, 1974). There are sobering implications of this finding for those concerned about the ability of another form of authority – government – to extract frightening levels of obedience from ordinary citizens. Furthermore, the finding tells us something about the sheer strength of authority pressures in controlling our behavior. After witnessing Milgram's subjects squirming and sweating and suffering at their task, could anyone doubt the power of the force that held them there?
>
> (Cialdini, 1993: 176; citing Milgram, 1974)

The 'squirming and sweating and suffering' subjects Cialdini is referring to are not the pretended victims in the experiment, but the experimental subjects, the individuals who believed that they were inflicting pain on the victim. Despite the stress they experienced in performing the task they were given, they nearly all went on with it. Their situation may well have been like that of individuals we have discussed above who experience stress from being confronted with conflicting obligations. It seems plausible to suggest that the experimental subjects continued with their task because they believed that they ought to. Perhaps they did not all formulate such a belief, but it seems plausible to suggest that many of them proceeded on that basis.

If so, the situation they found themselves in was very much like that of employees who are instructed to carry out some instruction that is ethically problematic, or a soldier's unease at orders that create some moral qualms. Something that such cases have in common is that individuals experience the situation as one where there are competing ethical calls on them. I noted in Chapter 4 above that members of organisations often experience bureaucratic authority as having legitimate force, as it grows out of the processes of an institutionalised group, involving scripts and role prescriptions that have normative force, which in some sense or other organisational members experience as statements of what they 'ought' to do. There is clear overlap amongst cases where individuals experience a tug from institutionalised authority, and the case where their social identity as a member of an abstract group also impels them towards acting on behalf of the group. In many cases, it will be hard to separate the two forces. Players on a football team will be driven partly by expectations that they have of one another, partly by their coach's instructions, reflecting the legitimised authority of the institutionalised group, and partly by their identification with the team and its efforts. In addition, of course, in the world of professional football, they may be motivated by financial reward, but the fact that this is not always a major consideration is clear both from the experiences many people have from their involvement with sporting teams, and from the efforts and achievements shown by members of amateur clubs. The fact that financial reward is not the only factor that can motivate people is one reason why commercial organisations and others may seek 'commitment' from their members and employees.

It is understandable that perceptions of legitimacy and social identity are such powerful influences on us. We can imagine various sorts of evolutionary explanation for the extent to which we are bewitched by social identity and perceptions of legitimacy. When a group is threatened, by natural forces or otherwise, it may be very important for its survival that its members pull together in a common cause. We can also see cognitive explanations, at least for the effect of social identity, since our own understanding of our place in the world is fundamental to our mental organisation of experience and action.

Because they create such powerful pressures on us, it is hardly surprising that perceptions of legitimacy and social identity are used as sources of influence. However, the use of perceptions of legitimacy is ethically all the more problematic because of the force it has. Earlier in the chapter I noted some ethical concerns about cases where a third party exploits the moral obligations and ethical commitments that people have to one another, and I contended that such actions are especially problematic because they use these obligations and commitments as means, rather than ends: we disregard the importance persons have as beings whose moral dimension is fundamental to who they are.

We may reasonably have similar concerns about influence that is based on people's social identity and perceptions of legitimate authority within an institutionalised group. Deliberate influence using such means can also disregard the importance of the ethical dimension of our existence, in the same way that a counterfeiter just like a burglar may disregard the importance of money to those who use it. Just as a counterfeiter gets us to commit ourselves to endeavours and actions through the use of false currency, so does exploitation of our beliefs and perceptions that we have obligations where in reality we have none. The outcome is a problem for the same reasons that counterfeiting is. Not only does counterfeit currency entice us into actions that fail to achieve what we think they do – payment in genuine coin – at the same time it undermines our faith in genuine currency.

Counterfeit efforts at influencing people that use their social identity and perceptions of legitimacy are problematic because they are effective, and cause us to wonder about the significance or worth of ethical action. To some extent, they can trade on the fact that sometimes there can be real conflict between different ethical obligations, as there are in the kinds of 'dirty hands' situations where we are 'damned if we do and damned if we don't'. Because there are situations where we face genuine conflicts between different obligations we have, we are all the more likely to accept that perceptions of legitimacy and calls of social identity have some genuine moral force when really they have none. It is notable that in the whistleblowing cases studied by Glazer and Glazer, they found that 'only those employees who have a highly developed alternative belief system can withstand the intense pressure to conform to the requirements of management' (Glazer and Glazer, 1989: 97). Sometimes such a belief system was rooted in employees' professional training; sometimes in religious belief. But they needed some clear vision to distinguish the perceptions of organisational legitimacy from genuine ethical demands. A clear vision of what is genuinely an ethical requirement is hugely important, not least because it has to stand up to the great pressures of perceived legitimacy within institutionalised groups, and of the individual's social identity. Certainly, it often had to do that, in Glazer and Glazer's studies: 'whistleblowers, we discovered, are conservative people devoted to their work and their organizations', they commented (Glazer and Glazer, 1989: 5). For such people, it took clear moral views to counteract the pressures on them. The conflict they had to deal with raises some general questions about moral decision making that we consider a little more in the next, concluding, chapter.

SUMMARY

In earlier parts of the book I have tried to analyse some of the logic of the obligations we have on account of our relations with social groups. In the previous chapter I drew out some of the implications for people's multiple and possibly conflicting obligations. In this chapter we have moved on to consider how people's actual or perceived obligations may be used by others to exploit or influence them. The initial sort of case we considered led on from one of the previous chapter's cases of people's multiple obligations, where people's mutual obligations yield benefit to their organisation.

Where people's mutual obligations are contrived or used for others' benefit, the critical issue is how far the arrangement has their informed consent. Where it does not, it may be problematic for a number of reasons, but the most prominent is a failure to respect others as responsible decision makers. While that may be a consideration whenever people's welfare or situation is affected without their informed consent, it is especially salient when their obligations are contrived or exploited, because the requirement on us to meet obligations we have is so clearly tied to our existence as responsible agents.

Although that point is a general one, the cases considered in that context were predominantly drawn from people's interpersonal relationships as members of common-bond groups like work teams. A different point arises in regard to people's roles and membership of common-identity groups. The point once again hinges on respect for people as responsible agents, but in this case the problematic cases are ones where people are influenced by appeal to obligations of loyalty they perceive themselves to have to the abstract group, even though I have argued that such obligations are illusory. Our felt allegiances to abstract groups affect us very much, but our genuine moral obligations are to other individuals and common-bond groups.

Not only our allegiances to abstract groups but also our perceptions of legitimate authority create pressures on us that others can turn to advantage. When that occurs, the ethical problems are extended, sometimes undermining the force of real ethical concerns. Our roles in institutionalised groups can certainly create real obligations for us, but these are grounded primarily in relationships with other individuals, and in the benefit or harm we assist in bringing about through actions by the group. It often requires good moral judgment to work out what our obligations actually are, just as it does to deal with conflicting obligations, as we saw in the previous chapter. In the next chapter I consider some general implications of the complexity of such moral judgment in organisational settings.

8　Decisions, groups and reasons

I began this book by accepting as given some moral and ethical principles that seem plausible and relatively uncontroversial. I identified some such principles in Chapter 1, like principles of beneficence, fairness and respect. Accepting those, I have gone on to consider the ethical implications of some well-attested findings about social life. These have included points about roles and social scripts, and about pressures towards social conformity and towards compliance with authority that is perceived as legitimate. It has been a central theme of our discussion that often these social influences on people can run counter to genuine ethical demands. On the other hand, business organisations and other institutionalised groups are complex social environments, with multiple factors affecting our genuine obligations, including others' expectations and our impact on organisational outcomes. As a result, there is ample scope for conflicts amongst such factors, and for confusion between genuine moral demands and other social pressures.

In this final chapter of the book it is therefore worthwhile to go a little further into the processes by which we make decisions in such situations. I have several times suggested that intuitive judgment is required to make good decisions when faced with the conflicting pressures that surround us in social groups. This idea is at odds with the sort of decision processes that have become common in business and government since the rise of neoliberalism in the 1970s. Neoliberalism has begun to fall into discredit after the global financial crisis that began in 2007, a crisis seen by many as tied to neoliberal laissez-faire policies, but approaches to decisions and organisational arrangements that have been fostered by neoliberalism still remain strong. I focus here on the nexus between neoliberalism and rational choice theory. Sometimes, neoliberalism is more directly associated with public choice theory, but there is a clear association amongst the theoretical approaches to social life that have been labelled 'rational choice', 'social choice' and 'public choice' (Udehn, 1996: 195–204, 251–54). In this chapter, before summarising the main points of the book, I discuss the relationships amongst moral judgment, rational choice theory and neoliberalism, considering as an example the sort of moral problem raised by members of organisations who conscientiously act contrary to official organisational policy. The calculative, result-oriented decision making fostered by neoliberalism has difficulty dealing with this sort of case. It needs reflection and dialogue, processes that can also improve the sort of intuitive moral judgment we need to use in many complex social situations.

RATIONAL CHOICE THEORY AND NEOLIBERALISM

Over the last few decades of the twentieth century, an array of linked views gained hegemony in public policy debate and decision making (Udehn, 1996; Pierre and Peters, 2000: 44). One is rational choice theory, the idea that by and large people's actions can be explained in terms of utility maximisation, and that choices that do not aim at utility maximisation are irrational (cf. Frank, 2004: 3–4). Rational choice theory is closely associated with techniques of economic analysis, and with efforts to apply economic analysis to a wide range of social phenomena, beyond the processes of exchange that have traditionally been thought of as 'economic'.[1]

Despite many theoretical problems, rational choice theory has been called on in some widely accepted approaches to public policy. These include the cousins of rational choice theory that are referred to as social choice theory and public choice theory. These focus especially on politics and organisational governance. Social choice theory addresses how individual preferences can be translated into a collective social preference (Elster and Hylland, 1986: 2). In doing so, it focusses on individual preferences, using economists' techniques to analyse their possible arrangements in social contexts. Similarly, public choice theory is distinguished by its use of economists' tools in analysis of political phenomena (Buchanan, 1991: 218; Self, 1993: 1).

In their approaches to politics and organisational governance, these views tend to focus especially on the so-called 'principal–agent problem', the idea that in general one person cannot trust another to act in accordance with requirements of social roles or agreements unless it is in the other's own interests so to act. This focus is a natural outcome of economic analysis that assumes that most behaviour is the result of self-interested preference. It means, however, that recommendations for organisational governance and management have two characteristics that have been very noticeable, and which can be explained by the support they have gained from rational choice views. First, they have implied that management primarily consists of implementing arrangements to get employees to act in accordance with organisational policy, rather than to engage in dialogue with employees about how best to achieve organisational aims. Second, they have encouraged a

1 For example, to religious belief: see Montgomery (1996) and references therein. Rational choice theory can also still be found as a recommended approach to business ethics (e.g. Hooker, 2011).

'results-based' focus so that employee performance can be most effectively monitored and audited. That is to say, rational choice views have supported 'managerialism' in organisations, especially in public sector organisations (Self, 1993: 157, 167). In addition, the same set of views has been associated with views that so far as possible social organisation should be constructed to allow the operation of free markets, since it is in free markets that individual preferences can best be satisfied. That is to say, rational choice views have supported 'neoliberalism' in public policy (Oatley, 2008: 139).

These approaches to theory and policy have great strengths, and can unquestionably point to worthwhile achievements. In addition, although there are some logical links amongst the views, as indicated, they do not all rely on the same evidence or support. For example, it is possible to argue for neoliberal trade policy on some quite specific economic grounds (Oatley, 2008: ch. 7), while some managerialist initiatives have been prompted by specific organisational inefficiencies (see e.g. Osborne and Gaebler, 1992). The argument I wish to put forward aims at just two points: one, the views I have mentioned have sometimes been extended and their application sought in areas and for purposes that go beyond the support they can reasonably be given; and, two, they distract us from good moral decision making as individuals in group contexts.

These points can be seen by considering the principal–agent problem, alluded to above. It can be stated in a more circumspect way than given above, as shown by Gottheil:

> If personal interests and motives are infused in the production process, then a **principal–agent problem** may arise, undermining the efficacy of labor markets.
>
> How so? Let's suppose you hire a gardener. Do you really know whether the gardener is giving you the full measure of his effort? Acting as principal, you hire the worker for a day, assuming 'an honest day's work.' Acting as agent, the gardener may have other ideas. If he is paid by the hour, it may be in his personal interest to work in slow motion. If he is paid by work done, he may find work where none is needed. You, as principal, are sometimes at a disadvantage not knowing what is slow or fast motion or what really needs to be done in the garden. The agent may be fully aware of and may take advantage of your disadvantage. Herein lies the problem.
>
> (Gottheil, 2008: 387–88, bold type in original; see also
> Bowie and Freeman, 1992)

Sorts of remedy that may be used to overcome the problem include closer monitoring of the agent's work, and closer specification of what it requires. The public sector in particular has been seen as an area where the principal–agent problem arises, because of the ill-defined connections between principals and agents (Hughes, 2003: 12). Remedies for the problem then include 'identifying or establishing accountable units within government departments – units where output can be measured as objectively as possible and where individuals can be held personally responsible for their performance' (Hughes, 2003, 247, quoting the 1968 UK Fulton Report; see also Power, 1997: 43–44).

The approach to management that calls forth such remedies to the principal–agent problem is consistent with some major aspects of rational choice theory. Rational choice theory revolves around decisions that seek to achieve certain outcomes or results, where different results have different utilities, typically to be determined by the extent to which they satisfy individuals' preferences. Remedies to the principal–agent problem typically take the form of defining results that individuals must achieve by their work.

A concrete example illustrates that these views have sometimes gone too far, and may distract us from good moral decision making. I still remember quite vividly some 'result-oriented job descriptions' being trialled in South Australian public administration in the late 1980s. One of them was a job description for a receptionist. The duties of the role had to be defined by the results to be achieved. One of the duties was therefore to 'ensure clients feel that they have been treated courteously'. Why might that seem better than including amongst the duties 'treat clients courteously'? The answer appears to be the need to fit within a 'results-based' framework, and a focus on definable outcomes of roles promoted by concern about the 'principal–agent problem'. It is anticipated that it will be easier to monitor results of agents' actions rather than the character of the action itself.

In fact, the receptionist example gives the lie to that line of argument. The effort to focus on results has been taken too far. This is an example of how reliance on results-oriented decision making over-simplifies and misleads. Assessing whether a client feels courteously treated is not more easily or reliably discovered than whether the treatment was actually courteous. More important from an ethical point of view, however, there is a real difference between treating someone courteously and getting them to feel courteously treated. Treating others courteously involves genuine attention to their concerns and expectations. Getting them to feel courteously treated might be contrived through distraction or otherwise.

Similar problems arise in other contexts where we try to discern obligations or evaluate actions on the basis of routine or stereotyped indicators (Power, 1997: 75, 115–21). In business and management, there are many roles where people's work is like that of the receptionist. In all the many jobs that involve 'emotional labour' (Hochschild, 1983), such as care work and many types of service delivery, it is likely to be the nature of an action itself that is really at issue, and an outcome it achieves only part of what ought to be evaluated. In ethical terms, in particular, respect for persons often involves behaviour of one type rather than another, and it is that we ought to focus on.

In other cases, outcomes may be at issue as much as a specific type of behaviour, but the effort to improve monitoring of employee performance in response to the principal–agent problem distorts and confuses organisational arrangements because of difficulties in defining outcomes in ways that are readily measurable, leading important outcomes to be pushed aside in favour of ones that are measurable. The child protection call centre studied by van den Broek (2003) was mentioned above, and her account vividly illustrates the point, as results like 'number of calls dealt with' or 'average call waiting times' are given priority, rather than difficult-to-define outcomes to do with children's well-being. Such moves to well-defined outcomes that do not require developed professional judgment are symptomatic of 'managerialism', the approach to management that sees similar techniques being applicable to widely different areas of work, so that a manager's finance industry call centre experience may be transferred to a child care protection call centre (van den Broek, 2003: 247).

Various studies have cast light on the extent to which the abstract principal–agent problem ought to shape thinking about organisational arrangements (see e.g. Miller and Whitford, 2002; James, 2005). Empirical studies suggest that individual agents often show concern about fair outcomes and interests of the principal, and simply want to do a good job. Just as focus on well-defined results can detract from good decision making in social contexts, so too can undue focus on individuals' personal preferences as their major motivation.

It is no novelty to suggest that aggregation of individuals' preferences is limited as a basis for decision making. Questions about how far all preferences ought to be given some weight are sometimes referred to as questions about 'consumer sovereignty'. There are complex and difficult issues about strategies to deal with the problems that arise in focussing on individuals' preferences as a basis for decisions (see e.g. Goodin, 1986; Brennan and Walsh, 1990). For us, the point is that rational choice theory and the array of views associated with it may detract from good ethical decision making in the sorts of situations we have been concerned with in this book. By focussing on preferences, these views obscure the need for dialogue and discussion about the sorts of ethical issues that arise in groups. I have argued that in social life, particularly in organisations, we face an array of conflicting factors. Some of these create genuine but conflicting obligations; others create illusory obligations, with a strong psychological pull but no genuine moral force. The need to separate genuine obligations from other influences highlights the shortcomings of preference aggregation as a basis of decision making.

ETHICS, CONSCIENCE AND INSTITUTIONALISED GROUPS

The need to deal with conflicting pressures on us, where we are not immediately sure what ethics requires, is shown most acutely in cases where people conscientiously disagree. In Chapter 4 we noted that authoritative instructions often do create obligations for members of organisations. In particular, they create expectations amongst people that allow them to coordinate their actions in complex situations, to pursue beneficial outcomes and avoid harmful ones. However, it is also true that we cannot simply assume that an organisational requirement or a supervisor's instructions to an employee automatically create a genuine moral obligation. They may just be expressions of power, calling on the additional force of social identification and perceptions of legitimacy within the institutional structure of the organisation. Sometimes their claim to moral authority is very slight.

The sorts of cases that are hard to deal with are those with a balance of considerations on each side. Consider a case reported from the Superior Court of New Jersey (see Beauchamp and Bowie, 2004: 310–14). The plaintiff, Corrine Warthen, was taking action for unfair termination of employment, termination caused by her refusal to dialyse a terminally ill double amputee patient.

> On two occasions plaintiff claims that she had to cease treatment because the patient suffered cardiac arrest and severe internal hemorrhaging during the dialysis procedure. ... She approached her head nurse and informed her that 'she had moral, medical, and philosophical objections' to performing this procedure on the patient because the patient was terminally ill and, she contended, the procedure was causing the patient additional complications.
>
> (Beauchamp and Bowie, 2004: 310, extracted from *Warthen v. Toms River Community Memorial Hospital*, Superior Court of New Jersey, 488 A.2d 299 [1985]; see also Provis, 2006)

Eventually, Warthen refused to dialyse the patient and was dismissed. Her (unsuccessful) lawsuit relied partly on reference to her general moral qualms, and partly on role prescriptions to be found in the American Nurses Association Code for Nurses.

What were the genuine ethical requirements in the situation? It may be that the instructions Warthen was given were in fact reasonable and appropriate ones, justified and given moral force by the needs of the patient. But there are plenty of cases where individuals have been victimised where they were plainly in the right (see e.g. Glazer and Glazer, 1989). The difficulty is to make that judgment. Sometimes, organisational requirements are legitimate, and the right thing to do is conform with them. But sometimes they are not, despite being supported by pressures of social identity and perceived legitimacy, and the right thing is to stand against them. The difficulty is a general one about discerning what is right. There is no simple rule, like saying that the organisation is always right, or always wrong. There are many cases where it is hard to make a judgment.

There are two sides to the coin. On the one hand, organisational requirements and instructions may be morally problematic, and the problem is how individuals can withstand influences of social identity and perceived legitimacy, reminding us of Glazer and Glazer's suggestion that individuals need well-developed belief systems and moral commitments to do so. On the other hand, organisational requirements and instructions may be ethically quite proper, and a problem arises if an individual refuses to comply, even if refusal is prompted by some sincerely held but mistaken beliefs.

The fact that an individual's commitment and belief system is strong enough to stand up against social influence pressures does not automatically mean it is correct. However, from the point of view of the individual making a decision, the situation is very much as Frankena described it, in his discussion of conscience:

> It remains true, nevertheless, that a man must in the moment of decision do what he thinks is right. He cannot do otherwise. This does not mean that what he does will be right or even that he will not be worthy of blame or punishment. He simply has no choice, for he cannot at that moment see any discrepancy between what is right and what he thinks is right. The life of man, even if he would be moral, is not without its risks.
>
> (Frankena, 1963: 46)

For each of us, as individuals, we may find ourselves in situations where we need to make a decision, confronted by some institutionalised imperatives, and then all we can do is take everything into account and decide accordingly. We cannot be enjoined in such a situation to set aside the call of conscience, because the call of conscience is by definition our belief about what it is best to do.

That was the point of view we adopted in considering Jean's situation, in the case of Jean and the new product in Chapter 5. We tried to consider things as they presented themselves to her. But there is another point of view: the observer of the other's action. This may be a colleague's point of view, or a manager's, like Corinne Warthen's head nurse. What should we do in the face of the other's conscientious objection to an organisational demand?

Whatever our organisational role, there is a demand on us to respect the conscience of the other individual, for the sort of reason we have turned to previously: the need to regard persons as moral beings in a community of moral beings. Toleration of another's conscience is not just respect for their rights or preservation of their freedom: it is respect for them as moral agents, capable of making choices on moral grounds.

The problem is the need to weigh organisational needs against the individual's commitment, when we ourselves disagree with their position, even if we respect it as genuine. In that case, we have to compare the force of our conflicting obligations: the obligation we have to assist the organisation, against the need to respect the individual we regard as sincere, but misguided. The process needs to be one of exploration and dialogue. It cannot only be one of aggregating preferences.

One motivation behind rational choice theory is that it can simplify the process of giving reasons to others. We noted in Chapter 1 that Mill proffered its 'tangible and intelligible mode of deciding' ethical differences as a merit of utilitarianism. With a tendency to focus on outcomes, rational choice theory can offer the same advantage, but in doing so falls foul of some of the same problems as classical utilitarianism. Difference is overcome by reducing problems to calculation in terms of a common currency, whether pleasure (Bentham), happiness (Mill) or utility (rational choice theory). However worthy its objective of promoting agreement, this approach actually pushes aside exploration of differences in dialogue and social exchange. As we have seen earlier, the ethical issues that arise in group contexts are often complex and difficult. In simplifying issues to become matters of preference, to allow agreement to be reached more easily, we put aside some of the complexities and difficulties that are actually very important.

Thus, proponents of public choice views have tended to identify 'political' as opposed to 'economic' behaviour merely by the fact that political behaviour involves voting rather than exchange (e.g. Brennan, 1990). To the extent that economic analysis focusses on the preferences that people display in choices they actually make, it is no surprise that it tends to focus on voting behaviour rather than the deliberative processes that occur in a lot of politics. In fact, however, it is characteristic of much political behaviour to involve discussion and argument in processes that gradually lead to more refined judgments and shared understandings, even if they do not result in full agreement. Indeed, McLean notes that 'Many people, including politicians and political theorists, are deeply suspicious of "government by opinion poll"' (1991: 188), adding that 'Voters' unconsidered opinions on the doorstep are no substitute for measured opinions reached after discussion.'

That leads to the second main effect of rational choice theory on public policy: to encourage populism in politics. The concept of 'right of choice', developed primarily in relation to its effect on the market, is extended from the economic to the political sphere, generating the idea that all preferences ought to be given equal weight in the realm of public policy. However, this tendency of rational choice theory to encourage populism can then be complemented by appeal to ingroup identification and the associated mechanism of influence: 'Populists speak in the name of the inclusive people while targeting a feared minority fit for exclusion' (Uhr, 2005: 96). The psychological mechanisms that draw us into such ingroup loyalties have been discussed above, together with the morally questionable potential they offer for exploitation by unscrupulous individuals.

The implication is that accounts of political behaviour that focus too exclusively on voting discourage good moral decision making, because they discourage the dialogue and exchange of views and ideas that are needed for people to arrive at a considered understanding of their obligations, and preferences that reflect respect for others as well as themselves. The remaining question then is whether we can say more about improving the processes of dialogue and exchange that are important for us to work out what we ought to do.

CONSCIENCE, MORAL EDUCATION AND RATIONAL CHOICE

Cases of conscientious disagreement raise problems for rational choice theory because aggregation of preferences and calculation of outcomes does not show us how to respect views we disagree with. It fails to distinguish between mere preference and conscientious moral commitment. Dealing with the latter requires us to engage in dialogue about others' reasons, not only considering the fact of their commitment and the force of their preference, but also considering the possibility that we ourselves may be wrong.

However, cases of conscientious disagreement also raise problems for the sort of intuitive decision making that I have suggested is often necessary in complex social situations. Different individuals may have conflicting intuitive moral judgments about an issue. This is unsurprising, since intuitive judgment is fallible. We may feel ourselves to have a clear intuitive judgment about an issue, where our judgment is actually unsound. Kahneman and Klein have noted that 'people, including experienced professionals, sometimes have subjectively compelling intuitions even when they lack true skill' (2009: 521). This is true of some areas where it is clear that there is expertise to be had: they mention the case of baseball scouts judging potential players. We might expect the problem to be even greater in matters of ethical judgment, where there are not such clear criteria to evaluate judgment as a player's subsequent performance can provide. It is highlighted in cases of conscientious action, where people are at odds over what to do.

While this is initially a problem about intuitive judgment, the fact that our intuitive judgment may be subjectively compelling, even though it is faulty, points the way to fuller understanding of how intuitive judgment is developed, and the role of social groups in developing it.

It is well attested that intuitive pattern recognition is the basis for expert decisions in chess and other such activities (Klein, 1998: ch. 10). Nevertheless, there have been substantial improvements in chess strategy since the middle of the nineteenth century, and problems have been identified with openings and endgame strategies that were previously well accepted. Often, such advances have occurred not through improved judgment during the play of a game, but through analysis before and after. By analogy, we can see how advances may occur in other areas that use intuitive pattern recognition, moral judgment included. Our ability to recognise patterns in events and situations is typically developed not only through exposure to a variety of instances with feedback about them, but also through opportunity to reflect on them. Modern work about development of people's decision making refers not only to processes of routine and formal analysis, but also to reflective thought and intuition (Smith, 2008). Intuition can certainly lead us astray, but through recognising how important it is, and understanding how it functions, we can improve many decisions (Haidt, 2001; Hogarth, 2008; Kahneman and Klein, 2009). Advances in moral understanding can emerge through reflection, even though on-the-spot judgment in complex situations may need to rely on intuition.

A basic account of the mechanisms by which intuitive judgment is developed can be given by the idea of repeated synaptic adjustment, in particular the idea of 'synaptic adjustment by the successive backpropagation of errors' (Churchland, 1995: 42), which has been modelled in artificial neural networks. The models show how such networks can develop abilities to recognise patterns such as human faces. Accounts of human neural mechanisms have begun to complement work on artificial neural mechanisms (Lehrer, 2009), and explain many cases where we can learn to recognise patterns through exposure to a variety of instances. That sort of mechanism is a key to explaining important basic cases. However, it is limited in how far it can go. It encounters difficulty in cases where feedback we receive is unreliable because it is vague or the product of 'wicked' environments in which our judgments are self-fulfilling prophecies. Hogarth gives the example of Anna, a waitress who develops an intuitive understanding of who will give the best tips, based on how well-dressed they are. The trouble is that she is more attentive to such customers, and may get better tips from them because of that extra attention she gives them.

Development of intuitive judgment is based not only on repeated exposure to relevant instances, but also to language-based social exchange: 'connections are established in people's minds not only by what they see but also by what they have been told by others' (Hogarth, 2001: 86). Others' advice could have encouraged Anna to believe that better-dressed customers would leave better tips, or others' advice could encourage her to see whether less well-dressed customers will leave equally good tips if given more attention.

The significance of language emerges clearly from studies of intuitive judgment in practical decision making. Most notably, Gary Klein and his colleagues have reported extensive studies on how intuitive expertise is developed and used in natural settings (see especially Klein, 1998). Unsurprisingly, it is based on experience. Unsurprisingly, too, this experience may develop abilities to make fine discriminations and detect salient cues (Klein, 1998: ch. 10). In addition, it commonly involves 'mental simulation' (Klein and Crandall, 1995; Klein, 1998: ch. 5), where we mentally project from a perceived present state of affairs into the future, and evaluate that hypothetical future. In the context of our present discussion, though, the crucial point is that often we retain memories of patterns and linkages through their embodiment in stories, rather than remembering abstract principles (Klein, 1998, ch. 11).

Stories are not always told in words, but most often they are. The idea that stories are important is tied to the point that in many contexts language use is integral to humans' development of good intuitive judgment. This point has been emphasised by a number of writers, including both Clark (2000) and Hogarth (2001). They show the links between language and intuition, and possibilities for overcoming limitations imposed by wicked learning environments: 'humans have evolved capacities for learning in wicked structures. These include the powers of imagination and communication through language' (Hogarth, 2001: 225). Clark has argued that

> human moral expertise is made possible only by the potent complementarity between two distinct types of cognitive resource ... One is, indeed, the broadly pattern-based, skill-learning capacity that we share with other animals and artificial neural networks. But the other is, precisely, the very special modes of learning, collaboration and reason made available by the tools, of words, rules, and linguistic exchange.
>
> (Clark, 2000: 269)

When we are dealing with complex social situations, we may not be able to analyse the details fully, but we can imagine alternatives, and we can continue to do so after judgment and action have given us more information than we had initially. Such reflection can help us for the future, and refine our intuitions. Use of language allows this reflection to be taken further, with analysis and dialogue that complement reflection on judgment and decisions. The fact that we retain memories in the form of stories suggests that the processes of social exchange by which more experienced individuals convey their experience to others ought to include stories as an important component. But language allows more than the embodiment of intuition in stories. It also allows critical scrutiny where step-by-step reasoning comes to the fore.

Such critical scrutiny is possible in cases where people conscientiously disagree. We can examine our own intuitions and others' to see how consistent they are with other beliefs we hold and with testimony from others about their own experiences. The process is typically a to-and-fro exchange, and participating in it is a sign of people's genuine respect for one another. Crucially, it takes place most often in face-to-face interaction, and that fact reflects the moral importance of small, face-to-face groups.

Development of moral intuition in small group interaction is the sort of process by which children develop understanding of social norms and standards. They get feedback through social exchange and dialogue, when they make judgments and decisions about what is appropriate in various different sorts of situations. Initially, that may just acquaint them with local community norms and standards, but through reflection and dialogue they can start to refine their intuitive judgment. This can happen especially as they become members of larger, institutionalised groups like schools, and then sporting clubs, business organisations and professional associations.

Professional associations in particular are a clear example of how larger institutionalised groups can assist in the development of good intuitive moral judgment, drawing on the effects of language-based dialogue as well as direct experience and feedback. Even here, though, face-to-face interaction is very important in developing professional expertise and judgment, as more experienced individuals pass on their knowledge and understanding. Explanation of our actions is a social process not just in being provision of information by one person to another, but as a process of mutual interaction based on shared understandings about the world and about people (Marková et al., 1995). It is because professionals develop their judgment in a social context, learning from others with more experience, as well as through 'book learning', that we may wish to refer to a profession as a 'community of practice' (see e.g. Duguid, 2005). The social context allows new members simultaneously to develop judgment and the ability to use relevant language. The language may then be used not only in social exchange but in codification of ethical standards. Often, professional associations show the effects of developing intuitive judgment through social interaction with other more experienced individuals, conjoined with institutionalised codes of professional practice, integrating language-based understanding and role expectations.

Thus, the use of intuitive judgment to make decisions in complex social situations is consistent with language-based reasoning and dialogue about our actions in those situations. In rejecting rational choice theory we are not rejecting reason. In situations of conscientious disagreement we are emphasising the importance of reasons, but their importance in processes of reflection and dialogue, not of calculation or rule following. The implication is a need for moral education that integrates experience and judgment with dialogue and rationality. Those points need emphasis at present because of the hegemony of rational choice theory, with its allied efforts to reduce decision making down to a series of rules and algorithms, eliminating the need for moral education.

Rational choice theory, neoliberalism and the ethics of groups

Rational choice theory has been associated with the neoliberalism promoted and implemented by politicians like Margaret Thatcher and Ronald Reagan (Considine, 2005: 71; Stoker, 2006: 122). If I am expressing doubts about rational choice theory, and aspects of neoliberalism that are associated with rational choice theory, it may be asked how those doubts fit with what has been said above about the question I labelled Thatcher's issue: how far we can ascribe ethical responsibility to society and social groups.

There is a link between rational choice theory and Thatcher's decrying of 'society' as a fiction, compared to individuals and families. Rational choice theory emphasises individual preference as a basis for calculation, aiming to aggregate preferences of different individuals to reach a decision, and minimising appeals to collective action to address social problems. The account given in this book goes along Thatcher's line, at least so far as I have argued that it is only individuals and small, face-to-face groups that have moral worth in their own right, in contrast with large, abstract collectives like corporations, nations and societies. Nevertheless, that line of argument is consistent with critiques of neoliberalism and rational choice theory, for two reasons. First, I have suggested in this chapter that in complex social situations decisions often need to be arrived at through collaborative processes, rather than through calculative preference aggregation. Second, large institutionalised groups like corporations or nations can often have great instrumental significance. They allow us to deliver products and services ranging from consumer goods to health, education and welfare.

In discussing options for regeneration of democratic politics, Stoker has suggested that we discard ways of thinking that so exaggerate regard for individuals that we cannot sustain our collective life (2006: 204), and goes on to discuss the ways in which neoliberal thinking has emphasised individuals and individual freedom, at the expense of collective action and public, social goods. As so often, the appropriate way forward here seems to be a mean between extremes. Face-to-face relationships with other individuals are crucially important for ethics, but the obligations we have to one another still go beyond obligations to known individuals. The emphasis of the discussion in Chapters 2 and 3 was that individuals have obligations to other individuals that they do not have towards abstract identity groups like nations and corporations. We can imagine obligations towards abstract identity groups that are not genuine obligations. But it is also possible to make an opposite mistake: focussing so much on our obligations to friends, family and acquaintances that we forget other obligations we have in terms of universal moral principles, obligations of beneficence, fairness, honesty and the like, to other individuals who are not personally known to us.

In addition, I have argued that individuals are obliged to assist good things that are done or attempted by groups of which they are members, just as we may be obliged to assist actions by other individuals. The question identified as Thatcher's issue then simply fades away. Thatcher's concern is that we may eschew responsibility as individuals because we expect action by society and social institutions like governments or welfare agencies. On the present account, we retain our individual obligations and responsibilities, without being committed to such a view as 'there is no such thing as society'. Both welfare agencies and business corporations may do good and productive things, in different contexts. That does not free us from individual responsibilities: we have responsibilities as individuals to assist their activities where practicable and appropriate.

This account harmonises with everyday, common-sense views. We can accept that institutionalised groups like societies, government, businesses and the like are important parts of our lives, without implying that our obligations or responsibilities vanish, being replaced by the responsibilities of societies and governments. The networks of interrelated roles that make up institutionalised groups are indispensable for coordinating social activities to produce modern goods and services. We have responsibilities by virtue of roles we play, but these are not separate kinds of responsibilities from others. We are constantly in situations where we have some requirements on us to meet others' reasonable expectations, but also to assess our possible actions in terms of their contributions to group actions and outcomes. We cannot take it for granted that those group actions and outcomes are good, but in many cases we have grounds to believe they are, and then we ought to do what we can to assist.

Thus, this account aims to find a middle point between individualist views that deny or deplore the significance of group activities, and collectivist views that subordinate individuals to groups. In the context of Thatcher's issue, we can accept that as individuals we have responsibilities that we cannot simply shift to abstract groups, but we can also accept that institutionalised groups are important in supporting our lives in a community, and we ought to assist institutionalised groups to provide that support.

At the same time, this account suggests a response to Kennedy's issue, which was juxtaposed with Thatcher's issue: whether we have moral obligations to groups. The simple answer was that we may have obligations to common-bond groups, for reasons that are tied to our obligations towards individuals: individuals' identities cannot be neatly separated from those of other individuals in small, common-bond groups. However, it is often hard to see what genuine responsibilities we have towards large, abstract groups: they are mental constructs we use to categorise ourselves and others, rather than objects of real moral worth. The exception is that on occasion such groups may also be institutionalised groups, and then we may have obligations towards them for instrumental reasons: we can assist or hinder what they do, for good or ill. When Kennedy enjoins us to think what we can do for our country, we can put his call aside so far as it suggests we aim to promote the interests of the country, but we can accept it so far as it asks us to consider how we may contribute to the good work done by its institutionalised groups, be they government, business, charitable organisations or others.

SUMMARY: THE MAIN POINTS

Rational choice theory underestimates the importance of reflection and dialogue, because it fails to appreciate the need for intuitive moral judgment and the way that reflection and dialogue can improve such judgment. In practical terms, rational choice theory also neglects details of the psychological factors that affect decision making, too often explaining poor decisions as the simple result of self-interest or reasoning error. Good decision making requires us to look more closely at some details of social life. That has been the aim of this book, and in this concluding section we can summarise the details we have considered.

The issues are difficult because we are not just subject to a variety of influences in groups and organisations. Many of the influences appear like obligations, but I have argued that in fact they are a mixture of genuine obligations with counterfeits, pressures that we can mistake for obligations but which lack real moral force. It is certainly true that we are prey to factors that have no semblance of obligation about them, such as greed, self-interest and laziness, but these do not provide great theoretical difficulty. The discussion here has focussed on factors that may sometimes influence us just as much, but which we may be more likely to confuse with genuine obligations. To make this case it has been necessary to consider what factors underlie genuine obligations, and I have located these primarily in such general moral principles as beneficence, justice and respect for persons. Accepting principles like these, we clearly have obligations to other people, but it is less clear what obligations we have to groups, and how our obligations are affected by membership of groups.

I have argued that we may have genuine obligations to small, face-to-face groups, because for relevant purposes it may be impossible to separate fully the identities of individuals within those groups. However, we can contrast such small, face-to-face groups with large, abstract groups like nations and major organisations. Minimal group experiments show that we tend to identify with abstract groups even when they are essentially fictional, and it is hard to see how such commitments reflect genuine obligations. More often, they are associated with ingroup–outgroup conflict that can degenerate into corporate scandal, violence, oppression or war. It is hard to see how large, abstract groups have separate interests or rights of their own that can be weighed against the interests or rights of individual human beings. However, large, abstract groups like nations or major organisations can be institutionalised through networks of roles and relationships amongst individuals, and we can treat those institutionalised groups as performing actions. Whatever the metaphysical status of the group action, relative to actions performed by individual group members, we can appraise individuals' actions by reference to whether they help or hinder the group action, coupled with evaluation of the group action itself.

However, individuals in groups do not only have obligations associated with their potential contribution to actions of the group as a whole. They have a multiplicity of other obligations, and in an institutionalised setting these emerge prominently from role requirements. Role scripts both predict and prescribe what role incumbents will do. Having a role implies that others expect one to act according to known scripts, and they base their own decisions and actions on these expectations.

The expectations others have of us often create genuine obligations. Failure to act as others expect can lead to their harm or discomfiture, potentially violating principles of beneficence or respect, at least. That is especially clear where we are responsible for others having the expectations they do, but is also true even in some cases where we have no responsibility for those expectations others have of us.

Within organisations and other institutionalised groups, the interwoven expectations people have of one another are a widespread source of obligations. The harm and discomfiture that others may experience when we fail to live up to the expectations that are tied to our roles can be both significant and extensive. However, the genuine obligations we have can easily be confused with obligations to comply with authority perceived as legitimate, like the authority of the experimenter in Milgram's studies. Just as we tend to identify with abstract groups, so we tend to heed authority that we perceive as legitimate, regardless of how far it reflects genuine obligations. We may indeed have obligations to act according to the requirements of our roles, but those obligations are created by the whole array of others' expectations. Organisational authority and others' expectations may often point in the same direction, but in terms of underlying moral principles, our obligations are created not by authoritative instructions so much as by the expectations these may create in others, together with the contribution our actions can make to worthwhile organisational outcomes.

In organisations we thus have many genuine obligations but other pressures on us also, which can masquerade as obligations. These include not only our tendencies to identify with abstract groups and to comply with authority that is perceived as legitimate; they also include the simple, well-known conformity pressures that operate within groups, pressures both to see things as others do and to act as they do. The result is complex and difficult ethical decision making, and one implication of the account given here is that shortcomings of our moral decision making in group situations are often too simply explained as being due to self-interest or lack of regard for moral requirements. The complexity of real decision making in organisations and other groups means that we must go beyond calculation of outcomes or uncritical rule following. Modern work on decision making recognises the importance of pattern recognition and intuition in many decisions, and that is what is required in cases like the hypothetical example of Jean and the new product, discussed in Chapter 5. However, the fact that intuitive judgment may be required to deal with the moral complexities that face us in groups and organisations does not entail that no judgments are better than others, and we may improve our judgment through experience, reflection and dialogue.

The case of Jean and the new product is one of several set in the fictional Endeavour organisation. They aim to illustrate some ideas discussed in earlier chapters, but also to provide an opportunity to look more closely at some of the points they raise. Discussion of Jean's conflicting responsibilities opened the way for subsequent examination of the conflicts of obligations that may confront us in organisations. Obligations we have as a result of others' expectations of us may be unsought and unwanted but may be genuine obligations nonetheless. The idea of role conflict is well known, but more often considered because of the stress it creates than because of the moral dilemma it often embodies.

It is fundamental to this account that the types of obligations we have are not of different basic types. The obligations we have as citizens, employees, parents or friends are all equally obligations that emerge from the sorts of considerations we noted in Chapter 1: beneficence, respect and so on. Role obligations or obligations as members of groups are not different types of obligations, but emerge from considerations similar to the obligations we have in all the other parts of our lives. If we are making decisions, the considerations we have to take into account when we are in groups are no different than elsewhere.

That does not mean that decision making is easy. Despite what proponents of rational choice theory may say to the contrary, we cannot simply calculate 'aggregate' preferences, and we shall be confronted with many situations like Jean's with the new product, where a number of considerations are entwined and opposed. To understand and support good decision making, we need to appreciate and combat the tendencies we have to favour simple, rule-based solutions, and also our human tendency to be influenced by factors like social identity and group conformity. It can assist if we understand that our decision making often is based on prototypes or exemplars.

We can then help ourselves by identifying and focussing on specific examples of good decisions, and contrast them with cases where we are affected by influences that run counter to good ethical decisions. Milgram's experiments provide one clear example of the tendency we all have to be unduly influenced by authority that we perceive as legitimate. Another is given by experiments where individuals embrace a social identity derived from an abstract group that is essentially a fictional construct. Apart from such examples of research, we can also bear in mind documented cases like Corinne Warthen's. We may not always have a clear view of the facts of such cases, but they can remind us of what is possible, and what may have to be considered in specific instances.

In addition, although there may be no rules or algorithms or universal safeguards that will allow us to approach such cases in a routine way, we can also remind ourselves of some of the general issues that arise, in simple terms. For example, some are conflicts between group requirements and individuals' moral commitments. Elsewhere, individuals performing roles in institutionalised groups confront inconsistent expectations from others and inconsistent obligations as a result. In either case, it is problematic to create or allow situations where individuals find themselves faced with such conflict.

We might like to separate cases where people wrongly believe themselves to be confronted by conflicting moral demands from cases where they are truly confronted by such conflict: for example, we might want to agree with the hospital against Corinne Warthen, if we knew all the facts of the case. However, in practical terms, the cases need to be dealt with similarly, if we accept that we may sometimes be mistaken and sometimes be correct about what are genuine moral requirements. It may assist if mechanisms or organisational processes are set in place to address questions about whether the conflicts of obligations are real or not. Initially, these may involve some cost, by way of time and delay, and probably the commitment of other people to consider issues thoughtfully or to arrange alternative courses of action that will free individuals from conflicting demands. But such processes are important, and the time spent on such issues is decreased by developing the moral judgment of people in the situation. If we fail to address such issues in one way or another, just assuming that all preferences and inclinations are equal, then we fail to notice things that set us apart as persons who have the capacity to be responsible decision makers.

We may also be able to make the process easier. We can foresee situations where people may be confronted by dilemmas, and try to structure arrangements differently to ease those dilemmas (as is done in cases of potential conflicts of interest). We may also be able to structure arrangements to assist moral decision making, not only to ease dilemmas, but also to make clearer what is required. For example, I argued above that in organisations we must be careful not to assign too much weight to official rule prescriptions or formal authority, needing to consider the parts our actions play in assisting or hindering good or bad actions by the organisation as a whole. In large modern organisations it may simply be difficult to assess what effects our own actions will have on the organisation as a whole, and it can assist us if organisational arrangements make that clearer, mitigating Thompson's 'many hands' problem, and allowing us a clear vision of the implications of our individual actions. Then we can truly accept responsibility, rather than falling into it, heedless or unknowing. The more that organisations permeate our lives, the more important that is.

References

Adobor, H. (2006) 'Exploring the Role Performance of Corporate Ethics Officers', *Journal of Business Ethics* 69(1): 57–75.

Albrow, M. (1970) *Bureaucracy*. Macmillan, London.

Allinson, R. E. (1998) Review of D. Vaughan, *The Challenger Launch Decision: Risky Technology, Culture and Deviance at NASA* (Chicago: University of Chicago Press, 1996). *Business Ethics Quarterly* 8(4): 743–56.

Anscombe, G. E. M. (1958) 'Modern Moral Philosophy', *Philosophy* 33: 1–19. Reprinted in R. Crisp and M. Slote, eds, *Virtue Ethics*. Oxford University Press, Oxford, 1997: 26–44.

Appelbaum, E. (2002) 'The Impact of New Forms of Work Organization on Workers', in G. Murray, J. Bélanger, A. Giles and P. Lapointe, eds, *Work and Employment Relations in the High Performance Workplace*. Continuum, London: 120–49.

Aristotle. (1934) *Nicomachean Ethics*, translated by H. Rackham. Harvard University Press, Cambridge, MA.

Atiyah, P. S. (1967) *Vicarious Liability in the Law of Torts*. Butterworths, London.

Austin, J. (1998) *The Province of Jurisprudence Determined*. Ashgate, Aldershot. First published 1832.

Baron, M. (1984) *The Moral Status of Loyalty*. Kendall/Hunt Publishing Co., Chicago.

Baron, R. S., N. L. Kerr and N. Miller. (1992) *Group Process, Group Decision, Group Action*. Open University Press, Buckingham.

Barrett, R. A. (1984) *Culture and Conduct*. Wadsworth, Belmont, CA.

Batson, C. D. (1998) 'Altruism and Prosocial Behavior', in D. T. Gilbert, S. T. Fiske and G. Lindzey, eds, *The Handbook of Social Psychology*, 4th edn, vol. 2. McGraw-Hill, Boston: 282–316.

Beauchamp, T. L. and N. E. Bowie (eds). (2004) *Ethical Theory and Business*, 7th edn. Pearson, Upper Saddle River, NJ.

Beaumont, P. B. (1993) *Human Resource Management: Key Concepts and Skills*. Sage, London.

Bélanger, J., A. Giles and G. Murray. (2002) 'Towards a New Production Model: Potentialities, Tensions and Contradictions', in G. Murray, J. Bélanger, A. Giles and P. Lapointe, eds, *Work and Employment Relations in the High Performance Workplace*. Continuum, London: 15–71.

Benn, S. I. (1988) *A Theory of Freedom*. Cambridge University Press, Cambridge.

Benn, S. I. and R. S. Peters. (1959) *Social Principles and the Democratic State*. George Allen &Unwin, London.

Bentham, J. (1962) 'Introduction to the Principles of Morals and Legislation', in M. Warnock, ed., *Utilitarianism, On Liberty, Essay on Bentham. Together with selected writings of Jeremy Bentham and John Austin.* Collins/Fontana, London: 33–77. First published 1789.

Betsch, T. (2008) 'The Nature of Intuition and Its Neglect in Research on Judgment and Decision Making', in H. Plessner, C. Betsch and T. Betsch, eds, *Intuition in Judgment and Decision Making.* Psychology Press, New York: 3–22.

Bettinghaus, E. P. and M. J. Cody. (1994) *Persuasive Communication*, 5th edn. Harcourt Brace, Fort Worth, TX.

Bicchieri, C. (2006) *The Grammar of Society: The Nature and Dynamics of Social Norms.* Cambridge University Press, Cambridge.

Biddle, B. J. (1986) 'Recent Developments in Role Theory', *Annual Review of Sociology* 12: 67–92.

Bloch, M. (1965) *Feudal Society*, translated by L. A. Manyon, vol. 1. Routledge & Kegan Paul, London.

Blum, L. A. (1980) *Friendship, Altruism and Morality.* Routledge & Kegan Paul, London.

Boatright, J. R. (2009) *Ethics and the Conduct of Business*, 6th edn. Pearson Prentice-Hall, Upper Saddle River, NJ.

Bok, S. (1984) *Secrets: On the Ethics of Concealment and Revelation.* Oxford University Press, Oxford.

Boulton, D. (1967) *Objection Overruled.* MacGibbon & Kee, London.

Bovens, M. (1998) *The Quest for Responsibility: Accountability and Citizenship in Complex Organisations.* Cambridge University Press, Cambridge.

Bowie, N. E. (1999) *Business Ethics: A Kantian Perspective.* Blackwell, Oxford.

Bowie, N. E. and R. E. Freeman (eds). (1992) *Ethics and Agency Theory: An Introduction.* Oxford University Press, New York.

Boxall, P. and J. Purcell. (2007) 'Strategic Management and Human Resources: The Pursuit of Productivity, Flexibility, and Legitimacy', in A. Pinnington, R. Macklin and T. Campbell, eds, *Human Resource Management Ethics and Employment.* Oxford University Press, Oxford: 66–80.

Brandt, R. B. (1959) *Ethical Theory.* Prentice-Hall, Englewood Cliffs, NJ.

Brennan, G. (1990) 'Irrational Action, Individual Sovereignty and Political Process: Why There *is* a Coherent "Merit Goods" Argument', in G. Brennan and C. Walsh, eds, *Rationality, Individualism and Public Policy.* Centre for Research on Federal Financial Relations, Australian National University, Canberra: 97–118.

Brennan, G. and C. Walsh (eds). (1990) *Rationality, Individualism and Public Policy.* Centre for Research on Federal Financial Relations, Australian National University, Canberra.

Brenner, S. N. and E. A. Molander. (1977) 'Is the Ethics of Business Changing?' *Harvard Business Review* (January-February): 57–71.

Brewer, A. M. (1993) *Managing for Employee Commitment.* Longman, Melbourne.

Brooke, C. (1975) *Europe in the Central Middle Ages*, revised edn. Longman, London.

Brown, A. D. (1995) *Organisational Culture.* Pitman, London.

Brown, R. (1988) *Group Processes: Dynamics Within and Between Groups.* Blackwell, Oxford.

Brown, R. W. (1986) *Social Psychology: The Second Edition.* The Free Press, New York.

Brysk, A. (1995) '"Hearts and Minds": Bringing Symbolic Politics Back In', *Polity* 27(4): 559–85.

Buber, M. (1957) 'The William Alanson White Memorial Lectures, Fourth Series', *Psychiatry* 20: 95–129.

Buchanan, J. M. (1991) 'Politics without Romance: A Sketch of Positive Public Choice Theory and Its Normative Implications', in P. Pettit, ed., *Contemporary Political Theory*. Macmillan, New York: 216–28. Originally published in *IHS Journal*, 1979.

Buunk, B. P. (2001) 'Affiliation, Attraction and Close Relationships', in M. Hewstone and W. Stroebe, eds, *Introduction to Social Psychology*. Blackwell, Oxford: 371–400.

Cappelli, P. (1999) *The New Deal at Work: Managing the Market-Driven Workforce*. Harvard Business School Press, Cambridge, MA.

Carr, A. Z. (1968) 'Is Business Bluffing Ethical?' *Harvard Business Review* Jan-Feb: 143–53.

Cassidy, J. (2009) *How Markets Fail: The Logic of Economic Calamities*. Farrar, Straus and Giroux, New York.

Chugh, D., M. H. Bazerman and M. R. Banaji. (2005) 'Bounded Ethicality as a Psychological Barrier to Recognizing Conflicts of Interest', in D. A. Moore, D. M. Cain, G. Loewenstein and M. H. Bazerman, eds, *Conflicts of Interest: Challenges and Solutions in Business, Law, Medicine, and Public Policy*. Cambridge University Press, Cambridge: 74–95.

Churchland, P. M. (1995) *The Engine of Reason, the Seat of the Soul*. MIT Press, Cambridge, MA.

Cialdini, R. B. (1993) *Influence: Science and Practice*, 3rd edn. Harper Collins, New York.

Clark, A. (2000) 'Word and Action: Reconciling Rules and Know-How in Moral Cognition', in R. Campbell and B. Hunter, eds, *Moral Epistemology Naturalized*. University of Calgary Press, Calgary: 267–89. *Canadian Journal of Philosophy* Supplementary Volume 26.

'Climber's Everest Decision Agony'. (2006) *BBC News*, 23 May, http://news.bbc.co.uk/1/hi/england/tees/5010348.stm, accessed 2 September 2006.

Clutterbuck, D. (2003) *Managing Work–life Balance*. CIPD, London.

Coady, C. A. J. (1990) 'Messy Morality and the Art of the Possible', *Proceedings of the Aristotelian Society* Supp. vol. 64: 259–79.

—— (1991) 'Politics and the Problem of Dirty Hands', in P. Singer, ed., *A Companion to Ethics*. Blackwell, Oxford: 373–83.

Cocking, D. and J. Kennett. (2000) 'Friendship and Moral Danger', *Journal of Philosophy* 97(5): 278–96.

Cohen, S. (2004) *The Nature of Moral Reasoning*. Oxford University Press, Melbourne.

Considine, M. (2005) *Making Public Policy*. Polity Press, Cambridge.

Considine, M. and M. Painter (eds). (1997) *Managerialism: The Great Debate*. Melbourne University Press, Melbourne.

Crane, A. and D. Matten (2007) *Business Ethics*, 2nd edn. Oxford University Press, Oxford.

Crisp, R. and M. Slote. (1997) 'Introduction', in R. Crisp and M. Slote, eds, *Virtue Ethics*. Oxford University Press, Oxford: 1–25.

Cross, R. and J. W. Harris. (1991) *Precedent in English Law*, 4th edn. Clarendon Press, Oxford.

Cullity, G. (2007) 'The Moral, the Personal and the Political', in I. Primoratz, ed., *Politics and Morality*. Palgrave Macmillan, New York: 54–75.

Dane, E. and M. G. Pratt. (2007) 'Exploring Intuition and Its Role in Managerial Decision Making', *Academy of Management Review* 32(1): 33–54.

Danley, J. R. (2005) 'Polishing Up the Pinto: Legal Liability, Moral Blame, and Risk', *Business Ethics Quarterly* 15(2): 205–36.

Davies, B. and R. Harré. (1999) 'Positioning and Personhood', in R. Harré and L. van Langenhove, eds, *Positioning Theory*. Blackwell, Oxford: 32–52.

Davis, M. and A. Stark (eds). (2001) *Conflict of Interest in the Professions*. Oxford University Press, Oxford.

Dawes, R. M. and R. H. Thaler. (1988) 'Anomalies: Cooperation', *Journal of Economic Perspectives* 2: 187–97.

Deal, T. E. and A. A. Kennedy. (1988) *Corporate Cultures: The Rites and Rituals of Corporate Life*. Penguin, Harmondsworth.

'Death on the Mountain'. (2006) ABC National Radio, *The Sports Factor*, 2 June, www.abc.net.au/rn/sportsfactor/stories/2006/1651512.htm#, accessed 2 September 2006.

Dees, J. G. and P. C. Cramton. (1991) 'Shrewd Bargaining on the Moral Frontier: Toward a Theory of Morality in Practice', *Business Ethics Quarterly* 1(2): 135–67.

Delbridge, R. (1998) *Life on the Line in Contemporary Manufacturing*. Oxford University Press, Oxford.

Delbridge, R. and P. Turnbull. (1992) 'Human Resource Maximization: The Management of Labour under Just-in-Time Manufacturing Systems', in P. Blyton and P. Turnbull, eds, *Reassessing Human Resource Management*. Sage, London: 56–73.

Doherty, N. and S. Tyson. (2000) 'HRM and Employee Well-Being: Raising the Ethical Stakes', in D. Winstanley and J. Woodall, eds, *Ethical Issues in Contemporary Human Resource Management*. Palgrave Macmillan, London: 102–15.

Donaldson, T. (1982) *Corporations and Morality*. Prentice-Hall, Englewood Cliffs, NJ.

Duggan, A., M. Bryan and F. Hanks. (1994) *Contractual Non-Disclosure*. Longman, Melbourne.

Duguid, P. (2005) '"The Art of Knowing": Social and Tacit Dimensions of Knowledge and the Limits of the Community of Practice', *The Information Society* 21(2): 109–18.

Dunfee, T. W. and D. E. Warren. (2001) 'Is Guanxi Ethical? A Normative Analysis of Doing Business in China', *Journal of Business Ethics* 32(3): 191–204.

Duska, R. (2004) 'Whistleblowing and Employee Loyalty', in T. L. Beauchamp and N. L. Bowie, eds, *Ethical Theory and Business*, 7th edn. Prentice-Hall, Upper Saddle River, NJ: 305–10.

Dworkin, R. (1989) 'The Original Position', in N. Daniels, ed., *Reading Rawls*, 2nd edn. Stanford University Press, Stanford, CA: 16–53. Reprinted from *University of Chicago Law Review*, 1973.

Eaton, J. (1966) *Political Economy: A Marxist Textbook*. International Publishers, New York.

Edelman, G. (1992) *Bright Air, Brilliant Fire: On the Matter of the Mind*. Penguin, London.

Edwards, P., J. Geary and K. Sisson. (2002) 'New Forms of Work Organization in the Workplace: Transformative, Exploitative, or Limited and Controlled?', in G. Murray, J. Bélanger, A. Giles and P. Lapointe, eds, *Work and Employment Relations in the High Performance Workplace*. Continuum, London: 72–119.

Edwards, P. and J. Wajcman. (2005) *The Politics of Working Life*. Oxford University Press, Oxford.

Elkington, J. (1999) *Cannibals with Forks: The Triple Bottom Line of 21st Century Business*. Capstone, Oxford.

Ellemers, N., S. A. Haslam, M. J. Platow and D. van Knippenberg. (2003) 'Social Identity at Work: Developments, Debates, Directions', in S. A. Haslam, D. van Knippenberg, M. J. Platow and N. Ellemers, eds, *Social Identity at Work: Developing Theory for Organizational Practice*. Psychology Press, New York: 3–26.

Elliot, N., E. Katz and R. Lynch. (1993) 'The Challenger Tragedy: A Case Study on Organizational Communication and Professional Ethics', *Business and Professional Ethics Journal* 12(2): 91–108.

Elster, J. (1989) *Nuts and Bolts for the Social Sciences*. Cambridge University Press, Cambridge.

Elster, J. and A. Hylland. (1986) 'Introduction', in J. Elster and A. Hylland, eds, *Foundations of Social Choice Theory*. Cambridge University Press, Cambridge: 1–10.

Erickson, M. H. (1967) 'The Confusion Technique in Hypnosis', in J. Haley, ed., *Advanced Techniques of Hypnosis and Therapy*. Grune & Stratton, New York: 130–57. Originally in *The American Journal of Clinical Hypnosis* 6 (1964): 183–207.

Feinberg, J. (1965) 'Action and Responsibility', in M. Black, ed., *Philosophy in America*. Allen & Unwin, London: 134–60. Reprinted in A. R. White, ed., *The Philosophy of Action*. Oxford University Press, Oxford, 1968: 95–119.

—— (1984) *Harm to Others*. Oxford University Press, New York. Vol. 1 of Feinberg's *The Moral Limits of the Criminal Law*.

—— (1986) *Harm to Self*. Oxford University Press, New York. Vol. 3 of Feinberg's *The Moral Limits of the Criminal Law*.

Fielder, J. H. (1992) 'Organizational Loyalty', *Business and Professional Ethics Journal* 11(1): 71–90.

Fiske, S. T. and S. E. Taylor. (1991) *Social Cognition*, 2nd edn. McGraw-Hill, New York.

Fletcher, G. (1993) *Loyalty: An Essay on the Morality of Relationships*. Oxford University Press, New York.

Forster, E. M. (1965) *Two Cheers for Democracy*. Penguin, Harmondsworth. First published 1951.

Forsyth, D. R. (1990) *Group Dynamics*, 2nd edn. Wadsworth, Belmont, CA.

Frank, R. H. (2004) *What Price the Moral High Ground? Ethical Dilemmas in Competitive Environments*. Princeton University Press, Princeton, NJ.

Frankena, W. K. (1963) *Ethics*. Prentice-Hall, Englewood Cliffs, NJ.

French, P. A. (1979) 'The Corporation as a Moral Person', *American Philosophical Quarterly* 16(3): 207–15.

—— (1984) *Collective and Corporate Responsibility*. Columbia University Press, New York.

—— (1995) *Corporate Ethics*. Harcourt Brace, Forth Worth, TX.

Friedman, M. (1970) 'The Social Responsibility of Business Is to Increase Its Profits', *New York Times Magazine*, 13 September.

Gilligan, C. (1982) *In a Different Voice*. Harvard University Press, Cambridge, MA.

Glazer, M. P. and P. M. Glazer. (1989) *The Whistleblowers*. Basic Books, New York.

Goffman, E. (1971) *The Presentation of Self in Everyday Life*. Penguin, Harmondsworth. First published 1959.

Golden-Biddle, K. and H. Rao. (1997) 'Breaches in the Boardroom: Organizational Identity and Conflicts of Commitment in a Nonprofit Organization', *Organization Science* 8(6): 593–611.

Goodin, R. E. (1986) 'Laundering Preferences', in J. Elster and A. Hylland, eds, *Foundations of Social Choice Theory*. Cambridge University Press, Cambridge: 75–101.

—— (1996) 'Institutions and Their Design', in R. E. Goodin, ed., *The Theory of Institutional Design*. Cambridge University Press, Cambridge: 1–53.

Goodpaster, K. E. (2007) *Conscience and Corporate Culture*. Blackwell, Oxford.

Gottheil, F. (2008) *Principles of Microeconomics*, 5th edn. Thomson, Mason, OH.

Grover, S. L. (1997) 'Lying in Organizations', in R. A. Giacalone and J. Greenberg, eds, *Antisocial Behavior in Organizations*. Sage, Thousand Oaks, CA: 68–84.

Grover, S. L. and R. Moorman. (2009) 'Challenges to Leader Integrity', in C. Garsten and T. Hermes, eds, *Ethical Dilemmas in Management*. Routledge, London: 53–63.

Haidt, J. (2001) 'The Emotional Dog and Its Rational Tail: A Social Intuitionist Approach to Moral Judgment', *Psychological Review* 108(4): 814–34.

Hardin, R. (1996) 'Institutional Morality', in R. E. Goodin, ed., *The Theory of Institutional Design*. Cambridge University Press, Cambridge: 126–53.

Harré, R. and L. van Langenhove. (1999) 'The Dynamics of Social Episodes', in R. Harré and L. van Langenhove, eds, *Positioning Theory*. Blackwell, Oxford: 1–13.

Hart, H. L. A. and A. M. Honoré. (1959) *Causation in the Law*. Oxford University Press, Oxford.

Herron, T. L. and D. L. Gilbertson. (2004) 'Ethical Principles vs. Ethical Rules: The Moderating Effect of Moral Development on Audit Independence Judgments', *Business Ethics Quarterly* 14(3): 499–523.

Hinde, R. A. (1987) *Individuals, Relationships and Culture*. Cambridge University Press, Cambridge.

Hobbes, T. (1968) *Leviathan*, edited by C. B. Macpherson. Penguin, Harmondsworth. First published 1651.

Hochschild, A. R. (1983) *The Managed Heart*. University of California Press, Berkeley.

Hogarth, R. M. (2001) *Educating Intuition*. University of Chicago Press, Chicago.

—— (2008) 'On the Learning of Intuition', in H. Plessner, C. Betsch and T. Betsch, eds, *Intuition in Judgment and Decision Making*. Psychology Press, New York: 91–105.

Homans, G. C. (1964) 'Bringing Men Back In', *American Sociological Review* 29(5): 809–18.

Hooker, J. (2011) *Business Ethics as Rational Choice*. Prentice-Hall, Boston.

Hughes, O. E. (2003) *Public Management and Administration: An Introduction*, 3rd edn. Palgrave Macmillan, London.

Ignatius Loyola, St. (1951) *The Spiritual Exercises of St. Ignatius*, translated by L. J. Puhl. Loyola University Press, Chicago.

Jackall, R. (1988) *Moral Mazes*. Oxford University Press, New York.

Jackson, F. (1987) 'Group Morality', in P. Pettit, R. Sylvan and J. Norman, eds, *Metaphysics and Morality: Essays in Honour of J. J. C. Smart*. Basil Blackwell, Oxford: 91–110.

Jackson, J. (1996) *An Introduction to Business Ethics*. Blackwell, Oxford.

James, H. S., Jr. (2005) 'Why Did You Do That? An Economic Examination of the Effect of Extrinsic Compensation on Intrinsic Motivation and Performance', *Journal of Economic Psychology* 26(4): 549–66.

Janis, I. L. (1972) *Victims of Groupthink*. Houghton Mifflin, Boston.

Jepperson, R. L. (1991) 'Institutions, Institutional Effects, and Institutionalism', in W. W. Powell and P. J. DiMaggio, eds, *The New Institutionalism in Organizational Analysis*. University of Chicago Press, Chicago: 143–63.

Johnson, M. (1993) *Moral Imagination*. University of Chicago Press, Chicago.

Jowett, G. S. and V. O'Donnell. (1986) *Propaganda and Persuasion*. Sage, Newbury Park, CA.

Kahneman, D. and G. Klein. (2009) 'Conditions for Intuitive Expertise', *American Psychologist* 64(6): 515–26.

Kant, I. (1964) *Groundwork of the Metaphysic of Morals*, translated by H. J. Paton. Harper & Row, New York. First published in German in 1785.

Katz, D. and R. L. Kahn. (1966) *The Social Psychology of Organizations*. John Wiley & Sons, New York.

Keay, D. (1987) 'AIDS, Education and the Year 2000', *Woman's Own*, 31 October, pp. 8–10.

Kelly, C. and J. Kelly. (1994) 'Who Gets Involved in Collective Action? Social Psychological Determinants of Individual Participation in Trade Unions', *Human Relations* 47(1): 63–88.

Kipnis, A. (2002) 'Practices of *Guanxi* Production and Practices of *Ganqing* Avoidance', in T. Gold, D. Guthrie and D. Wank, eds, *Social Connections in China: Institutions, Culture, and the Changing Nature of Guanxi*. Cambridge University Press, Cambridge: 21–34.

Kiss, E. (2006) 'Combining Clarity and Complexity: A Layered Approach to Cross-Cultural Ethics', in R. Grant, ed., *Naming Evil, Judging Evil*. University of Chicago Press, Chicago: 139–73.

Klein, G. (1998) *Sources of Power: How People Make Decisions*. MIT Press, Cambridge, MA.

Klein, G. and B. W. Crandall. (1995) 'The Role of Mental Simulation in Problem Solving and Decision Making', in P. Hancock, J. Flach, J. Caird and K. Vicente, eds, *Local Applications of the Ecological Approach to Human-Machine Systems*. Lawrence Erlbaum: Hillsdale, NJ: 324–358.

Knoke, D. (1990) *Organizing for Collective Action*. Aldine de Gruyter, New York.

Kohlberg, L. (1976) 'Moral Stages and Moralization: The Cognitive-Developmental Approach', in T. Lickona, ed., *Moral Development and Behavior: Theory, Research and Social Issues*. Holt, Rinehart and Winston, New York: 31–53.

Kopala, B. (2004) 'The Influence of Pressure on Nurses' Moral Capacity', in D. C. Thomasma and D. N. Weisstub, eds, *The Variables of Moral Capacity*. Kluwer, Dordrecht: 159–71.

Kutz, C. (2000) *Complicity: Ethics and Law for a Collective Age*. Cambridge University Press, Cambridge.

Ladd, J. (1970) 'Morality and the Ideal of Rationality in Formal Organizations', *Monist* 54(4): 488–516.

—— (1984) 'Corporate Mythology and Individual Responsibility', *International Journal of Applied Philosophy* 2(1): 1–21.

Lahiry, S. (1994) 'Building Commitment Through Organizational Culture', *Training and Development* 48(4): 50–52.

Lai, K. (2006) *Learning from Chinese Philosophies*. Ashgate, Aldershot.

Laing, R. D. (1969) *Self and Others*, 2nd edn. Tavistock Publications, London.

Laslett, P. (1956) 'The Face to Face Society', in P. Laslett, ed., *Philosophy, Politics and Society: First Series*. Basil Blackwell, Oxford: 157–84.

Latham, M. (1998) *Civilising Global Capital*. Allen & Unwin, Sydney.

Lehrer, J. (2009) *How We Decide*. Houghton Mifflin Harcourt, Boston.

Leidner, R. (1993) *Fast Food, Fast Talk: Service Work and the Routinization of Everyday Life*. University of California Press, Berkeley.

Leung, T. K. P. and Y. H. Wong. (2001) 'The Ethics and Positioning of *Guanxi* in China', *Marketing Intelligence and Planning* 19(1): 55–64.

Levine, J. M. (1999) 'Solomon Asch's Legacy for Group Research', *Personality and Social Psychology Review* 3(4): 358–64.

Lewis, D. (1969) *Convention: A Philosophical Study*. Harvard University Press, Cambridge, MA.

Luban, D. (1989) *Lawyers and Justice*. Princeton University Press, Princeton, NJ.

—— (2001) 'Law's Blindfold', in M. Davis and A. Stark, eds, *Conflict of Interest in the Professions*. Oxford University Press, Oxford: 23–48.

Lukes, S. (1973) *Individualism*. Basil Blackwell, Oxford.

Luo, Y. (2000) *Guanxi and Business*. World Scientific Publishing Co., Singapore.

Maciejewski, J. J. (2005) 'Reason as a Nexus of Natural Law and Rhetoric', *Journal of Business Ethics* 59(3): 247–57.

Marková, I., C. F. Graumann and K. Foppa (eds). (1995) *Mutualities in Dialogue*. Cambridge University Press, Cambridge.

Martin, R. and M. Hewstone. (2003) 'Social-Influence Processes of Control and Change: Conformity, Obedience to Authority, and Innovation', in M. A. Hogg and J. Cooper, eds, *The Sage Handbook of Social Psychology*. Sage, London: 347–66.

May, L. (1987) *The Morality of Groups*. University of Notre Dame Press, Notre Dame, IN.

McLean, I. (1991) 'Forms of Representation and Systems of Voting', in D. Held, ed., *Political Theory Today*. Polity Press, Cambridge: 172–96.

McShane, S. and T. Travaglione. (2003) *Organisational Behaviour on the Pacific Rim*. McGraw-Hill, Sydney.

Michael, M. L (2006) 'Business Ethics: The Law of Rules', *Business Ethics Quarterly* 16(4): 475–504.

Milgram, S. (1974) *Obedience to Authority*. Harper & Row, New York.

Mill, J. S. (1968) *Utilitarianism, Liberty, Representative Government*. Dent, London. Originally published 1859–63.

Miller, G. J. and A. B. Whitford. (2002) 'Trust and Incentives in Principal-Agent Negotiations', *Journal of Theoretical Politics* 14(2): 231–67.

Montgomery, J. D. (1996) 'Contemplations on the Economic Approach to Religious Behavior', *The American Economic Review* 86(2): 443–47.

—— (1998) 'Toward a Role-Theoretic Conception of Embeddedness', *American Journal of Sociology* 104(1): 92–125.

—— (2000) 'The Self as a Fuzzy Set of Roles, Role Theory as a Fuzzy System', *Sociological Methodology* 30: 261–314.

—— (2005) 'The Logic of Role Theory: Role Conflict and Stability of the Self-Concept', *Journal of Mathematical Sociology* 29(1): 33–71.

Moore, D. A., D. M. Cain, G. Loewenstein and M. H. Bazerman (eds). (2005) *Conflicts of Interest: Challenges and Solutions in Business, Law, Medicine, and Public Policy*. Cambridge University Press, Cambridge.

Moore, D. A., G. Loewenstein, D. M. Cain and M. H. Bazerman. (2005) 'Introduction', in D. A. Moore, D. M. Cain, G. Loewenstein and M. H. Bazerman, eds, *Conflicts of Interest: Challenges and Solutions in Business, Law, Medicine, and Public Policy*. Cambridge University Press, Cambridge: 1–9.

Morris, C. (1972) *The Discovery of the Individual: 1050–1200*. Harper & Row, New York.

Moskowitz, G. B. (2005) *Social Cognition*. The Guilford Press, New York.

Murphy, J. G. (1971) 'Involuntary Acts and Criminal Liability', *Ethics* 81(4): 332–42. Reprinted in Jeffrie G. Murphy, *Retribution, Justice and Therapy*. Dordrecht, Reidel, 1979.

Nagel, T. (1986) *The View from Nowhere*. Oxford University Press, New York.

Newton, T. (1995) *'Managing' Stress: Emotion and Power at Work*. Sage, London.

Noddings, N. (1984) *Caring: A Feminine Approach to Ethics and Moral Education*. University of California Press, Berkeley.

Nowak, A., R. R. Vallacher and M. E. Miller. (2003) 'Social Influence and Group Dynamics', in T. Millon and M. J. Lerner, eds, *Handbook of Psychology*, vol. 5. John Wiley & Sons, Hoboken, NJ: 383–417.

Oatley, T. (2008) *International Political Economy*, 3rd edn. Pearson, New York.

Oliver, N. and A. Davies. (1990) 'Adopting Japanese-Style Manufacturing Methods: A Tale of Two (UK) Factories', *Journal of Management Studies* 27(5): 555–70.

Orts, E. W. (2001) 'Conflict of Interest on Corporate Boards', in M. Davis and A. Stark, eds, *Conflict of Interest in the Professions*. Oxford University Press, Oxford: 129–55.

Osborne, D. and T. Gaebler. (1992) *Reinventing Government*. Addison-Wesley, Reading, MA.

Osborne, R. (2004) *Greek History*. Routledge, London.

Owen, W. (1963) *The Collected Poems of Wilfred Owen*, edited by C. Day Lewis. Chatto & Windus, London.

Parfit, D. (1984) *Reasons and Persons*. Clarendon Press, Oxford.

Parker, M. and J. Slaughter. (1988) *Choosing Sides: Unions and the Team Concept*. Labor Notes, Boston.

Peck, M. S. (1990) *The Road Less Travelled*. Arrow Books, London. First published 1978.

Pettit, P. (1988) 'The Paradox of Loyalty', *American Philosophical Quarterly* 25(2): 163–71.

—— (1997) 'The Consequentialist Perspective', in M. Baron, P. Pettit and M. Slote, *Three Methods of Ethics: A Debate*. Blackwell, Oxford: 92–174.

—— (2007) 'Responsibility Incorporated', *Ethics* 117(2): 171–201.

Phillips, A. (1993) *Democracy and Difference*. Polity Press, Cambridge.

Pierre, J. and B. G. Peters. (2000) *Governance, Politics and the State*. Macmillan, London.

Plessner, H., C. Betsch and T. Betsch (eds). (2008) *Intuition in Judgment and Decision Making*. Psychology Press, New York.

Pocock, B. (2003) *The Work/Life Collision*. Federation Press, Sydney.

Pollock, S., H. K. Bhabha, C. A. Breckenridge and D. Chakrabarty. (2002) 'Cosmopolitanisms', in C. A. Breckenridge, S. Pollock, H. K. Bhabha and D. Chakrabarty, eds, *Cosmopolitanism*. Duke University Press, Durham, NC: 1–14.

Popper, K. (1957) *The Poverty of Historicism*. Routledge and Kegan Paul, London. First published in *Economica*, 1944–45.

Postmes, T. and J. Jetten (eds). (2006) *Individuality and the Group*. Sage, London.

Power, M. (1997) *The Audit Society: Rituals of Verification*. Oxford University Press, Oxford.

—— (2004) 'Counting, Control and Calculation: Reflections on Measuring and Management', *Human Relations* 57(6): 765–83.

Prentice, D. A., D. T. Miller and J. R. Lightdale. (1994) 'Asymmetries in Attachments to Groups and to Their Members: Distinguishing Between Common-Identity and Common-Bond Groups', *Personality and Social Psychology Bulletin* 20(5): 484–93.

Provis, C. (2004) *Ethics and Organisational Politics*. Edward Elgar, Cheltenham and Northampton.

—— (2006) 'Industrial Relations, Ethics and Conscience', *Business Ethics: A European Review* 15(1): 64–75.

—— (2007) 'Ethics, Groups and Belief', *Australian Journal of Professional and Applied Ethics* 9(2): 4–13.

—— (2010a) 'The Ethics of Impression Management', *Business Ethics: A European Review* 19(2): 199–212.

—— (2010b) 'Virtuous Decision Making for Business Ethics', *Journal of Business Ethics* 91(1): 3–16.

Provis, C., J. McKay and J. Tomaino. (1998) 'Whistleblowing and Organisational Strategy', *Journal of Contemporary Issues in Business and Government* 4(1): 43–51.

Provis, C. and S. Stack. (2004) 'Caring Work, Personal Obligation and Collective Responsibility', *Nursing Ethics* 11(1): 5–14.

Rabin, M. (1998) 'Psychology and Economics', *Journal of Economic Literature* 36(1): 11–46.

Rachels, J. (1995) *The Elements of Moral Philosophy*, 2nd edn. McGraw-Hill, New York.

Rawls, J. (1972) *A Theory of Justice*. Clarendon Press, Oxford.

Raz, J. (2000) 'The Truth in Particularism', in B. Hooker and M. O. Little, eds, *Moral Particularism*. Clarendon Press, Oxford: 48–78.

Riley, P. (1983) 'A Structurationist Account of Political Culture', *Administrative Science Quarterly* 28: 414–37.

Robbins, S. P., T. Waters-Marsh, R. Cacioppe and B. Millett. (1994) *Organisational Behaviour: Concepts, Controversies and Applications; Australia and New Zealand*. Prentice-Hall, Sydney.

Rogers, T. B. (1981) 'A Model of the Self as an Aspect of the Human Information Processing System', in N. Cantor, ed., *Personality, Cognition, and Social Interaction*. Lawrence Erlbaum, Hillsdale, NJ: 193–214.

Ross, L. and A. Ward. (1995a) 'Naive Realism in Everyday Life: Implications for Social Conflict and Misunderstanding', in T. Brown, E. Reed and E. Turiel, eds, *Values and Knowledge*. Erlbaum, Hillsdale, NJ: 103–35.

—— (1995b) 'Psychological Barriers to Conflict Resolution', in M. P. Zanna, ed., *Advances in Experimental Social Psychology*, vol. 27. Academic Press, San Diego, CA: 255–304.

Ross, W. D. (1930) *The Right and the Good*. Clarendon Press, Oxford.

Rothschild, J. and T. D. Miethe. (1994) 'Whistleblowing as Resistance in Modern Work Organizations', in J. M. Jermier, D. Knights and W. R. Nord, eds, *Resistance and Power in Organizations*. Routledge, London: 252–73.

Sadler-Smith, E. and P. R. Sparrow. (2008) 'Intuition in Organizational Decision Making', in G. P. Hodgkinson and W. H. Starbuck, eds, *The Oxford Handbook of Organizational Decision Making*. Oxford University Press, Oxford: 305–24.

Sally, D. (1995) 'Conversation and Cooperation in Social Dilemmas: A Meta-Analysis of Experiments from 1958 to 1992', *Rationality and Society* 7: 58–92.

Samuels, S. M. and L. Ross. (1993) 'Reputations versus Labels: The Power of Situational Effects in the Prisoner's Dilemma Game'. Unpublished manuscript, Stanford University.

Sandler, T. (1992) *Collective Action: Theory and Applications*. University of Michigan Press, Ann Arbor.

Scanlon, T. M. (1998) *What We Owe to Each Other*. Harvard University Press, Cambridge, MA.

Schaefer, R. T. and R. P. Lamm. (1995) *Sociology*, 5th edn. McGraw-Hill, New York.

Schank, R. C. and R. P. Abelson. (1977) *Scripts, Plans, Goals and Understanding*. Lawrence Erlbaum, Hillsdale, NJ.

Scheffler, S. (1995) 'Individual Responsibility in a Global Age', *Social Philosophy and Policy* 12: 219–36.

—— (1997) 'Relationships and Responsibilities', *Philosophy and Public Affairs* 26(3): 189–209.

Scheffler, S. (ed.). (1988) *Consequentialism and Its Critics*. Oxford University Press, Oxford.

Schein, E. H. (1992) *Organizational Culture and Leadership*, 2nd edn. Jossey-Bass, San Francisco.

Schiffer, S. R. (1972) *Meaning*. Clarendon Press, Oxford.

Schoemaker, P. J. H. and J. E. Russo. (1993) 'A Pyramid of Decision Approaches', *California Management Review* (Fall): 9–31.

Schroeder, D. A., L. A. Penner, J. F. Dovidio and J. A. Piliavin. (1995) *The Psychology of Helping and Altruism: Problems and Puzzles*. McGraw-Hill, New York.

Self, P. (1993) *Government by the Market? The Politics of Public Choice*. Macmillan, London.

Sennett, R. (1998) *The Corrosion of Character*. W. W. Norton & Co., New York.

Shaw, W. H. (2005) *Business Ethics*, 5th edn. Wadsworth, Belmont, CA.

Sherif, C. W. (1976) *Orientation in Social Psychology*. Harper & Row, New York.

Sherif, M. (1936) *The Psychology of Social Norms*. Harper & Row, New York.

—— (1966) *In Common Predicament: Social Psychology of Intergroup Conflict and Cooperation*. Houghton Mifflin, Boston.

Sherman, N. (1989) *The Fabric of Character: Aristotle's Theory of Virtue*. Clarendon Press, Oxford.

Sidgwick, H. (1907) *The Methods of Ethics*, 7th edn. Macmillan, London.

Sims, R. R. and J. Brinkmann. (2009) 'Thoughts and Second Thoughts about Enron Ethics', in C. Garsten and T. Hermes, eds, *Ethical Dilemmas in Management*. Routledge, London: 103–16.

Singer, P. (1981) *The Expanding Circle: Ethics and Sociobiology*. Clarendon Press, Oxford.

Smiley, M. (2005) 'Collective Responsibility', *Stanford Encyclopedia of Philosophy*, available at http://plato.stanford.edu/archives/fall2005/entries/collective-responsibility/

Smith, E. E., C. Langston and R. E. Nisbett. (1992) 'The Case for Rules in Reasoning', *Cognitive Science* 16(1): 1–40.

Smith, G. F. (2008) 'Teaching Decision Making', in G. P. Hodgkinson and W. H. Starbuck, eds, *The Oxford Handbook of Organizational Decision Making*. Oxford University Press, Oxford: 455–74.

Smith, P. B. and M. H. Bond. (2003) 'Honoring Culture Scientifically when Doing Social Psychology', in M. A. Hogg and J. Cooper, eds, *The Sage Handbook of Social Psychology*. Sage, London: 43–61.

Solomon, R. C. (1992) *Ethics and Excellence*. Oxford University Press, New York.

—— (1994) *Above the Bottom Line: An Introduction to Business Ethics*, 2nd edn. Harcourt Brace, Fort Worth, TX.

Solso, R. L. (1995) *Cognitive Psychology*, 4th edn. Allyn and Bacon, Boston.

Stansbury, J. and B. Barry (2007) 'Ethics Programs and the Paradox of Control', *Business Ethics Quarterly* 17(2): 239–61.

Staw, B. M. (1991) 'Organizational Psychology and the Pursuit of the Happy/Productive Worker', in R. M. Steers and L. W. Porter, eds, *Motivation and Work Behavior*, 5th edn. McGraw-Hill, New York: 264–77. Originally published in *California Management Review* 28(1986): 40–53.

Stocker, M. (1976) 'The Schizophrenia of Modern Ethical Theories', *Journal of Philosophy* 73: 453–66. Reprinted in R. Crisp and M. Slote, eds, *Virtue Ethics*. Oxford University Press, Oxford, 1997: 66–78.

—— (1987) 'Duty and Friendship', in E. F. Kittay and D. T. Meyers, eds, *Women and Moral Theory*. Rowman & Littlefield, Totowa, NJ: 56–68.

—— (1990) *Plural and Conflicting Values*. Clarendon Press, Oxford.

Stoker, G. (2006) *Why Politics Matters: Making Democracy Work*. Palgrave Macmillan, Basingstoke.

Stone, L. (1972) *The Causes of the English Revolution 1529–1642*. Routledge and Kegan Paul, London.

Stone, R. J. (2008) *Managing Human Resources*, 2nd edn. John Wiley & Sons Australia, Milton, QLD.

Stroebe, W. and K. Jonas. (2001) 'Health Psychology: A Social-Psychological Perspective', in M. Hewstone and W. Stroebe, eds, *Introduction to Social Psychology*. Blackwell, Oxford: 519–57.

Swann, W. B., Jr and R. J. Ely. (1984) 'A Battle of Wills: Self-Verification Versus Behavioral Confirmation', *Journal of Personality and Social Psychology* 46(6): 1287–1302.

Tan, D. and R. S. Snell. (2002) 'The Third Eye: Exploring *Guanxi* and Relational Morality in the Workplace', *Journal of Business Ethics* 41(4): 361–84.

Tawney, R. H. (1938) *Religion and the Rise of Capitalism*. Penguin, Harmondsworth. First published 1926.

Taylor, C. (1991) *The Ethics of Authenticity*. Harvard University Press, Cambridge, MA.

Thomas, E. J. (1960) 'Effects of Facilitative Role Interdependence on Group Functioning', in D. Cartwright and A. Zander, eds, *Group Dynamics*, 2nd edn. Tavistock Publications, London: 449–71. Reprinted from *Human Relations* 4 (1951): 39–56.

Thompson, D. (1980) 'Moral Responsibility of Public Officials: The Problem of Many Hands', *American Political Science Review* 74(4): 905–16.

—— (1983) 'Ascribing Responsibility to Advisers in Government', *Ethics* 93(3): 546–60.

Thompson, P. and D. McHugh. (1995) *Work Organisations: A Critical Introduction*, 2nd edn. Macmillan, London.

Thomson, R. M. (ed.). (1974) *The Chronicle of the Election of Hugh, Abbot of Bury St. Edmunds and Later Bishop of Ely*. Clarendon Press, Oxford. Translation of *Cronica de Electione Hugonis Abbatis Postea Episcopi Eliensis*, c. 1222–29.

Treviño, L. K. and K. A. Nelson. (2007) *Managing Business Ethics: Straight Talk About How To Do It Right*, 4th edn. John Wiley & Sons, New York.

Treviño, L. K., G. R. Weaver and S. J. Reynolds. (2006) 'Behavioral Ethics in Organizations: A Review', *Journal of Management* 32(6): 951–90.

Turner, J. C. (1982) 'Towards a Cognitive Redefinition of the Social Group', in H. Tajfel, ed., *Social Identity and Intergroup Relations*. Cambridge University Press, Cambridge: 15–40.

Udehn, L. (1996) *The Limits of Public Choice: A Sociological Critique of the Economic Theory of Politics*. Routledge, London.

—— (2001) *Methodological Individualism: Background, History and Meaning*. Routledge, London.

Uhr, J. (2005) *Terms of Trust*. University of New South Wales Press, Sydney.

Van Avermaet, E. (2001) 'Social Influence in Small Groups', in M. Hewstone and W. Stroebe, eds, *Introduction to Social Psychology*. Blackwell, Oxford: 403–43.

van den Broek, D. (2003) 'Selling Human Services: Public Sector Rationalisation and the Call Centre Labour Process', *Australian Bulletin of Labour* 29(3): 236–52.

Vaughan, D. (1996) *The Challenger Launch Decision*. University of Chicago Press, Chicago.

Waley, D. (1975) *Later Medieval Europe: From Saint Louis to Luther*, revised edn. Longman, London.

Wang, L. (2002) *Grass Fortune*. Penguin, Camberwell, VIC.

Watson, J. (1988) *Nursing: Human Science and Human Care*. National League for Nursing, New York.

Weaver, G. R. (2006) 'Virtue in Organizations: Moral Identity as a Foundation for Moral Agency', *Organization Studies* 27(3): 341–68.

Weber, M. (1930) *The Protestant Ethic and the Spirit of Capitalism*, translated by T. Parsons. Allen & Unwin, London. First published in German in 1904–5.

—— (1947) *The Theory of Social and Economic Organization*, translated by A. M. Henderson and T. Parsons. The Free Press, New York. Translation of part I of *Wirtschaft und Gesellschaft*, c. 1915.

—— (1968) *Economy and Society*, vol. 1. Bedminster Press, New York. German original c. 1914–20.

Werhane, P. H. (1999) *Moral Imagination and Management Decision-Making*. Oxford University Press, New York.

Williams, B. (1979) 'Internal and External Reasons', in R. Harrison, ed., *Rational Action*. Cambridge University Press, Cambridge: 17–28.

Wittgenstein, L. (1958) *Philosophical Investigations*, 2nd edn, translated by G. E. M. Anscombe. Basil Blackwell, Oxford.

Wolfe, A. (1989) *Whose Keeper? Social Science and Moral Obligation*. University of California Press, Berkeley.

Wolgast, E. (1992) *Ethics of an Artificial Person: Lost Responsibility in Professions and Organizations*. Stanford University Press, Stanford, CA.

Wueste, D. E. (1994) 'Role Moralities and the Problem of Conflicting Obligations', in D. E. Wueste, ed., *Professional Ethics and Social Responsibility*. Rowman & Littlefield, Lanham, MD: 103–20.

Young, J., C. J. Thomsen, E. Borgida, J. L. Sullivan and J. H. Aldrich. (1991) 'When Self-Interest Makes a Difference: The Role of Construct Accessibility in Political Reasoning', *Journal of Experimental Social Psychology* 27(3): 271–96.

Index

advertising 101–2
Aristotle 10, 25, 27, 32, 65n6, 116, 117
Asch, Solomon 69–70
Auden, W. H. 33
Austin, John 76
authority, legitimacy of 77–9, 141–4, 151–2

Barrett, Richard A. 52–3
beneficence 10–11, 14–15, 35, 63–4
Benn, Stanley 137, 139
Bentham, Jeremy 11, 37, 153
Biddle, Bruce J. 53–4, 56
Bloch, Marc 112, 122–3
Blum, Lawrence A. 117
Broek, Diane van den 119–20, 122, 150
Brown, Roger 39n8, 136
Brown, Rupert 40, 43, 70, 74, 76, 98, 100, 133, 135
bureaucracy 35, 51, 73–4, 81, 120

Challenger disaster 96, 98
Churchland, Paul 23–4
Clark, Andy 98, 156
Coady, Tony 21, 113
codes of conduct 98, 120, 151
coercion 16; *see also* informed consent
conflict of interest 34n5, 111–12, 117
conflicting obligations 4, 21–2, 26, 107–125, 162; duty to avoid 114–15, 121–3, 131; in Endeavour organisation 103–5; perceived 142–3, 162; and self-defence 131; and stress 109–10, 113–14, 121–2, 142
conformity effects 69–70, 74–5, 82–3, 86–7, 97–100
Confucianism 24, 32, 135n1
conscience 19, 69, 73, 152, 154, 157

consequentialism 11, 22, 97; *see also* utilitarianism
conventions 75–6
corporate ethics programmes 120–1
corporate social responsibility *see* responsibility
cosmopolitanism 136–8

Delbridge, Rick 127, 130, 132, 133, 140
'dirty hands' problem *see* conflicting obligations

emotional labour 149; *see also* nurses
Erickson, Milton 58–9
expectations: to act unethically 79; based on roles or social conventions 14–15, 57–9, 64, 72, 104–5; and communication 101–2; created by institutional authority 80, 82; deliberately induced 13–14; that generate obligations 3, 12–13, 58, 79–81, 93, 160–1; and obligations in Endeavour organisation 99–102; from third party actions 14, 128–32; widespread 101–2
exploitation 129

fairness 11–12, 15
families 34, 36, 38, 41, 43–4, 51–2, 117–18
feudalism 31–2, 112, 122–3
Ford Pinto case 95
Forster, E. M. 28–9
Forsyth, Donelson R. 39–40, 109, 119
French, Peter A. 49–50
friendship 32–5, 37–8, 117–18, 120

Gilligan, Carol 37
Glazer, Myron P. and Penina M. 72–3, 83, 95, 98, 144, 152

For Product Safety Concerns and Information please contact our
EU representative GPSR@taylorandfrancis.com Taylor & Francis
Verlag GmbH, Kaufingerstraße 24, 80331 München, Germany